Tcl Scripting for Cisco IOS

Ray Blair, CCIE No. 7050
Arvind Durai, CCIE No. 7016
John Lautmann

D1245697

Cisco Press

800 East 96th Street

Indianapolis, IN 46240

Tcl Scripting for Cisco IOS

Ray Blair, Arvind Durai, John Lautmann

Copyright © 2010 Cisco Systems, Inc.

Published by:
Cisco Press
800 East 96th Street
Indianapolis, IN 46240 USA

Printed in the United States of America

First Printing   June 2010

Library of Congress Cataloging-in-Publication Data:

Blair, Ray, 1965—
  Tcl scripting for Cisco IOS / Ray Blair, Arvind Durai, John Lautmann.
    p. cm.
  ISBN-13: 978-1-58705-945-2 (pbk.)
  ISBN-10: 1-58705-945-2 (pbk.)
  1. Tcl (Computer program language) 2. Cisco IOS. I. Durai, Arvind.
II. Lautmann, John. III. Title.

  QA76.73.T44B58 2010
  005.13'3—dc22

                                        2010015179

ISBN-13: 978-1-58705-945-2

ISBN-10: 1-58705-945-2

Warning and Disclaimer

Trademark Acknowledgments

Corporate and Government Sales

The publisher offers excellent discounts on this book when ordered in quantity for bulk purchases or special sales, which may include electronic versions and/or custom covers and content particular to your business, training goals, marketing focus, and branding interests. For more information, please contact: U.S. Corporate and Government Sales   1-800-382-3419   corpsales@pearsontechgroup.com

For sales outside the United States, please contact: **International Sales**   international@pearsoned.com

Feedback Information

At Cisco Press, our goal is to create in-depth technical books of the highest quality and value. Each book is crafted with care and precision, undergoing rigorous development that involves the unique expertise of members from the professional technical community.

Readers' feedback is a natural continuation of this process. If you have any comments regarding how we could improve the quality of this book, or otherwise alter it to better suit your needs, you can contact us through e-mail at feedback@ciscopress.com. Please make sure to include the book title and ISBN in your message.

We greatly appreciate your assistance.

Publisher: Paul Boger

Associate Publisher: Dave Dusthimer

Executive Editor: Brett Bartow

Managing Editor: Sandra Schroeder

Senior Development Editor: Christopher Cleveland

Project Editor: Mandie Frank

Editorial Assistant: Vanessa Evans

Cover Designer: Sandra Schroeder

Indexer: Tim Wright

Cisco Representative: Eric Ullanderson

Cisco Press Program Manager: Anand Sundaram

Copy Editor: Keith Cline

Proofreader: Sheri Cain

Technical Editors:
Joe Marcus Clarke, Greg S. Thompson

Book Designer: Louisa Adair

Composition: Mark Shirar

CISCO.

Americas Headquarters
Cisco Systems, Inc.
San Jose, CA

Asia Pacific Headquarters
Cisco Systems (USA) Pte. Ltd.
Singapore

Europe Headquarters
Cisco Systems International BV
Amsterdam, The Netherlands

Cisco has more than 200 offices worldwide. Addresses, phone numbers, and fax numbers are listed on the Cisco Website at www.cisco.com/go/offices.

CCDE, CCENT, Cisco Eos, Cisco HealthPresence, the Cisco logo, Cisco Lumin, Cisco Nexus, Cisco StadiumVision, Cisco TelePresence, Cisco WebEx, DCE, and Welcome to the Human Network are trademarks; Changing the Way We Work, Live, Play, and Learn and Cisco Store are service marks; and Access Registrar, Aironet, AsyncOS, Bringing the Meeting To You, Catalyst, CCDA, CCDP, CCIE, CCIP, CCNA, CCNP, CCSP, CCVP, Cisco, the Cisco Certified Internetwork Expert logo, Cisco IOS, Cisco Press, Cisco Systems, Cisco Systems Capital, the Cisco Systems logo, Cisco Unity, Collaboration Without Limitation, EtherFast, EtherSwitch, Event Center, Fast Step, Follow Me Browsing, FormShare, GigaDrive, HomeLink, Internet Quotient, IOS, iPhone, iQuick Study, IronPort, the IronPort logo, LightStream, Linksys, MediaTone, MeetingPlace, MeetingPlace Chime Sound, MGX, Networkers, Networking Academy, Network Registrar, PCNow, PIX, PowerPanels, ProConnect, ScriptShare, SenderBase, SMARTnet, Spectrum Expert, StackWise, The Fastest Way to Increase Your Internet Quotient, TransPath, WebEx, and the WebEx logo are registered trademarks of Cisco Systems, Inc. and/or its affiliates in the United States and certain other countries.

All other trademarks mentioned in this document or website are the property of their respective owners. The use of the word partner does not imply a partnership relationship between Cisco and any other company. (0812R)

About the Authors

Ray Blair, CCIE No. 7050, is a Vertical Solutions Architect and has been with Cisco Systems for more than 10 years, working primarily with large network designs. He has almost 22 years of experience with designing, implementing, and maintaining networks that have included nearly all networking technologies. During the early stages of his career, he wrote many applications using Assembly language and C. Mr. Blair maintains three CCIE certifications in Routing and Switching, Security, and Service Provider. He is also a Certified Information Systems Security Professional (CISSP) and coauthor of the *Cisco Secure Firewall Services Module* book.

Arvind Durai, CCIE No. 7016, is an Advanced Services Technical Leader for Cisco Systems. His primary responsibility in the past 10 years has been in supporting major Cisco customers in the enterprise sector, including financial, manufacturing, e-commerce, state government, utility (smart grid networks) and health-care sectors. Some of his focuses have been on security, multicast, network virtualization, and he has authored several white papers and design guides in various technologies. He has leveraged Embedded Event Manager (EEM) and Tool Command Language (Tcl) scripts in various customer designs. Mr. Durai maintains two CCIE certifications: Routing and Switching, and Security. He holds a Bachelor of Science degree in electronics and communication, a master's degree in electrical engineering (MS), and master's degree in business administration (MBA), and is a coauthor of *Cisco Secure Firewall Services Module.*

John Lautmann is a Software Engineer for Cisco Systems. He has developed and enhanced network management software for nearly 14 years. Before joining Cisco, he held positions in customer support and software testing. With six networking patents, John has been involved in the development of new Cisco IOS features such as data-link switching, syslog, configuration rollback and archiving, IOS Tcl interpreter, digitally signed Tcl scripts, and Multiprotocol Label Switching (MPLS) ping and trace. Mr. Lautmann holds a Bachelor of Science degree in computer science and master's degrees in both business and engineering.

About the Technical Reviewers

Joe Marcus Clarke, CCIE No. 5384, is a distinguished support engineer working in Technical Services and specializing in network management. In his 11+ years at Cisco, he has handled worldwide escalations for network management problems relating to SNMP, CiscoWorks, and embedded management technologies. He has also helped customers design and implement embedded management solutions using the Embedded Event Manager, Embedded Syslog Manager, and the Tcl shell in IOS. He works closely with the embedded management technology teams to improve and extend the capabilities in Cisco products. Joe is also extremely active on the Cisco Support Communities (aka NetPro) network management forum where he provides assistance to customers on a wide variety of network management issues.

Greg S. Thompson is a senior software engineer with more than 25 years of experience working in networking/telecommunications. He has spent the past several years at Cisco Systems, Inc. implementing Tcl and Tcl-based features in Cisco IOS, such as ESM (Embedded Syslog Manager) and EMM (Embedded Menu Manager).

Dedications

Ray Blair   As with everything in my life, I thank my Lord and Savior for his faithful leading that has brought me to this place. This book is dedicated to my wife, Sonya, and my children, Sam, Riley, Sophie, and Regan. You guys mean the world to me!

Arvind Durai   This book is dedicated to my wife, Monica, and my son, Akhhill. Thank you for everything!

To my parents, for providing me with values.

To my brother and family, my parents-in-law, and brother-in-law and family for all their good wishes.

Thank you, God!

John Lautmann   I dedicate this book to my family: my wife, Susana, my daughter, Kate, and my son, Rhys. You are all very special!

Acknowledgments

Ray Blair   This project was a significant undertaking, and without the partnership of Arvind and John, and the support of those mentioned here and many others, this would not have been an achievable goal. I am very grateful for all your help and support in completing this book!

Thanks to my wife, Sonya, and my children, Sam, Riley, Sophie, and Regan, for your patience in the many hours I spent working on this book.

Arvind and John, your excellent technical knowledge and dedication to the accuracy of the content made writing this book a pleasure. I look forward to many more years as your colleague and friend.

Arvind Durai   Thanks to my wife, Monica, and my son, Akhhill, for your support and tolerance with my long working hours.

Thanks to my director, Andrew Maximow, and my manager, Shibu Nair, for supporting me in this effort.

As always, it is great working with Ray and John, who have immaculate technical knowledge and dedication. You both have made the experience of writing this book a pleasure. Thank you!

John Lautmann   I would like to thank my family members for their support during the writing of this book. I could not have done it without you. Thank you Susana, Kate, Rhys, Judith, and Ron.

Thank you Arvind and Ray for your excellent support and motivation during the writing of the book. As a team, we can achieve anything!

Our special thanks to:

We are very grateful to Joe Marcus Clarke and Greg S. Thompson for their valuable input in providing direction and maintaining accuracy of the material in this book. Without the talent of these two technical reviewers, the book would not have been possible.

The Cisco Press team was very helpful in providing excellent feedback and direction, many thanks to Brett Bartow, Christopher Cleveland, and Dayna Isley.

Thanks to all of our customers with whom we have worked. Each customer scenario inspired us to write this book.

Contents at a Glance

Contents

Command Syntax Conventions

The conventions used to present command syntax in this book are the same conventions used in the IOS Command Reference. The Command Reference describes these conventions as follows:

- **Boldface** indicates commands and keywords that are entered literally as shown. In actual configuration examples and output (not general command syntax), boldface indicates commands that are manually input by the user (such as a **show** command).

- *Italic* indicates arguments for which you supply actual values.

- Vertical bars (|) separate alternative, mutually exclusive elements.

- Square brackets ([ ]) indicate an optional element.

- Braces ({ }) indicate a required choice.

- Braces within brackets ([{ }]) indicate a required choice within an optional element.

Introduction

Embedded Event Manager (EEM) along with Tool Command Language (Tcl) and applets enable you to customize the operation of the IOS device. These powerful tools can be leveraged when the normal operation of IOS is not suitable for your specific requirements.

This book was written to provide an understanding of the operation of EEM, Tcl, and applets. It begins with the fundamentals of Tcl and provides practical examples of how to create your own application.

Who Should Read This Book?

This book is targeted at individuals who manage, maintain, or operate a network that contains IOS devices. To get the most value from the material, you should have at least a basic knowledge of programming.

How This Book Is Organized

This book is organized into seven chapters and one appendix and includes an introduction to Tcl, language basics, Cisco IOS device support, how Tcl functions in IOS, the use of EEM, and practical examples. After absorbing the material in this book, you will be well qualified to write your own programs. The chapters in this book cover the following topics:

■ **Chapter 1, "The Origin of Tcl":** This chapter introduces Tcl, EEM, and how you can use them to enhance Cisco IOS.

■ **Chapter 2, "Tcl Interpreter and Language Basics":** This chapter provides an overview of the basic command syntax for Tcl.

■ **Chapter 3, "Tcl Functioning in Cisco IOS":** This chapter examines how Tcl functions in Cisco IOS.

■ **Chapter 4, "Embedded Event Manager (EEM)":** This chapter explains the various EEM versions, platform considerations, and applets.

■ **Chapter 5, "Advanced Tcl Operation in Cisco IOS":** This chapter covers Embedded Syslog Manger (ESM), Embedded Menu Manager (EMM), and includes myriad Tcl examples.

■ **Chapter 6, "Tcl Script Examples":** This chapter explains how to write a Tcl script from start to finish.

■ **Chapter 7, "Security in Tcl Scripts":** This chapter introduces public key infrastructure (PKI) and covers how to secure Tcl scripts.

■ **Appendix A, "Cisco IOS Tcl Commands Quick Reference":** This appendix covers Tcl commands specific to Cisco IOS.

TCL Scripting Examples

To register this product and gain access to sample Tcl scripts, go to www.ciscopress.com/tclscripting to sign in and enter the ISBN. After you register the book, a link to the bonus content will be listed on your Account page, under Registered Products.

Chapter 3:

- **chap3e1.tcl**—Verifies if the 10.0.0.x network is associated with any local interfaces.

- **chap3e2.tcl**—Parses the running-configuration and looks for and displays the time-zone parameter. This script is helpful to parse parameters or text from the Cisco CLI **show** command and derive the desired value as an output.

Chapter 4:

- **cpu_threshold_email.tcl**—Sends an email in the event the CPU utilization is over 60%.

- **interface_errors_email.tcl**—Sends an email in the event interface errors are detected.

Chapter 5:

- **syslogd_book.tcl**—This is a syslog daemon script application that displays the syslog messages at the terminal.

- **syslogd_book2.tcl**—This is a syslog daemon script application used to collect and store information locally on an IOS device. There are two input parameters: tcp port and file name to write syslog messages.

- **filter.tcl, filter2.tcl, filter3.tcl, filter4.tcl**—Performs embedded syslog manager message processing.

- **my.mdf , my2.mdf, my3.mdf**—Examples of Embedded Menu Manager menu definition files.

- **chap5e1.tcl, chap5e2.tcl, chap5e3.tcl, chap5e4.tcl, clock.tcl, ipsla.tcl, ipsla1.tcl, ipsla1.5.tcl, ipsla2.tcl, ipsla3.tcl, ipslaresult1.tcl**—Examples of Tcl scripts that generate web pages.

Chapter 6:

- **MPLS-VPN.tcl**—This provisions MPLS VPN on a router through a GUI. (This application was tested on an ISR2800.)

- **Remote-SNMP.tcl**—Collects SNMP data from a remote device and displays it to the user as a graph on web page.

Chapter 7:

- **my_append**—An expect script that assists in converting and generating the correct format for signed Tcl script.

- **myscript**—Raw Tcl script to be signed.

- **myscript.hex, myscript.hex_sig, myscript.pk7**—Intermediate files generated in the process of signing a Tcl script.

- **myscript.tcl**—The final signed Tcl script in the correct format.

- **myscript-changed1char.tcl**—The final signed Tcl script with one modified character to illustrate the security violation being detected.

Appendix A:

- **arg-demo.tcl**—Illustrates the use of input arguments to a Tcl script.

- **count-to-one.tcl**—A Tcl script that counts to 1.

- **count-to-ten.tbc**—A Tcl script that counts to 10, in byte-code format.

- **count-to-ten.tcl**—A Tcl script that counts to 10.

- **debugging-tcl_trace**—Example procedures used to understand debugging using tcl_trace.

- **int.tcl**—A Tcl script the prints the value of tcl_interactive.

- **mypackages/**—directory.

- **pkgIndex.tcl**—File that assists in loading the correct package when a Tcl script requires a package.

- **circle.tcl, square.tcl, triangle.tcl**—Tcl files that provide some example packages.

## Chapter 1

The Origin of Tcl

This chapter covers the following topics:

- Tcl and Cisco IOS Software

- Using Tcl Scripts in the Network

Tool Command Language (Tcl), invented in the late 1980s by John K. Ousterhout of the University of California, Berkeley, is a dynamic programming or scripting language, an interpreter, and a C library. Tcl helps users control other applications or utilities using basic flow control. Tcl is pronounced "tickle" or "tee-cee-ell." One of the original suggestions for a title of this book was *How to Tickle Your Router*, which, although inappropriate, is quite descriptive.

Tcl is an interpreted programming language versus a compiled programming language. One advantage of an interpreted language is speed in the development process. A programmer can make changes quickly as the script is being developed and rapidly run the script to see the changes. Another advantage is that the script is available for any users to modify because it is written in a plain text format, with the exception of precompiled byte-code. As the requirements change over time, various changes can easily be made to modify the script to suit customer needs.

Note Precompiled byte-code enables you to hide the implementation details of a TCL script and is discussed in greater detail in Chapter 7, "Security in Tcl Scripts."

The disadvantage of an interpreted programming language is performance. The speed of execution is reduced slightly because of the overhead of interpreting the script commands first. The execution speed depends on the operating system, processor, programming language, and so on, but will typically be in the range of a few seconds. At runtime, the Tcl script must first be parsed before execution can begin. In contrast, a compiled language is written and compiled ahead of time. At runtime, the machine language (compiled code) is run without the interpretation step. Another disadvantage for commercial applications is the difficulty hiding the contents of the script. Because the script is plain text, a software company will be reluctant to release their work in an open format that can be seen and copied. The code can be obfuscated through the process of byte-code compilation, but this is not a completely secure method, because compiled byte-code can be reverse-engineered. This also makes it difficult to protect the intellectual property rights of the software they develop.

Besides performance, the memory requirements are generally greater for an interpreted language because the entire contents of the script itself, the compiled version of the script, and all the script variables are held in memory. Do not allow this to discourage you from writing Tcl scripts, however; they still are very usable and have a relatively small memory footprint.

Key benefits of Tcl include the following:

- Used to manipulate and display information that can be obtained from other devices, a user interface, a database, and so on.

- The automation of complex tasks.

- There are many commands for the manipulation of information, including integers and strings.

- Simple language to learn.

Another component of Tcl is Tool Kit (Tk). Tk is a library of procedures written to create graphical user interfaces (GUI). Tk includes commands to create GUI widgets, windows, buttons, text boxes, and so on. Tk also provides a GUI for the host operating system where the script is executed. Tk is not covered in this book because Tk support is not available in Cisco IOS Software.

The usage of Tcl can be seen in the following areas:

- **Testing and automation:** Use of this language is commonly seen in testing environments to leverage the capability of the language to interact with various software and hardware devices.

- **Web applications:** Tcl has Tcllib libraries, including a number of Common Gateway Interface (CGI) libraries and can also be used as a conventional web programming language.

- **Desktop GUI applications:** With the help of Tk, Tcl has been used to write GUI applications. The dynamic approach of Tcl makes it easy to develop GUIs.

- **Databases:** Tcl extensions are available to use for all standard databases, such as Oracle, Sybase, and so on.

- **Embedded development:** Tcl is a compact language and is popular with embedded development. Tcl scripts are hidden in many hardware devices for user-defined functionality.

Tcl/Tk has been gaining popularity and interest among users from the time it was introduced. This is primarily because it is fast, powerful, easy to learn, and can run on almost all computing platforms. The Tcl language is different from many other scripting languages in that it can embed into other applications. These applications can easily add a full-feature Tcl interpreter and macro language.

Note   Another offshoot of Tcl is Expect. Expect is highly specialized to match output strings. The primary use of Expect is to automate interactive user sessions such as Telnet, Secure Shell (SSH), File Transfer Protocol (FTP), Secure FTP (SFTP), and so on. For additional information about Expect, refer to *Exploring Expect*, by Don Libes (O'Reilly, 1994; ISBN 1-56592-090-2).

Tcl and Cisco IOS Software

By now, you probably have a general understanding of Tcl, but you may be thinking, "What's it gonna do for me?" The combination of Tcl with Cisco IOS Software is a powerful tool, one that enables you to enhance the operation of Cisco IOS. With the addition of Tcl, you can customize IOS to execute unique procedures specific to your environment. Maybe you would like to create a menu for the help desk to make VLAN changes on defined ports, but disallow any other changes. Are you thinking of other applications?

If you are considering running Tcl, you might also be wondering what devices are supported. The Tcl shell was first introduced in 12.3(2)T and 12.2(25)S and was merged into the Catalyst 6500 in version 12.2.(18)SX4 for modular IOS and 12.2(18)SX5 for IOS. In the desktop switching space, Tcl shell was added in 12.2(40)SE.

Note   If you do not have access to a router or switch that supports Tcl, you can start practicing on your computer. Windows, Mac OS X, and UNIX operating systems all support Tcl. You can download and install/compile Tcl to run on your computer. You can access the official Tcl/Tk distribution site at http://www.tcl.tk/.

This is probably a better place to start, rather than practicing on production equipment, especially if you want to keep your job!

Embedded Event Manager and Tcl

Embedded Event Manager (EEM) is a powerful tool available in Cisco IOS Software that enables users to run Tcl programs/scripts or applets directly on Cisco routers or switches. An applet is a single or series of IOS commands, similar to a macro. The support for EEM helps users to manage Cisco devices through event detectors. Event detectors monitor both the hardware and software components on specific platforms.

Examples of EEM functionality include the following:

- Event detectors monitor specific conditions of the device, and based on those parameters, event triggers can initiate a script to perform a predefined task.

- EEM can take actions based on syslog messages. For example, after detecting a CPUhog syslog message, EEM could take particular **show** command output and send an e-mail to the user.

- EEM can be used to influence the route forwarding based on an IOS trigger.

EEM has the capability to trigger or initiate two unique functions:

- **Create applet policies:** This is an easy-to-use interface using IOS command-line interface (CLI) commands. The user does not need to know the details of a scripting language; the familiarity with IOS is sufficient to create an applet policy.

- **Write user-defined policies with Tcl scripts:** This is more flexible because it is not constrained by IOS commands only and has extensive capabilities; however, the user should know how to use the Tcl language.

Note   Chapter 4, "Embedded Event Manager (EEM)," covers EEM in more detail.

Figure 1-1 offers a graphical example of the relationship of event detectors, EEM, Tcl scripts, and applets.

Restriction of Tcl in IOS

Before getting into the details of writing Tcl scripts, you should be familiar with Tcl programming and Cisco IOS commands.

Tcl code can be executed from the Tcl parser shell mode in the Cisco IOS CLI. The execution of Tcl in the CLI can be done *only* from privileged EXEC mode.

For example:

```
R1>en
Password:
R1#tclsh
R1(Tcl)#
```

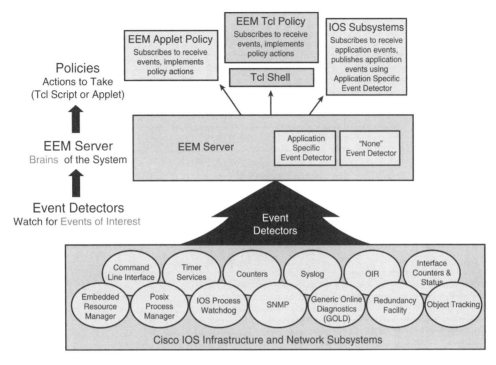

Figure 1-1   *EEM's Relationship with Other Functions*

Certain functionality of Cisco IOS uses Tcl subsystems such as Embedded Syslog Manager (ESM), Embedded Menu Manager (EMM), and Interactive Voice Response (IVR). These topics are covered in greater detail in Chapter 5, "Advanced Tcl Operation in Cisco IOS." These subsystems integrate proprietary commands and keywords not available in a Tcl shell.

A Tcl shell can be enabled, and Tcl commands can be executed, in IOS. The Tcl interpreter checks whether the entered Tcl commands are valid, and if so, the result is sent to the tty. Tcl commands that are not recognized as valid are sent to the Cisco IOS CLI parser.

Tcl with EEM Support in IOS

Tcl commands from version 8.3.4 are available in Cisco IOS. Table 1-1 shows support for Tcl with EEM in specific Cisco IOS code versions.

Table 1-1   *Tcl with EEM Support by Cisco Device/IOS Release*

Platform	IOS Release (Beginning With)
10000-PRE2	12.2(28)SB
10000-PRE3	12.2(31)SB2
10000-PRE4	12.2(33)SB
1700 series	12.3(14)T1
1800 series	12.3(14)YT
2600XM	12.3(14)T1
2691	12.3(14)T1
2800 series	12.3(14)T
3270	12.4(24)T
3600 series	12.3(14)T1
3700 series	12.3(14)T1
3800 series	12.3(14)T1
7200	12.2(25)S
7200-NPE-G2	12.2(31)SB2
7201	12.2(31)SB5
7301	12.2(31)SB3
7500	12.2(25)S
7600-RSP720-10GE	12.2(33)SRC
7600-RSP720/MSFC4	12.2(33)SRB
7600-SAMI	12.2(33)SRD
800 series	12.4(6)XE3
AS5350XM	12.4(20)T
AS5400XM	12.4(20)T
ASR1000-RP1	2.1.0
ASR1000-RP2	2.3.0
Cat 6500-Sup720	12.2(33)SXH
CAT3560E	12.2(35)SE1
CAT3750E	12.2(35)SE1

Platform	IOS Release (Beginning With)
CAT3750Metro	12.2(40)SE
CAT4500E-SUP6E	12.2(50)SG
CAT4948	12.2(44)SG
CAT4948-10GE	12.2(44)SG
CAT6000-SUP32/MSFC2A	12.2(33)SXH
CAT6000-VS-S720-10G/MSFC3	12.2(33)SXH
CBS3000 series	12.2(40)EX2
CBS3100 series	12.2(40)EX2
CRS-1	3.5.4
IAD2400 series	12.4(22)T
IAD2801	12.4(11)XJ2
IAD880 series	12.4(20)T
ME3400	12.2(40)SE
ME3400E	12.2(44)EY
ME4900	12.2(40)SG
ME6524	12.2(33)SXH
UBR10K-PRE2	12.2(33)SCB2
UBR10K-PRE4	12.2(33)SCB2
UBR7200	12.2(33)SCB2
UBR7200-NPE-G2	12.2(33)SCB2
UC520	12.4(20)T1
VGD-1T3	12.4(22)T
XR 12000-PRP	3.5.4
Nexus 7000	*Applets only

*Applets are covered in Chapter 4. This is not a comprehensive list. Consult the documentation on your specific device and version requirements.

Using Tcl Scripts in the Network

Network administrators can leverage Tcl scripts to provide enhanced functionality. Scripts can be used for troubleshooting, monitoring, and increasing the intelligence of IOS, as described in the sections that follow.

Troubleshooting Problems

Network administrators use different methods to analyze and troubleshoot problems in the network. Some of these tools and technologies consist of packet-capture devices or sniffers, Remote Monitoring (RMON) probes, NetFlow collectors, Simple Network Management Protocol (SNMP), IP service level agreement (IP SLA) measurements, network management system (NMS) tools, and so on. These tools help in gathering information about the condition or health of the network. Collection of information is accomplished through the monitoring or analysis of the packet passing to or through an interface. The problems that are more difficult to detect are those that do not break the network or node and are often referred to as *silent drops*. Some of the examples of silent drops are as follows:

- Packets dropped because of an incorrect quality of service (QoS) implementation

- Application slowness in the network

- High CPU usage

- Faulty cable infrastructure

Tcl scripts can be used to collect information based on an event. For example, if drops in the QoS queue or drops on the interfaces increase, a script can be executed to collect the interface statistic and send an e-mail with the pertinent information. You might find yourself troubleshooting an issue that occurs infrequently, in which case, the capability to execute a script to collect relevant information might just prove invaluable.

Monitoring the Network

Normally, NMS tools are used to monitor networks. NMS tools have the capability to receive SNMP traps, configuration management information, syslog monitoring messages, interface statistics, and traffic profiles. The raw data is then presented to the user in a graphical or user-defined format. These tools are expensive, and the cost factor mainly depends on the network size. In small networks, network administrators can use a Tcl script on a UNIX box to query the basic functionality of network gear. This functionality can be used as a substitute for a more expensive NMS product; however, Tcl scripts cannot be used to substitute an enterprise NMS solution. Tcl scripts can monitor particular SNMP traps; perform configuration assessment; parse severity 0 (emergencies), 1 (alerts), and 2 (critical) syslog information; and monitor the traffic profile for the local node.

Adding Intelligence to Cisco IOS Protocols

While designing networks, you may need to address a predetermined requirement, or you might need to address a requirement change because of new applications or services (sometimes referred to as *scope creep*). For example, when designing a network using Open Shortest Path First (OSPF), a remote site might have a requirement to load balance or install routes based on specific conditions. This requirement might need to be accomplished using features unavailable with OSPF. As a network administrator, you can create a Tcl script that aligns itself to the routing features of OSPF and uses other IOS features to influence the routing decision on how the packets are sent. Tcl script examples are included in Chapter 6, "Tcl Script Examples."

Summary

As you read through this chapter, you might have already begun thinking of applications that you could create to make managing your network infrastructure much easier using Tcl scripts. This could be task automation, building a user interface for the help desk, or notification of a change or problem in the network.

Our intent is for this first chapter to pique your interest in developing your own Tcl scripts. Now, continue reading. The following chapters walk you through the process of becoming an efficient Tcl programmer.

References

Tcl Developer Xchange: http://www.tcl.tk

EEM: http://www.cisco.com/go/eem

IP SLA: http://www.cisco.com/go/ipsla

RFC 1157, *Simple Network Management Protocol (SNMP)*: http://tools.ietf.org/html/rfc1157

RFC 3577, *Introduction to the Remote Monitoring (RMON) Family of MIB Modules*: http://www.ietf.org/rfc/rfc3577.txt

RFC 3954, *Cisco Systems NetFlow Services Export Version 9*: http://www.ietf.org/rfc/rfc3954.txt

"History of Tcl": http://home.pacbell.net/ouster/tclHistory.html

Chapter 2

Tcl Interpreter and Language Basics

This chapter covers the following topics:

- Simple Variables in Tcl

- Procedures

- Arrays

- **if** Command

- **switch** Command

- Files

This is where the rubber meets the road. Without a fundamental understanding of the command syntax, you will be unsuccessful in writing any programs whatsoever. Reading and attempting to memorize command syntax can be arduous and boring. To really get an idea of how to use commands in this chapter, a better solution is to use them in practice.

Tcl interpreters are supported on Mac, UNIX/Linux, Windows, and other operating systems. You can visit the Tcl Developer Xchange website at http://www.Tcl.tk/ or perform a search for the latest Tcl interpreters.

Note To determine the version of Tcl you are using on your IOS device, use the following commands:

```
Router#tclsh
Router(tcl)#info patchlevel
8.3.4
```

> **Note**   The examples in this chapter were created using Tcl version 8.3.4.

Simple Variables in Tcl

A variable is data (information) stored in memory and referenced by a name. Variables are one of the fundamental building blocks of any programming language. Many types of information can all be stored in a variable, including an input received from the keyboard, external I/O card, other applications, or a placeholder for the results of an equation. In addition, variables can be referenced later for display or further processing. Strings are ordered sets of characters or symbols.

> **Note**   Tcl supports only the single data type of a string. Many other programming languages require the initialization and specification of variables used when programming (for example, integers, characters, long integers). This makes the process of assigning variable types much simpler in Tcl.

Storing Variables

Storing variables in the Tcl interpreter is accomplished using the **set** command.

For example, to store the value of **100** in the variable **x**, enter the following:

```
Router(tcl)#set x 100
100
```

To use the value of a variable in a script, you must precede the variable with the dollar symbol, **$**. In the example that follows, the command **expr** evaluates the expression and returns the result. The **expr** command performs mathematical computations, comparison of operands, conditional checks, and so on. Because **x** has a value of **100** and **10** was added, the result is **110**:

```
Router(tcl)#expr $x+10
110
```

Table 2-1 provides some examples of setting variables. Consider practicing storing some variables to get a better understanding of how they can be referenced.

Table 2-1   *Storing Values in a Variable*

Variable	Result
set x 100	100
set y x	X
set y $x	100
set y $x+$x+$x	100+100+100
set y $x.3	100.3

Did you expect a different result from the variable **set y $x+$x+$x?** Remember that the **set** command is used to store variables and not perform any mathematic functions.

Viewing Variables

Viewing variables in the Tcl interpreter is accomplished using the **puts** command. There are three standard channels: **stdin**, **stdout**, and **stderr**. The default channel **stdout** provides the output to the display.

For example, to print the value of **x** on the screen, use the **puts** command as follows:

```
Router(tcl)#puts $x
100
```

Did you notice that the variable **x** was preceded with a **$** symbol? If you forget, the output will be **x**. In this case, the output is the value stored in **x**, which is **100**.

The append Command

The **append** command is another key feature used in Tcl to append or concatenate strings. The next example assigns strings to two variables, **a** and **b**, and displays the output on the screen:

```
Router(tcl)#set a "This is my"
This is my
Router(tcl)#set b " favorite book"
 favorite book
Router(tcl)#append a $b
This is my favorite book
Router(tcl)#puts $a
This is my favorite book
```

The **append** command is useful to add a command-line interface (CLI) statement.

Do you remember your high school math class? The teacher would always have you solve equations the hard way and then show you the easy method. As a shortcut, you can also use the following command with the previously defined variables:

```
Router(tcl)#puts "$a$b"
This is my favorite book
```

The incr Command

The **incr** command is used to increment or add 1 to an integer variable in a Tcl script, and is especially helpful when loops are being used. The following is a simple example of incrementing a variable:

```
Router(tcl)#set x 1
1
Router(tcl)#incr x
2
```

The **incr** command can also be used with a numeric value. The expression will be evaluated with either positive or negative values, as shown:

```
Router(tcl)#set x 10
10
Router(tcl)#incr x -2
8
Router(tcl)#incr x 13
21
```

Note   The **incr** command is applicable only for numeric values.

You can also use the **expr** command to accomplish the same result, but notice that it does require some additional characters and will make the script slightly more difficult to read. The next example provides the same results using the **expr** command:

```
Router(tcl)#set x 1
1
Router(tcl)#expr $x+1
2
```

Representation of Variables in Tcl

A few key elements necessary for scripting in Tcl are as follows:

- **Words:** White space separates words in a command.

- **Double quotes:** If the first character of a word is double quote ("), the word is terminated by the next double-quote character. Quotes allow for substitutions within a group.

- **Braces:** An open brace ({) needs to be matched by a close brace (}), and do not allow substitutions within a group.

Command Substitution

The open bracket ([) is used for command substitution. This is done by invoking the Tcl interpreter to process the characters between the open and closed brackets (]).

> **Note**   Command and variable substitution is not performed by words in braces.

Variable Substitution

When a variable is preceded by a dollar sign ($), the Tcl interpreter will execute the contents of the entire variable, by dereferencing the contents of the variable. Variable substitution can take any of the following forms:

- **$*name*:** The *name* is a sequence of one or more characters that are a alphanumeric, underscore, or namespace separators. Anything other than :: can be used.

- **$*name*(*index*):** The *name* denotes the name of the variable (obviously), and the *index* provides the name of an element within that array. Scalar variables contain strings (for example, a list).

The following example uses an array variable called **x,** which contains multiple subelements. The index of **1** is used to store **100:**

```
Router(tcl)#set x(1) 100
100
```

The index of **2** is used to store **200:**

```
Router(tcl)#set x(2) 200
200
```

The variables are displayed using the **puts** command:

```
Router(tcl)#puts $x(1)
100
Router(tcl)#puts $x(2)
200
```

> **Note**   If you are still using the variable **x** from an example, you might receive the following message: "Cannot set "x(1)": variable is not array." In this case, you can use the **unset** command as follows, or exit the Tcl shell using the **exit** command and return using the **tclsh** command:
>
> ```
> Router(tcl)#unset x
> ```

Index values of an array are not limited to numeric values. The following uses **y** to store the value of **1000**:

```
Router(tcl)#set x(y) 1000
1000
```

The output of **$x(y)** is **1000**:

```
Router(tcl)#puts $x(y)
1000
```

Alternatively, and in more common practice, you can use numeric values as index variables, as shown in the following example:

```
Router(tcl)#set x(23) 1000
1000
```

The output of **$x(y)** is **1000**:

```
Router(tcl)#puts $x(23)
1000
```

Lastly, if an element in the array has not been initialized, you will get an error when you attempt to reference it. The following message will display. In this case, you have not initialized the index of **3**:

```
Router(tcl)#puts $x(3)
cannot read "x(3)": no such element in array
```

For **${*name*}**, the *name* can contain any characters whatsoever, except for closed braces. For example, you could use the entire string of **I love-this book! @@** as a variable:

```
Router(tcl)#set {I_love-this book! @@} WOW
WOW
Router(tcl)#puts ${I_love-this book! @@}
WOW
```

Note There might be any number of variable substitutions in a single string. A string enclosed in braces is considered one element of the string.

For example:

```
Router(tcl)#set x substitution
```

substitution

```
Router(tcl)#puts "Quotes with $x"
```

Quotes with substitution

```
Router(tcl)#puts {Curly braces with $x}
```

Curly braces with

```
$x
```

Lists

A list is not a new data type but a collection of values separated by white space. An example of a list is as follows:

```
Router(tcl)#list red green blue orange purple black
red green blue orange purple black
```

You can also use the **set** command:

```
Router(tcl)#set COLORS "red green blue orange purple black"
red green blue orange purple black
```

Lists can be manipulated in different ways. Some of the more common methods that will be explained are as follows:

- lappend
- lindex
- linsert
- llength
- lrange
- lreplace
- lsearch
- lset
- lsort

lappend

This command appends a variable to a string. The **lappend** command is similar to **append**, except with **lappend**, elements are added to the list separated with white space. These values can be manipulated with the previously mentioned list-related commands, as compared to **append** where the values are added to the string.

The following example describes the use of **lappend**:

```
Router(tcl)#lappend tcl_book this book
this book
Router(tcl)#lappend tcl_book is great
this book is great
Router(tcl)#puts $tcl_book
this book is great
```

lindex

The command **lindex** returns an element from a list, but does not change the list. Using **lindex**, the specified element in the list is extracted, as follows:

```
Router(tcl)#set $tcl_book "this book is great"
this book is great
Router(tcl)#index $tcl_book 3
great
```

As seen from the output, the third element from the list is extracted, with the following command showing that the string has not changed:

```
Router(tcl)#puts $tcl_book
this book is great
```

linsert

The **linsert** command enables you to insert new elements in a list. These new elements can either be inserted before or after any element in the list.

Consider this continuation of the previous example:

```
Router(tcl)#puts $tcl_book
this book great
Router(tcl)#set tcl_book [linsert $tcl_book 2 is]
this book is great
Router(tcl)#puts $tcl_book
this book is great
```

This example used the **tcl_book** list, and added an element to the second position. The elements in the string are counted from the left, starting with 0. Because we used **2**, the **is** would be inserted between **book** and **great**.

llength

The **llength** command enables you to count the number of elements in a list.

Consider this continuation of the previous example:

```
Router(tcl)#puts $tcl_book
this book is great
Router(tcl)#llength $tcl_book
4
```

Notice that this command provides and actual count of the number of elements.

lsearch

The **lsearch** command enables you to search a list for a pattern match. The following example will attempt to search for the letter *i* in the string:

```
Router(tcl)#puts $tcl_book
this book is great
Router(tcl)#lsearch $tcl_book i
-1
```

The **-1** indicates that a match was not found. In looking at the list, you can clearly see that there is an *i* in *this* and *is*. What happened?

The **lsearch** command is looking for an exact match. When attempting to match an entire element, as the following example shows, a match will be found in element 2. Remember 0, 1, 2:

```
Router(tcl)#lsearch $tcl_book is
2
```

If you were interested in locating the first occurrence of the letter *i*, you could use a regular expression, as follows:

```
Router(tcl)#lsearch -regexp $tcl_book i
0
```

The **0** indicates that i is present in the first element.

The **lsearch** command has three options that you can use:

- **-exact:** The list element must contain exactly the same string as the pattern.
- **-glob:** The pattern is a glob-style pattern that is matched against each list element using the same rules as the string match command.
- **-regexp:** The pattern is treated as a regular expression and matched against each list element using the rules described in the re_syntax reference page (http://www.tcl.tk/man/tcl8.3/TclCmd/re_syntax.htm).

> **Note**   Regular expressions provide a method of matching strings through patterns and are commonly used when configuring Border Gateway Protocol (BGP) to match attributes in routing information. Many books and much material online have been published on regular expressions, and that particular topic is beyond the scope of this book.

lreplace

The **lreplace** command enables you to replace an element or elements in a list. As you will see in the example, elements can be added or removed.

The following example changes the list from **this book is great** to **this book is really awesome,** by starting (the first instance of 3) and ending with the third (3 3) element (the second instance of 3) **great**. Remember that the count starts with 0:

```
Router(tcl)#puts $tcl_book
this book is great
Router(tcl)#set tcl_book [lreplace $tcl_book 3 3 really awesome]
this book is really awesome
```

This next command manipulates the third and fourth (3 4) elements, by replacing both **really** and **awesome** with **spectacular:**

```
Router(tcl)#set tcl_book [lreplace $tcl_book 3 4 spectacular]
this book is spectacular
```

lrange

The **lrange** command selects a contiguous group of elements from a list based on the starting and ending index values.

The following example changes the **tcl_book** string from four elements to two. The element values of 2 and 3 specify the range. In this case, it is the last two elements in the string, **is spectacular:**

```
Router(tcl)#puts $tcl_book
this book is spectacular
Router(tcl)#set tcl_book [lrange $tcl_book 2 3]
is spectacular
```

lsort

The **lsort** function arranges elements within a list based on the following parameters in Table 2-2.

The **lsort** command enables you to arrange strings of text, as shown in the following example:

```
Router(tcl)#puts $tcl_book
this book is spectacular
Router(tcl)#set tcl_book [lsort $tcl_book]
book is spectacular this
```

Table 2-2   *lsort Parameters*

Options for lsort	Explanation
-ascii	Use a string comparison with Unicode code. This is the default.
-dictionary	Use dictionary-style comparison.
-integer	Use integer comparison
-real	Convert elements in a list to floating-point values and use floating comparison.
-command	Use command as a comparison. Used to evaluate Tcl scripts consisting of commands with the elements appended as additional arguments.
-increasing	Sort the list in ascending order, which means smallest items first. This is the default.
-decreasing	Sort the list in decreasing order, which means largest items first.
-index	Sort based on the specified element.
-unique	Only the last set of duplicate elements will be kept.

The output of **lsort** is used to modify the original string in alphabetic order.

This next example shows how numeric values (integers) in a string can be sorted from largest to smallest:

```
Router(tcl)#set numbers "34 2 42 9 192 3 8"
34 2 42 9 192 3 8
Router(tcl)#lsort -integer -decreasing $numbers
192 42 34 9 8 3 2
```

As you can see from the output, it worked as advertised. You might also notice that the **lsort** command was used alone. Any of the previous list-related commands can be used in conjunction with other commands or by itself. In this example, the output is sent only to the screen and not stored as another variable or modified the original variable.

Procedures

A procedure can be called in a Tcl script using the **proc** command. When the procedure is invoked, the contents will be executed by the Tcl interpreter.

The syntax for the **proc** command includes the following arguments:

```
proc name args body
```

In the following example, the procedure **myproc** is called. A **for** loop executes until variable **z** is less than 10 (variable **z** is initialized to 0):

```
Router(tcl)#proc myproc {} {
    puts "this is myproc"
}
% set  z {0}
0
Router(tcl)#puts $z
0
Router(tcl)#for {set z 0} {$z<10} {incr z} {
myproc
}
this is myproc
this is myproc
this is myproc
this is myproc
this is myproc
this is myproc
this is myproc
this is myproc
this is myproc
this is myproc
```

The result, **this is myproc**, is printed 10 times on the screen, starting at 0 and ending at 9.

for Command

The **for** command enables you to perform repetitive procedures to minimize the number of lines in a Tcl script. When this command is invoked, it evaluates an expression, and based on that condition, the body of the program is executed. This is similar to the **for** statement in the C programming language.

The syntax for the **for** command includes the following arguments:

for *start test next body*

In the following example

- *start* sets the variable **z** to 0.

- *test* evaluates the variable to determine whether it is less than 3 (if not, the **for** loop ends).

- *next* increments the variable **z.**

- *body* displays variable **z** along with the text **Enjoy your reading**, using the **puts** command.

```
Router(tcl)#for {set z 0} {$z<3} {incr z} {
+>puts " $z. Enjoy your reading"
+>}
 0. Enjoy your reading
 1. Enjoy your reading
 2. Enjoy your reading
```

As an alternative, the commands can also be placed on a single line, as follows:

```
Router(tcl)#for {set z 0} {$z<3} {incr z} {puts " $z. Enjoy your reading"}
 0. Enjoy your reading
 1. Enjoy your reading
 2. Enjoy your reading
```

foreach Command

The **foreach** command is also used to execute loops in Tcl scripts, and can be directed to one or more lists. A counter is not required to keep track of **foreach** loops. This is done internally, and as long as there are elements left in the list, the loop will continue.

The syntax for the **foreach** command includes the following arguments:

```
foreach varList list ?varList list ...? command
```

In the following example, we place several elements in a list that represents router names and the CPU utilization collected twice:

```
Router(tcl)#set cpuinfo  {r1 50 90 r2 20 10 r3 17 21}
r1 50 90 r2 20 10 r3 17 21
```

With that information entered into the **cpuinfo** list, we will parse through the list and glean the router name and the CPU information. We will then take an average of the first and second CPU values (divide by 2) and display the information:

```
Router(tcl)#foreach {router CPU1 CPU2} $cpuinfo { set CPUavg [expr ($CPU1
  +$CPU2)/2] ; puts "$router $CPUavg" }
r1 70.0
r2 15.0
r3 19.0
```

From the output, you can see that the average utilization of r1 was 70 percent, r2 was 15 percent, and r3 was 19 percent.

while Command

The **while** command is also used to create loop functions in Tcl scripts. The command evaluates a test expression, and based on the result of the expression, the body is executed. When the test expression is no longer true, the loop is complete.

The syntax for the **while** command contains only two arguments:

```
while test command
```

In the example that follows, the variable **y** is initialized to 0. The **while** loop runs while the variable **y** is less than 5. The body executes the expression (**expr**) of multiplying variable **y** by 2, and displays that information. Finally, variable **y** is incremented by 1 before the script performs the evaluation test:

```
Router(tcl)#set y 0 ; while {$y < 5}  { set T [expr ($y*2)] ; puts "$y. twice $y
  is $T" ;
incr y }
0. twice 0 is 0
1. twice 1 is 2
2. twice 2 is 4
3. twice 3 is 6
4. twice 4 is 8
```

Arrays

Arrays are a structured collection of variables. The **array** command provides a way to access the information stored within the array.

The syntax for the **array** command is as follows:

```
array option arrayName ?arg arg ...?
```

The example that follows begins by creating an array and populating the variables with the interface names along with the bits/second count:

```
Router(tcl)#set InterfaceCount(GigabitEthernet0/0) {221343 39387 313423}
382212 5133 125233
Router(tcl)# set InterfaceCount(GigabitEthernet0/1) {221343 39387 313423}
221343 39387 313423
Router(tcl)#set InterfaceCount(Serial0/0/0) {336373 383 27383}
336373 383 27383
```

Using the **get** command, you can display the entire array:

```
Router(tcl)#array get InterfaceCount
GigabitEthernet0/0 {382212 5133 125233} GigabitEthernet0/1 {382212 5133 125233}
Serial0/0/0 {336373 383 27383}
```

The variables associated with an element can also be displayed:

```
Router(tcl)#array get InterfaceCount Serial0/0/0
Serial0/0/0 {336373 383 27383}
```

The count of the number of items within the array can be viewed with the following command:

```
Router(tcl)#array size InterfaceCount
3
```

There are three elements within the array:

- GigabitEthernet0/0

- GigabitEthernet0/1

- Serial0/0/0

You can also search through the array; however, a token must be generated as the first step in the process. You can do so using the following command:

```
Router(tcl)#array startsearch InterfaceCount
s-1-InterfaceCount
```

Depending on how many times you generate a token and what the array name is, you will receive a different output. In a "real" script, this is a good opportunity to store it as a variable for future reference.

Using the previously generated token, you can begin searching through the list using the **nextelement** command:

```
Router(tcl)#array nextelement InterfaceCount s-1-InterfaceCount
GigabitEthernet0/0
```

To determine whether the array contains additional elements, use the **anymore** command, as follows:

```
Router(tcl)#array anymore InterfaceCount s-1-InterfaceCount
1
```

The result of **1** indicates that other elements are available.

You would use the **nextelement** command to display the next element in the array:

```
Router(tcl)#array nextelement InterfaceCount s-1-InterfaceCount
GigabitEthernet0/1
```

To terminate the search, use the **donesearch** command with the token. This command destroys all state information associated with the search:

```
Router(tcl)#array donesearch InterfaceCount s-1-InterfaceCount
```

Lastly, you have the capability to remove elements from the array using the **unset** command. For example, you can remove the element **GigabitEthernet0/1** as follows:

```
Router(tcl)#array unset InterfaceCount GigabitEthernet0/1
```

You can see that the element **GigabitEthernet0/1** has been removed from the array:

```
Router(tcl)#array get InterfaceCount
GigabitEthernet0/0 {382212 5133 125233} Serial0/0/0 {336373 383 27383}
Router(tcl)#
```

To see a list of the names of all the elements in an array, use the **names** command:

```
Router(tcl)#array names InterfaceCount
GigabitEthernet0/0 Serial0/0/0 GigabitEthernet0/1
Router(tcl)#
```

if Command

The **if** command evaluates an expression in a Tcl script, resulting in a Boolean value. If the value of the expression is true, the block of code is executed. If the value is false, the code block is ignored and another code block is executed.

The following example sets the variable **drops** to 0 and uses an **if-else** statement to verify the value.

```
Router(tcl)#set drops {0}
0
```

In the following statements, the **if** command checks whether the values of **drops** is absolutely equal to 0. In this case, the evaluation is true, and the **puts** command displaying **interface has no drops, and the value is 0** is executed, and the **else** section of the script is never executed:

```
Router(tcl)#if {$drops == 0} {
puts "interface has no drops, and the value is $drops"
} else {
puts "interface has drops and the value for the drops is $drops"}
interface has no drops, and the value is 0
```

In this example, the value of **drops** will be set to 23:

```
Router(tcl)#set drops {23}
23
```

Because the value of **drops** is not absolutely equal to 0, the **else** statement is evaluated and the output of the **puts** command is **interface has drops and the value for the drops is 23**:

```
Router(tcl)#if {$drops == 0} {
puts "interface has no drops, and the value is $drops"
```

```
} else {
puts "interface has drops and the value for the drops is $drops"}
interface has drops and the value for the drops is 23
```

switch Command

The **switch** command is a powerful conditional command in the Tcl scripting language. This command evaluates a pattern match on a string and runs the associated commands. The *default* variable can be used to run a command set in the event that there was not a specific string match.

The syntax for the **switch** command is as follows:

```
switch ?switches? string pattern body ... ?default body?
```

The *?switches?* parameter consists of the following options:

- **-exact:** Compares the exact string pattern and is the default match pattern used.
- **-glob:** Matches filenames.
- **-regexp:** Matches regular expression match criteria.

The following example sets the value of **drops** to 1 and uses the **switch** command to evaluate the condition:

```
Router(tcl)#set drops 1
```

Using the **switch** command, the evaluation matches 1 and the **put** command displays a 1:

```
Router(tcl)#switch $drops {
    "0" {
      puts "0"
     }
    "1" {
      puts "1"
     }
    default {
      puts "default"
    }
}
}
1
```

Any value other than a **0** or **1** will cause the **default** section to execute. It is a good practice to always include the **default** in all **case** statements, because if no matching value is found, an empty string is returned.

In Tcl, no **break** statement is needed, and each case will not result in a fall through as it does in the C programming language.

Files

Opening a file inside a program, or script in this case, requires much more attention to detail! Not only do you have to open the file for reading/writing, but you need to make sure that you close the file when you are finished with it; otherwise, you will waste resources. In addition, when a file is open, you have to know the location of the pointer to either read from or write to the contents.

The following example takes you through several commands in listing files, creating a file, writing information to that file, reading the contents, moving the pointer, closing the file, and finally deleting the file.

The first example begins by getting a list of the files that currently exist in the flash: file system of the router. You can do so using the **dir** command, which provides a list of files in the specified directory:

```
Router(tcl)#dir flash:
Directory of flash:/
    1  -rw-     31261340  Dec 31 1983 00:01:00 +00:00  c2800nm-ipbasek9-mz.124-
       24.T1.bin
    2  -rw-         3660  Jul 21 2009 20:28:04 +00:00  interface_errors_email.tcl
```

> **Note**   The **dir** command is not a Tcl command. This is an example where the Tcl inter-
> preter does not recognize the command and so sends it to the Cisco IOS exec-mode parser.

The output indicates that there are two files: the IOS image and a file called interface_errors_email.tcl. Notice on the left the letters *rw*. This indicates that the files can be opened for reading or writing. The file size is also shown, along with the creation date.

Next, create a file called IntStats.dat, which will be used to store information about (you guessed it) interface statistics. When opening a file, you have several options, including the following:

- **r:** Open for reading

- **r+:** Open for reading and writing

- **w:** Open for writing, overwrite existing file, or create a new one

- **w+:** Open for reading and writing, overwrite existing file, or create a new one

- **a:** Open for writing and append to file

- **a+:** Open for reading and writing and append to file

The following example creates a file called IntStats.dat for writing and declares a variable called IntStats to reference the open file handle:

```
Router(tcl)#set IntStats [open IntStats.dat w]
file7
```

Using information from the example on arrays, you will populate the file:

```
Router(tcl)#puts $IntStats "GigabitEthernet0/0 {382212 5133 125233}"
Router(tcl)#puts $IntStats "GigabitEthernet0/1 {382212 5133 125233}"
Router(tcl)#puts $IntStats "Serial0/0/0 {336373 383 27383}"
```

Notice that the **puts** command is used to send information to the file rather than to the terminal.

To close the file, enter the following:

```
Router(tcl)#close $IntStats
```

To verify that the file has been created, enter the following:

```
Router(tcl)#dir flash:
Directory of flash:/
    1  -rw-     31261340  Dec 31 1983 00:01:00 +00:00  c2800nm-ipbasek9-mz.124-
       24.T1.bin
    2  -rw-         3660  Jul 21 2009 20:28:04 +00:00
       interface_errors_email.tcl
    4  -rw-          111  Jul 28 2009 04:02:42 +00:00  IntStats.dat
       31885312 bytes total (616448 bytes free)
```

The file IntStats is in the flash: directory with a file size of 111 bytes.

To open the file you just created for reading only, use the **r** option:

```
Router(tcl)#set IntStats [open IntStats.dat r]
file7
```

Now you can get some data from the open file using the **gets** command as demonstrated in the following example, and place that information in the variable **data**:

```
Router(tcl)#gets $IntStats data
39
```

What in the world is 39? That is not the data that you stored! The number 39 indicates where the pointer resides in the file. Look at the collected data using the **puts** command:

```
Router(tcl)#puts $data
GigabitEthernet0/0 {382212 5133 125233}
```

As you can see from the output, you have just the first line of data. If you count the number of characters starting from the left (do not forget to start with 0), you will see that you collected 38 characters plus newline (**\n**).

You can also determine where the pointer is by using the **tell** command as follows:

```
Router(tcl)#tell $IntStats
40
```

Now that you know the pointer is on the first character of the second line, you can gather some additional information using the **read** command. In this case, get the next 18 bytes:

```
Router(tcl)#read $IntStats 18
GigabitEthernet0/1
```

No surprise here: The output is **GigabitEthernet0/1**, as expected.

With the **read** command, you can read the rest of the file, as follows:

```
Router(tcl)#read $IntStats
 {382212 5133 125233}
GigabitEthernet0/1 {382212 5133 125233}
```

Now when you check to see where the pointer is, you can see that it is at the end of the file (EOF):

```
Router(tcl)#tell $IntStats
111
```

The file pointer can be moved to any location using the **seek** command. To direct the pointer to the beginning of the file, use the following command statement:

```
Router(tcl)#seek $IntStats 0
```

> **Note** Not all Cisco IOS File System (IFS) devices support the **seek** operation. Some older flash types might not be supported.

You can use other methods covered earlier in the chapter to manipulate or search through the file for specific information.

When you have finished pulling information from the file, you should close it. Otherwise, you are wasting valuable memory resources. To close the file, simply use the following command:

```
Router(tcl)#close $IntStats
```

Finally, when you need to delete file, use the following command (with extreme caution):

```
Router(tcl)#file delete IntStats.dat
```

This should really be said for any of the **file** commands. You could inadvertently open or overwrite the IOS image or other files located on the flash, so always use care when manipulating files. In addition, files can be opened on remote devices. For example, you can open a file on a TFTP server using the following command:

```
Router(tcl)#open tftp://192.168.0.182/file.dat "w"
```

Summary

One of the best ways to familiarize yourself with the commands and procedures discussed in this chapter is hands-on practice. If you do not have access to a router, you can perform most of what you previously read about on your own personal computer. Just install the appropriate Tcl shell software if it is not already there.

One last note of caution: When cutting and pasting information into a Tcl shell, you might be challenged with formatting errors. For example, quotes might not paste properly and may cause some interesting issues.

References

Tcl Command Reference: http://www.tcl.tk/man/tcl8.3/TclCmd/contents.htm

## Chapter 3

Tcl Functioning in Cisco IOS

This chapter covers the following topics:

- Understanding the Tcl Interpreter in Cisco IOS

- Using Tcl to Enter Commands

- Copying a Tcl Script to an Cisco IOS Device

- Using Tcl to Examine the Cisco IOS Device Configuration

- Using Tcl to Modify the Router Configuration

- Using Tcl with SNMP to Check MIB Variables

Tcl operates as a process within IOS. It provides the capability of running Tcl scripts natively within IOS. As you will discover throughout this book, Tcl scripts can simplify repetitive tasks, automate processes, provide notification about specific events, or even be used to create a graphical user interface (GUI). Tcl is one of those tools that you need to have readily available in your tool bag. The more you understand how to leverage Tcl, the more powerfully it will enable you to operate and troubleshoot your network infrastructure. Tcl interpreters might be in several processes depending on the features being used. A Tcl shell can spawn a server process for each vty entering tclsh parser mode. Interactive Voice Response (IVR) maintains a cache of Tcl interpreters/processes to service incoming calls.

Understanding the Tcl Interpreter in Cisco IOS

The Tcl interpreter is available for use in certain IOS software images. See Table 1-1 in Chapter 1, "The Origin of Tcl," to determine which platform and IOS images are supported, or see the appropriate documentation for the specified device. You can also verify that the image you are using has the Tcl interpreter by just entering the command **tclsh** at the router prompt. Be sure that you are first in enable mode, which you can determine by looking at the command prompt:

```
Router>
! this is not yet in enable mode
Router>enable
Router#
! now we have entered enable mode
```

You might also be required to enter the enable mode password or username and password if additional authentication has been configured.

To check whether the Tcl interpreter is present, enter **tclsh** and observe if the command prompt changes:

```
Router#tclsh
Router(tcl)#
```

You can now see the command prompt has changed to show that you are in Tcl mode. Commands entered at the (tcl) prompt will be first handled by the Tcl interpreter, if it understands them. If the Tcl interpreter does not understand the commands, they will be passed along to the device's normal command handler.

Lastly, you can do an alternative check to see whether the image you are running has the Tcl interpreter, without actually entering the Tcl interpreter. Use the following command:

```
Router#show subsys name tcl
Name            Class        Version
tcl             Library      2.000.001
```

In the preceding example, you can see the Tcl library is present. This means the device software version you are using does have the capability to run the Tcl interpreter. If the device does not have a Tcl interpreter, the output would appear as follows:

```
Router#show subsys name tcl
Name            Class     Version
```

Using Cisco IOS Exec-Mode Parser in the Tcl Shell

The Tcl shell is not only used to process Tcl commands on Cisco IOS, it can also be use to send commands to the Cisco IOS exec-mode parser. As stated previously, all commands are first handled by the Tcl interpreter, unless the interpreter does not recognize the command. In that case, the command is passed along to the IOS command handler. The following examples explain how the interpreter functions.

Enter **info** at the Tcl command interpreter prompt, as follows:

```
Router(tcl)#info
wrong # args: should be "info option ?arg arg ...?"
```

Notice that you have provided the proper Tcl command, but have neglected to enter the appropriate options for which Tcl is looking. In this case, Tcl provides a brief help string about what went wrong.

In this example, you see that **info** must be followed by a valid option or options. If you are not familiar with all the options, you can simply enter one and see how it works. This example arbitrarily uses the word **games** as an option, as follows:

```
Router(tcl)#info games
bad option "games": must be args, body, cmdcount, commands, complete, default,
    exists, globals,
hostname, level, library, loaded, locals, nameofexecutable, patchlevel, procs,
    script, sharedlibextension, tclversion, or vars
```

The output of the Tcl interpreter has provided all the possible options associated with the base command. As you can see, you have quite a few choices!

The next example uses the option **tclversion** to display the current version:

```
Router(tcl)#info tclversion
8.3
```

If you are interested in more detailed information about the patch level of the Tcl interpreter, you can choose the **patchlevel** option, as follows:

```
Router(tcl)#info patchlevel
8.3.4
```

From the preceding output, you can see that the router has patch level 8.3.4 of the Tcl interpreter.

Note   There were also a few images that contained code for parser mode in Tcl 7.1, although this was not officially supported.

Entering an IOS Command into the Tcl Command Interpreter

Now that you have seen how a Tcl command behaves, you will next see how an IOS command that is entered into the Tcl command interpreter can be used. If the command is not recognized by the Tcl interpreter, it is passed along to the standard IOS command processor. This is similar to how Tcl behaves in a host-based environment.

The following IOS command, used to view the IP status of the interfaces, is entered into the Tcl command interpreter:

```
Router(tcl)#show ip interface brief
Interface            IP-Address      OK? Method Status                Protocol
Ethernet0/0          192.168.1.1     YES manual up                    up
Ethernet0/1          10.0.0.1        YES manual administratively down  down
Ethernet0/2          unassigned      YES NVRAM  administratively down  down
Ethernet0/3          unassigned      YES NVRAM  administratively down  down
```

In the preceding example, the IOS command **show ip interface brief** is not understood by the Tcl interpreter, even though it was entered at the (tcl) prompt. Because the command is not understood, it is passed to the normal IOS command handler, which provides the results.

As you can see, the ability to have commands "fall through" to the underlying operating system can be powerful. This is quite handy for collecting information from the router and acting on the output within a Tcl script. (You are probably already thinking of all the intelligent Tcl scripts that you could write.)

Using Tcl to Enter Commands

This section covers how to write a script that collects the output from an IOS command so that you can make a decision based on the output.

Suppose you want to know whether the router has any interfaces with an IP address in the 10.0.0.0/24 network.

Although commands that the Tcl interpreter does not recognize are passed along to the normal IOS interpreter, you do not have to or should not rely on this, because it will consume additional processing resources. If you know in advance that you want to send the command directly to the IOS command processor, you can use a special Tcl command named **exec**. To pass a command directly to the IOS command processor while in the Tcl shell, enter the command in quotes after the Tcl **exec** command:

```
Router(tcl)#exec "show ip interface brief"
Interface              IP-Address      OK? Method Status                Protocol
Ethernet0/0            192.168.1.1     YES manual up                    up
Ethernet0/1            10.0.0.1        YES manual administratively down down
Ethernet0/2            unassigned      YES NVRAM  administratively down down
Ethernet0/3            unassigned      YES NVRAM  administratively down down
```

Although you are still in the Tcl shell, the output of the **show ip interface brief** command is displayed.

To save the output of the command, the collected information can now be stored in a variable, namely **mybuffer**, as the following example shows:

```
Router(tcl)#set mybuffer [exec "show ip interface brief"]
Interface              IP-Address      OK? Method Status                Protocol
Ethernet0/0            192.168.1.1     YES manual up                    up
Ethernet0/1            10.0.0.1        YES manual administratively down down
Ethernet0/2            unassigned      YES NVRAM  administratively down down
Ethernet0/3            unassigned      YES NVRAM  administratively down down
Router(tcl)#
```

Note   You can suppress the output of the command results using the **log_user** command. To suppress the results, use the follow command:

```
Router(tcl)#log_user 0
0
```

Note   To display the results (default behavior), use the following command:

```
Router(tcl)#log_user 1
1
```

You can verify that **mybuffer** contains the contents you are interested in. The Tcl command **puts** will display the contents of any text buffer:

```
Router(tcl)#puts $mybuffer
Interface            IP-Address      OK? Method Status                Protocol
Ethernet0/0          192.168.1.1     YES manual up                    up
Ethernet0/1          10.0.0.1        YES manual administratively down down
Ethernet0/2          unassigned      YES NVRAM  administratively down down
Ethernet0/3          unassigned      YES NVRAM  administratively down down
```

Now that the command has been captured in a buffer, you can run a Tcl command against it for further processing.

The following command determines how many bytes are contained in the string:

```
Router(tcl)#string bytelength $mybuffer
430
```

All the characters can be changed to uppercase, as follows:

```
Router(tcl)#string toupper $mybuffer
INTERFACE            IP-ADDRESS      OK? METHOD STATUS                PROTOCOL
ETHERNET0/0          192.168.1.1     YES MANUAL UP                    UP
ETHERNET0/1          10.0.0.1        YES MANUAL ADMINISTRATIVELY DOWN DOWN
ETHERNET0/2          UNASSIGNED      YES NVRAM  ADMINISTRATIVELY DOWN DOWN
ETHERNET0/3          UNASSIGNED      YES NVRAM  ADMINISTRATIVELY DOWN DOWN
```

Returning to the original intention of the exercise (to determine whether the router has an interface in the 10.0.0.0/24 network), begin the script with a command to save the output of **show ip interface brief** into a buffer:

```
Router(tcl)#set mybuffer [exec "show ip interface brief"]
```

With the information stored in a variable, you can use the **string first** command to search the string named **mybuffer** for **10.0.0**. If the search string is found, the Tcl command will return a byte count number, corresponding to the first occurrence of the search string. Use the following command:

```
Router(tcl)#string first "10.0.0." $mybuffer
201
```

If the search string "**10.0.0.**" is found, the Tcl interpreter returns an integer value of the character number corresponding to the beginning of the search string. If the search string is not found, a **-1** is returned. Based on the returned value, you can make a decision whether the text buffer contains the network of interest "**10.0.0.***".

You can save the position of "**10.0.0.***" in the variable **foundposition** as follows:

```
Router(tcl)#set foundposition [string first "10.0.0." $mybuffer]
201
```

Next, you can determine whether the network was present in our router, by using the following command:

```
Router(tcl)#if {$foundposition > -1} {
puts "We found the 10.0.0.* network!"
}
We found the 10.0.0.* network!
```

Combining the previous commands, the entire script would appear as follows:

```
set mybuffer [exec "show ip interface brief"]
set foundposition [string first "10.0.0." $mybuffer]
if {$foundposition > -1} {
    puts "We found the 10.0.0.* network!"
}
```

The script is now finished. You can either enter the commands line by line at the Tcl prompt or save the script on the IOS device to be used later.

Copying a Tcl Script to a Cisco IOS Device

Entering Tcl commands on a line-by-line basis is an arduous task. To take advantage of the real power of Tcl, the script needs to reside on the IOS device or server.

You can copy the script to the IOS device in several different ways. Scripts can be transferred using Trivial File Transfer Protocol (TFTP), File Transfer Protocol (FTP), Secure

Copy Protocol (SCP), Hypertext Transfer Protocol (HTTP), Hypertext Transfer Protocol Secure (HTTPS), XModem, Ymodem, Remote File Copy (RCP), or even using "sneaker-net" (copying the script to removable media and walking it to the device).

To transfer scripts to an IOS device, other than sneakernet, a server must be configured to host the file-transfer service. This could be your PC, a UNIX host, or an IOS device that contains the script.

TFTP is one of the more common methods. As previously noted, a TFTP server must first be configured. Several commercial, free, and integrated applications are readily available for most operating systems. It is beyond the scope of this book to provide installation and configuration documentation on file server applications.

After the TFTP server has been set up and configured properly, the procedure to copy the Tcl script to the IOS device (flash:) is as follows:

```
Router#copy tftp: flash:
Address or name of remote host []? 192.168.1.17
Source filename []? chap3e1.tcl
Destination filename [chap3e1.tcl]? myscript.tcl
Accessing tftp://192.168.1.17/chap3e1.tcl...
Loading chap3e1.tcl from 192.168.1.17 (via Tunnel1): !
[OK - 170 bytes]
170 bytes copied in 0.100 secs (1700 bytes/sec)
```

Caution   Be aware, there are no inherent mechanisms within TFTP to validate a login, and the data (script) is sent across the network in clear text. Someone with a packet sniffer could easily capture the information you are retrieving from the TFTP server, or log in to the TFTP server and download data.

FTP provides an alternative to transfer a Tcl script to an IOS device. Many FTP software applications are available. Use the following command on the IOS device to copy a file via FTP, and follow the prompts:

```
Router#copy ftp: flash:
```

Although FTP has a mechanism for username and passwords, the information is sent in the clear across the network. Consequently, passwords and data can be easily captured.

A more secure method to transfer a script to an IOS device is using SCP. SCP uses the Secure Shell (SSH) protocol to securely transfer information. Unlike TFTP and FTP, the passwords and actual data transferred during the interactive session are all encrypted. To begin a secure copy, follow the prompts after entering the following command:

```
Router#copy scp: flash:
```

Cisco IOS devices also can transfer files using either HTTP or the secure HTTPS protocol. HTTP is the protocol used by web browsers, and HTTPS builds on top of that protocol by adding security. Follow the prompts after entering the following command on the IOS device:

```
Router#copy http: (or https:) flash:
```

After the script has been copied to the IOS device, it can now be executed. Before starting the script, you must validate that the script is present, using the following command:

```
Router#dir flash:chap3e1.tcl
Directory of flash:/chap3e1.tcl
   18  -rw-        170  Sep 16 2009 23:56:48 +00:00  chap3e1.tcl
```

The script is located in the local flash.

To start the script, you must enter Tcl mode and start the script using the **source** command as follows:

```
Router(tcl)#source flash:chap3e1.tcl
We found the 10.0.0.* network!
```

The preceding example is interactively running a Tcl interpreter. The Tcl interpreter exists both before the **source** command is entered and continues to run after the **source** command finishes. Why is this important? The Tcl script will have access to any variables or procedures that may exist before the Tcl script is "sourced," and you can examine any variables or procedures left behind by the **source** command.

For example:

```
Router(tcl)#puts $foundposition
201
```

The variable **foundpostion** did not exist in the running Tcl interpreter until you sourced the Tcl script and created the variable. To get a list of all variables known by the current Tcl interpreter, you can enter the following:

```
Router(tcl)#info vars
mybuffer tcl_interactive tcl_version sys_type argv argv0 tcl_traceCompile
   tclDefaultLibrary
foundposition tcl_pkgPath tcl_patchLevel argc tcl_traceExec tcl_platform
```

Most of the variables are created automatically for you. However, you can see other variables in the list created from the previous script, **mybuffer** and **foundposition**. When you exit the Tcl interpreter, these variables will be destroyed and will not persist after the exit, as shown here:

```
Router(tcl)#exit
Router#tclsh
Router(tcl)#info vars
tcl_version sys_type argv argv0 tcl_interactive tclDefaultLibrary tcl_pkgPath
   tcl_patchLevel argc
tcl_traceExec tcl_platform
```

The preceding examples demonstrated how a Tcl script can be run interactively using the **source** command. Alternatively, the Tcl script can be run one time and then immediately exit the Tcl interpreter. This could be done to run a more complicated script where you are only interested in the end result and do not want to examine any variables after the script completes. For this reason, IOS provides additional parameters to the **tclsh** command, similar to what is provided in a UNIX environment:

```
Router#tclsh flash:chap3e1.tcl
We found the 10.0.0.* network!
```

From the preceding output, you can see that a new Tcl interpreter is started, and it immediately "sourced" the script named **flash:chap3e1.tcl** and presented the output. In the end, the Tcl interpreter was destroyed when the Tcl script completed.

Fetching a Cisco IOS Tcl Script from a Remote Device

As a further convenience, Tcl on IOS can fetch a script from a remote device and immediately execute the script. This obviates the need to copy the script to the IOS device. Yes, all that work for nothing! All the other previously mentioned methods used to copy the Tcl script are supported. For example, if you do not want to maintain files local to the IOS device, a Tcl script located on a remote server can easily be initiated. You can tell Tcl to fetch the script and run it, as follows:

```
Router#tclsh tftp://192.168.1.17/chap3e1.tcl
Loading chap3e1.tcl from 192.168.1.17 (via Tunnel1): !
[OK - 170 bytes]
We found the 10.0.0.* network!
```

As long as a valid path is provided to Tcl, a script can be downloaded and run.

Note   You can also pass arguments to the Tcl script using the **tclsh** syntax as follows:

```
Router#tclsh tftp://192.168.1.17/chap3e1.tcl passed_arguments
```

Using Tcl to Examine the Cisco IOS Device Configuration

Tcl on IOS extends the Tcl interpreter with some unique functionality that makes it easier to examine and modify the router configuration. As you can imagine, this feature can be powerful.

The running-configuration contains all the settings and customization that has been done to the IOS device, from the initial state. The configuration is generally viewed using various commands, such as **show running-config**, to display the current state of the configuration.

On entering the following command, the entire running configuration will be stored in a variable called **config**:

```
Router(tcl)#set config [exec "show running"]
```

After the information has been saved in a variable, you can view that variable for any configuration commands of interest. For example, suppose you are interested in checking what time zone has been configured. A simple script that will display the time zone is as follows:

```
set runconfig [exec "show running-config"]
set foundposition [string first "clock timezone" $runconfig]
set cutoff [string length "clock timezone"]
if {$foundposition > -1} {
    set cutoff [string length "clock timezone"]
    set begin [expr $foundposition + $cutoff]
    set end [string first "\n" $runconfig $begin]
    set timezone [string range $runconfig $begin $end]
    puts "We found the timezone!"
    puts -nonewline "The current timezone is"
    puts $timezone
}
```

The following list describes the script:

1. The entire configuration is stored in a variable called **runconfig** with the **set runconfig [exec "show running-config"]** command.

2. Using the following **string** command locates the integer position of the configuration command **clock timezone**:

    ```
    Router(tcl)#set foundposition [string first "clock timezone" $runconfig]
    393
    ```

3. If the **clock timezone** string is not present, **if {$foundposition > -1}**, the commands following are not processed and the script will be completed.

4. The string length of **clock timezone** is calculated and stored in a variable using the following command:

    ```
    Router(tcl)#set cutoff [string length "clock timezone"]
    14
    ```

5. To glean the contents of the **timezone** variable and not include the keywords **clock timezone**, the following command is used to populate a variable with the beginning location of the contents:

    ```
    Router(tcl)#set begin [expr $foundposition + $cutoff]
    407
    ```

6. The following statement sets the variable **end** to the first newline (**\n**) occurrence in the string (**runconfig**) starting at the location **begin**:

    ```
    Router(tcl)#set end [string first "\n" $runconfig $begin]
    414
    ```

7. The following command collects the time zone information from the **runconfig** string and stores it in the **timezone** variable:

```
Router(tcl)#set timezone [string range $runconfig $begin $end]
 PST -8
```

8. Using the following statement displays a message indicating that the time zone was found:

```
Router(tcl)#puts "We found the timezone!"
We found the timezone!
```

9. The **puts -nonewline "The current timezone is"** and the **puts $timezone** commands display the time zone:

```
Router(tcl)#puts $timezone
The current timezone is PST -8
```

Using Tcl to Modify the Router Configuration

Tcl can also be used to add or modify any setting in the IOS device. This section explains how to change the hostname of the device.

Using the **ios_config** command, a one-line statement is used to change the hostname of the router, as follows:

```
Router(tcl)#ios_config "hostname TCLRouter"
TCLRouter(tcl)#
```

To make the changes permanent, you must copy the running-config to the startup-config and add one line to the script:

```
exec "copy running-config startup-config"
```

Now you can run the script and see that IOS has saved its configuration permanently as indicated by **[OK]** in the output, and notice that the hostname has changed:

```
Router#tclsh tftp://192.168.0.186/chap3e2.tcl
Loading chap3e2.tcl from 192.168.0.186 (via GigabitEthernet0/0): !
[OK - 73 bytes]
TCLRouter#
```

Note   It is not a recommended practice to enter configuration mode from the Tcl shell because this has been known to cause collisions between configuration commands and Tcl commands.

Using Tcl with SNMP to Check MIB Variables

One little-known tool available within Tcl on IOS is the ability to check any Simple Network Management Protocol (SNMP) Management Information Base (MIB) variable. SNMP is a protocol that enables system administrators to check various counters and information about devices connected to a network. Some standard MIBs define what variables mean and how to interpret the data. The data can come as simple variables, such as textual or numeric, or it can be tabular, too.

SNMP is typically used by a graphical network management application that can be used to check on various devices throughout the network. Many commercial and free software packages can be used to examine the network and troubleshoot issues that may arise.

One common use for SNMP is in developing graphical maps that show an overall picture of the network, showing connections between devices and the overall topology diagrams.

Other Uses of SNMP

SNMP can also be used to collect information, such as interface errors, interface input/output statistics, CPU utilization, memory usage, and so on, from devices on the network. This information can be saved over a period of time to develop trend statistics that will help in determining what resources need to be allocated to meet the changing demands. As an alternative to the CLI or graphical network configuration tools, SNMP is also used to make configuration changes on network devices.

Another widespread use of SNMP is to troubleshoot network issues. Suppose a device on the network has been determined to be causing problems on the network. Various MIBs exist on the device for different networking protocols and interface counters. When additional information is required from a "device of interest," you can drill down and view MIB information for a closer look at to how the device is performing.

One common question a system administrator may ask is this: What is this device, and how long has it been up and running? In the SNMP world, you would examine objects within the SNMPv2-MIB file, and look at the object sysDescr for more information about the device. Of course, someone needs to enter this information in the device for it to be useful. Another MIB object to determine how long the system has been running is the sysUpTime.

A typical IOS device will have many interfaces connected to the network. You can check each of these interfaces at the router prompt by typing commands such as **show interface**. Although it is convenient for a human to examine interfaces in this way, it is not so easy for a graphical network management application to understand the output. For this reason, an "interfaces" MIB was designed to standardize the information available for various types of interfaces and collect all the pertinent information in one place. The "interfaces MIB" is shortened to just IF-MIB in the actual names of objects within it.

Another common question to answer is this: What interfaces are present on this device? If you were connected to the IOS device, you could simply enter **show interfaces** and look at the output. With SNMP, you need to send a packet or series of packets requesting the information from the device, the ifTable of the IF-MIB.

Every item defined in the MIB has an object identifier (OID). It is just a numeric representation of what piece of information you are looking at, and can be thought of as a very long telephone number that gives us an exact item we are interested in. It also represents a hierarchy, in that related information is within the same MIB.

Cisco provides an "SNMP object navigator" to help understand where a given object fits in the hierarchy:

http://tools.cisco.com/Support/SNMP/do/BrowseOID.do?local=en

When you are searching the IF-MIB, the specific object information is shown as follows:

- **Object:** IF-MIB.

- **OID:** 1.3.6.1.2.1.31.

- **MIB:** IF-MIB.

- **Description:** This MIB describes the generic objects for a network interface sublayer and is an updated version of MIB-II's ifTable. It incorporates the extensions defined in RFC 1229.

In addition, a hierarchy diagram shows where it fits in with the all MIBs, as shown in Figure 3-1.

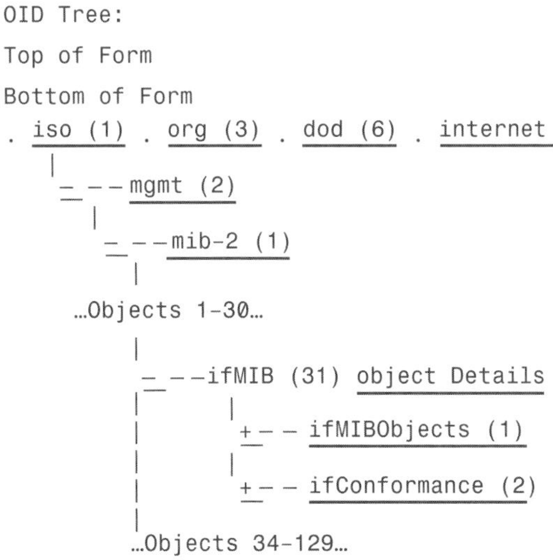

```
OID Tree:
Top of Form
Bottom of Form
 . iso (1) . org (3) . dod (6) . internet (1)
     |
     _ − −mgmt (2)
        |
        _ − −mib-2 (1)
           |
    …Objects 1−30…
          |
          _ − −ifMIB (31) object Details
          |      |
          |      +− − ifMIBObjects (1)
          |      |
          |      +− − ifConformance (2)
          |
    …Objects 34−129…
```

Figure 3-1 *IF-MIB Hierarchy*

At the top of the hierarchy, the highest-level organization (iso.org.dod.internet) defines objects. Most of the standard MIBs developed by the IETF will fall somewhere below this level, and therefore their individual OIDs will begin with the same number (1.3.6.1…).

As you progress lower in the hierarchy, suborganizations may define their own MIBs within the tree. An organization such as Cisco Systems is free to define its own custom MIBs, such as the CISCO-DLSW-MIB, as shown here:

■   **Object:** ciscoDlswMIB.

■   **OID:** 1.3.6.1.4.1.9.10.9.

■   **MIB:** CISCO-DLSW-MIB.

■   **Description:** This MIB module contains objects to manage data-link switches.

Figure 3-2 illustrates the Cisco MIB hierarchy.

```
OID Tree:
Top of Form
Bottom of Form
. iso (1) . org (3) . dod (6) . internet (1) . private (4).
enterprises (1)
    |
    _ -- cisco (9)
       |
    …Objects 1-9…
       |
       _ ---ciscoExperiment (10)
       |
    …Objects…
       |
       |                 _ ---ciscoDlswMIB (9) object Details
       |        |        |
       |        |        +-- ciscoDlswMIBObjects (1)
       |        |        |
       |        |        +-- ciscoDlswDomains (2)
       |        |        |
       |        |        +-- ciscoDlswConformance (3)
    …Objects continue…
       |
       +-- ciscoAdmin (11)
       |
    …Objects continue…
```

Figure 3-2   *Cisco MIB Hierarchy*

Most of the MIBs defined by Cisco Systems will fall below the level iso.org.dod.internet.private.enterprises.cisco, and therefore, their individual OIDs will all begin with the same number (1.3.6.1.4.1.9…).

The root item in the IF-MIB is ifMIBObjects, and the first item we can use is ifTableLastChange. This item fits in the hierarchy of the MIB as ifMIBObjects.5. In this case, ifTableLastChange is the fifth item underneath ifMIBObjects.

The description of ifTableLastChange is "the value of sysUpTime at the time of the last creation or deletion of an entry in the ifTable." It tells you what time the interface table was last changed. The next example queries the ifTableLastChange to see how you can use the information.

Enabling SNMP on a Cisco IOS Device

Before any SNMP queries can be performed on an IOS device, the SNMP protocol needs to be enabled. When enabling SNMP, a community string is specified, which essentially acts as a primitive layer of security. The correct community string must be provided in any incoming SNMP request. Without the correct string, no response will be provided. In addition, many community strings may be entered, each with their own security level. For now, we simply configure one SNMP community with the default access, read-only (RO). This prevents any changes to the configuration of the router being performed from within SNMP. Enter the following command in configuration mode:

```
Router(config)#snmp-server community public RO
```

Note   It is not a recommended to use **public** as the read community string for production networks, because this is the default value that many devices use.

Now you are able to make SNMP requests from within the Tcl interpreter. You have the ability to query the ifTableLastChange by fully specifying its location in the IF-MIB hierarchy:

```
Router(tcl)#snmp_getone public ifMIB.1.5.0
{<obj oid='ifTableLastChange.0' val='121'/>}
```

From the output, the value of **121** represents the elapsed time in SNMP. It shows you that the last time anything changed in the Interfaces Table was 121 ms after the router started.

The object that was returned in response to the query was changed from **ifMIB.1.5.0** to **ifTableLastChange.0**. The IOS device has simplified the request, because it has changed the OID to the more specific one. In the future, you can simply query **ifTableLastChange.0**.

Note   Every SNMP must have an instance, indicated as 0 in **ifTableLastChange.0**. Scalar objects (for example, ifTableLastChange) will always have a 0 index, and tabular objects (for example, ifDescr) will always have at least one non-0 index.

The router has also answered the SNMP request by placing the response in XML encoding. OIDs are noted with **obj oid**, and MIB values are shown using **val**. The XML encoding can be used by Tcl to recognize elements parsing the response data.

Querying the Configuration of a Cisco IOS Device Using SNMP

The next example adds a new interface called Loopback 3 to the IOS device and queries the SNMP MIB. Adding a new interface will cause the device to modify the Interfaces Table. Therefore, the last update time will change to reflect the change:

```
Router(tcl)#ios_config "int Loopback 3" "end"
*Aug 10 20:23:17.987: %LINEPROTO-5-UPDOWN: Line protocol on Interface Loopback3,
    changed state to up
Router(tcl)#snmp_getone public ifMIB.1.5.0
{<obj oid='ifTableLastChange.0' val='811373'/>}
```

> **Note**   To minimize locking of the configuration, use the **"end"** parameter as the final statement in the **ios_config** command.

Notice the value has changed from **121** to **811373**, which indicates the Interfaces Table has been modified. Whenever this value has increased from the last time you checked it, you can be sure the Interfaces Table has been modified, indicating that an interface was either added or removed.

The **sysUpTime** parameter is a 32-bit numeric value that indicates the time a change was made in reference to the system uptime, with the least significant number being .01 seconds. You can determine the time as follows:

811373/100 = seconds

    8113.73 seconds

811373/60 = minutes

     135.22 minutes

135.22/60 = hours

     2.25 hours

The last change was 2.25 hours after the system started.

SNMP MIB objects are kept in a particular order. It is possible to request information about the next object after the current object. You might wonder why SNMP needs this capability and why **getone** is insufficient? There are two reasons. The first is that there may be gaps in a particular implementation of a MIB. Certain objects are optional, and a particular vendor such as Cisco might choose to or not to implement a specific object. Objects might be left unimplemented if they are too difficult or CPU intensive to calculate. The second reason is that **getone** is not sufficient because of tables, as explained next.

You can query the next object after ifTableLastChange using **snmp_getnext** command:

```
Router(tcl)#snmp_getnext public ifTableLastChange.0
{<obj oid='ifStackLastChange.0' val='811373'/>}
```

The ifStackLastChange is the next object after ifTableLastChange. If the process is continued, the entire MIB tree can be "walked":

```
Router(tcl)#snmp_getnext public ifTableLastChange.0
{<obj oid='ifStackLastChange.0' val='326343004'/>}
Router(tcl)#snmp_getnext public ifStackLastChange.0
{<obj oid='atmTrafficDescrParamEntry.2.0' val='mib-2.37.1.1.1'/>}
Router(tcl)#snmp_getnext public atmTrafficDescrParamEntry.2.0
{<obj oid='atmTrafficDescrParamEntry.3.0' val='0'/>}
Router(tcl)#snmp_getnext public atmTrafficDescrParamEntry.3.0
{<obj oid='atmTrafficDescrParamEntry.4.0' val='0'/>}
```

Caution   Entering the **snmp_getnext** command in repetition through a script will essentially perform a "MIB walk" and might cause high CPU utilization. Exercise caution when using this command.

The following example displays every MIB variable, and yes, this will drive up the CPU:

```
set MIB_Object [snmp_getnext public 1.0]
set Start_Position [string first "'" $MIB_Object]
set Number_of_MIBS 0
set Valid_Data -1
while {$Valid_Data == -1} {
    puts $MIB_Object
    set End_Position [string first "' val" $MIB_Object]
    set Next_MIB [string range $MIB_Object [expr $Start_Position + 1] [expr
$End_Position - 1]]
    set MIB_Object [snmp_getnext public $Next_MIB]
    set Start_Position [string first "'" $MIB_Object]
    incr Number_of_MIBS
    set Valid_Data [string first "END_OF_MIB" $MIB_Object]
}
puts "This is the total number of MIB objects: $Number_of_MIBS"
...output suppressed...
{<obj oid='internet.6.3.12.1.4.0' val='0'/>}
{<obj oid='internet.6.3.12.1.5.0' val='0'/>}
This is the total number of MIB objects: 24759
```

The following shows high CPU utilization because of Tcl script:

```
Router#show processes cpu | exclude 0.00
CPU utilization for five seconds: 99%/1%; one minute: 56%; five minutes: 26%
 PID Runtime(ms)     Invoked     uSecs    5Sec    1Min    5Min TTY Process
   2         292      657979         0   0.08%   0.03%   0.02%   0 Load Meter
 115       28460      248046       114   0.48%   0.29%   0.15%   0 IP Input
 231      504916        3819    132211  97.14%  54.48%  25.01% 515 Tcl Serv-tty51
```

In addition to simple objects, SNMP allows for tables to be built that store data. One example is the actual Interfaces Table. If you want to get all the elements from the Interfaces Table, you can repeatedly use **snmp_getnext** until you have passed the last element in the table.

In the Interfaces Table definition, there is an object that stores the name of a particular interface on the router. This object is called ifDescr. The following example will "walk" through all the objects in this table one by one, until you realize you have all of them:

```
Router(tcl)#snmp_getnext public ifDescr.0
{<obj oid='ifDescr.1' val='Ethernet0/0'/>}
Router (tcl)#snmp_getnext public ifDescr.1
{<obj oid='ifDescr.2' val='Ethernet0/1'/>}
Router (tcl)#snmp_getnext public ifDescr.2
{<obj oid='ifDescr.3' val='Ethernet0/2'/>}
Router (tcl)#snmp_getnext public ifDescr.3
{<obj oid='ifDescr.4' val='Ethernet0/3'/>}
Router (tcl)#snmp_getnext public ifDescr.4
{<obj oid='ifDescr.5' val='VoIP-Null0'/>}
Router (tcl)#snmp_getnext public ifDescr.5
{<obj oid='ifDescr.6' val='Null0'/>}
Router (tcl)#snmp_getnext public ifDescr.6
{<obj oid='ifDescr.7' val='Loopback3'/>}
Router (tcl)#snmp_getnext public ifDescr.7
{<obj oid='ifType.1' val='6'/>}
```

From the last line of the output, you see that the device returned the next object after the one you asked it for. The response coming back from the router is simply fed back into the next request. The process continues, until you realize you have walked past the objects you are interested in. When the last response came back, the router responded with ifType.1, which is past the last ifDescr object in the Interfaces Table. As you can see, there are four Ethernet interfaces in the router, plus the loopback interface created earlier. This matches other **show** commands, such as **show ip interface brief**:

```
Router(tcl)#show ip interface brief
Interface        IP-Address      OK? Method Status                 Protocol
Ethernet0/0      unassigned      YES NVRAM  administratively down  down
Ethernet0/1      unassigned      YES NVRAM  administratively down  down
Ethernet0/2      unassigned      YES NVRAM  administratively down  down
Ethernet0/3      unassigned      YES NVRAM  administratively down  down
Loopback3        unassigned      YES NVRAM  up                     up
```

You may have noticed two other interfaces: VoIP-Null0 and Null0. VoIP-Null0 is purely cosmetic and will be enabled when Cisco Express Forwarding (CEF) is turned on, and Null0 is the bit bucket or garbage can for discarding traffic.

Because of the complexity of tables in SNMP, there are other methods besides **snmp_getone** and **snmp_getnext** that can fetch multiple items at once. For convenience, there is also **snmp_getbulk**, which provide a particular number of MIB objects simultaneously.

For example:

```
Router(tcl)#snmp_getbulk public 0 10 ifDescr.0
{<obj oid='ifDescr.1' val='Ethernet0/0'/>}
{<obj oid='ifDescr.2' val='Ethernet0/1'/>}
{<obj oid='ifDescr.3' val='Ethernet0/2'/>}
{<obj oid='ifDescr.4' val='Ethernet0/3'/>}
{<obj oid='ifDescr.5' val='VoIP-Null0'/>}
{<obj oid='ifDescr.6' val='Null0'/>}
{<obj oid='ifDescr.7' val='Loopback3'/>}
{<obj oid='ifType.1' val='6'/>}
{<obj oid='ifType.2' val='6'/>}
{<obj oid='ifType.3' val='6'/>}
```

The output shows 10 of the objects within the Interfaces Table, starting from the first interface description. Besides the usual community string and object names, two numeric values are passed into **snmp_getbulk**.

The first is **non_repeaters**, which will be used to limit the responses and can be set to 0 or 1. The second is **max_repetitions**, which will also limit the number of **get-next** attempts that will be made within the table. Setting these values will limit how many objects will be returned in the response. In practice, when you are setting the **max_repetitions** to an extremely high value, the responses are limited by the maximum SNMP packet size, which is configured using the **snmp-server packetsize** command.

Modifying the Configuration of a Cisco IOS Device Using SNMP

You have seen how to query SNMP MIB variables with Tcl. Next, you will change one of them. Remember you have created a new interface in the Interfaces Table, Loopback 3? By default, when a new loopback interface is created, it is enabled. However all interfaces in the router can be shut down. The identifier for this new Loopback 3 interface is 7, from the previous interface description.

To determine the interface status, you must query the interface with the following command:

```
Router(tcl)#snmp_getone public ifAdminStatus.7
{<obj oid='ifAdminStatus.7' val='1'/>}
```

The current value is **1**, indicating **up** from the MIB definition.

To shut the interface down, you can set it to **2** or **down** from the MIB definition:

```
Router(tcl)#snmp_setany public ifAdminStatus.7 -i 2
{<snmp error type='tcl_snmp_processing_error' value='6' text='NO_ACCESS_ERROR:
   1.' />}
```

The specified variable of **-i** indicates an integer. Other options include the following:

- **-u:** A 32-bit number representing a decimal value

- **-c:** A 32-bit counter

- **-g:** A 32-bit number (gauge) that can be incremented or decremented

- **-o:** An octet string in hex notation

- **-d:** An octet string in text notation

- **-ipv4:** An IP Version 4 address

- **-oid:** An OID

Unfortunately, the attempt to shut down the loopback interface has failed! This is evident from the "snmp error" message. In reviewing the parameters for the **snmp_setany** command, the community string is provided, followed by the object you want to change, and finally a type and value for the object.

In reviewing the parameters that were sent to the **snmp_setany** command. The community string is provided, followed by the object you want to change, and finally a type and value for the object. In this case, you specify an integer of value **2**.

Why did the attempt fail? Remember, you previously configured a community string at the beginning that has just read-only access. In this case, you tried to change an object and SNMP refused, because the **public** community was not granted permission to write to a MIB object. Instead, define a community string that will provide the capability to write to MIB objects:

```
Router(config)#snmp-server community private rw
```

Note   It is not recommended to use **private** as the write community string for production networks, because this is the default value that many devices use.

Now that the community string is set to read-write, you can once again attempt to shut down the interface from within Tcl:

```
PE11(tcl)#snmp_setany private ifAdminStatus.7 -i 2
{<obj oid='ifAdminStatus.7' val='2'/>}
*Aug 10 22:29:58.447: %LINK-5-CHANGED: Interface Loopback3, changed state to
   administratively down
```

After a brief delay, the interface has been shut down. To verify this, you can double-check the router's running-configuration:

```
Router(tcl)#show running-config interface Loopback3
Building configuration...
Current configuration : 52 bytes
!
interface Loopback3
 no ip address
 shutdown
end
```

To make the configuration changes permanent, you must copy the running-configuration to the startup-configuration.

The preceding output verifies that the interface has been shut down.

SNMP MIB access is a powerful tool that can be used from within the Tcl interpreter in IOS. It provides valuable management information that can help you understand what is occurring on the device.

Summary

Tcl is implemented in many flavors of Cisco IOS, and as you have seen in this chapter, it enables you to interact with the command line directly. Scripts can be downloaded directly to the IOS device or be initiated from a central server using TFTP, FTP, SCP, HTTP, and so on. SNMP combined with Tcl can be used to glean pertinent information from the device for monitoring or troubleshooting and for making configuration changes.

References

RFC 2863, *The Interfaces Group MIB* (June 2000): http://www.ietf.org/rfc/rfc2863.txt?number=2863

"Cisco IOS Scripting with Tcl": http://tinyurl.com/47gv9v

Chapter 4

Embedded Event Manager (EEM)

This chapter covers the following topics:

- EEM Architecture

- Software Release Support for EEM

- Writing an EEM Applet

- Using EEM and Tcl Scripts

Embedded Event Manager (EEM) enables you to run user-defined scripts (Tcl scripts) in Cisco IOS. EEM consists of three components:

- **Event detectors:** Event detectors are used as a trigger based on certain conditions. Some of these conditions include, monitoring for syslog events, online insertion and removal (IOR), command-line interface (CLI) input, timers, and so on.

- **EEM server:** The EEM server is the director of EEM. When configured events occur, the associated action is implemented.

- **Policies:** Policies or scripts are either applets or Tcl scripts configured by the administrator.

This chapter explains the architecture of EEM. In this chapter, you will learn about event detectors, which platforms are supported, and see some examples of implementation. By the time you finish this chapter, you should be well on your way to customizing the operation of a Cisco IOS device.

EEM Architecture

Figure 4-1 illustrates the relationship of the three primary building blocks of the EEM architecture (policies, the EEM server, and event detectors).

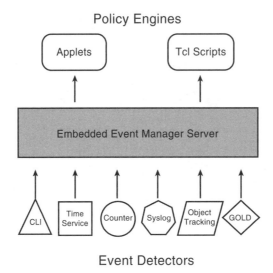

Figure 4-1   *EEM Architecture Framework*

Policies

Policies or scripts are either applets or Tcl scripts configured by the administrator:

- **Applets:** Users do not need to know how to write Tcl scripts. Policies can be defined through the IOS CLI. The body of applets also appear in the configuration of the Cisco IOS device.

- **Tcl scripts:** Actions can also be defined through Tcl scripts. Scripts provide an extensive control as compared to applet policies. Applets were designed to provide a simpler interface for EEM.

EEM Server

The EEM server is a bridge between the policies and internal Cisco IOS subsystems used within the event detectors. Some of the functionality of the EEM server is to register events seen in the IOS subsystems, store information about an event, publish an event, request additional information about an event, register internal script directories, register Tcl scripts and applets, and process actions taken by user-defined scripts. The version of EEM is based on the IOS release cycle. It is important to understand the functionality of EEM based on the IOS image, so that you fully understand the features and functionality of the event detectors and what is supported. The specifics about EEM versions are covered in the section "Software Release Support for EEM."

Event Detectors

Event detectors monitor the operational state of processes on an IOS device. These processes run at medium priority, are always operational, and on detecting an event, the event detector sends an alert that provides information about the specific event. The list that follows describes some of the event detectors in Cisco IOS (for a current and complete list, refer to the appropriate documentation for the specific platform):

- **Syslog event detector:** Triggered when a syslog message match is seen in the output of the console. Additional granularity can be achieved based on number of occurrences for any given message. Console logging does not have to be active for the syslog event detector to generate events; this is completely independent of which logging targets are configured.

- **SNMP event detector:** A specific Simple Network Management Protocol (SNMP) variable can be polled, and if the SNMP variable reaches a threshold, a trigger can be generated.

- **SNMP notification event detector:** This event detector provides the capability to intercept SNMP trap messages sent into the IOS device.

- **Timer event detector:** Generates an event at a specific time interval. This can be used to run a task after a period of time, at a specific time, or at selected intervals. This is similar to KRON on Cisco IOS or CRON in UNIX:

  - **Absolute time of day:** Publishes an event when a specified absolute date and time occur.

  - **Countdown time:** Publishes an event when timer counts to zero.

  - **Watchdog timer:** Publishes an event when a timer counts down to zero. The timer will automatically resets itself to the initial value and start the countdown sequence again.

  - **CRON timer:** Publishes an event using the UNIX standard CRON specifications to indicate when the event is to be published.

- **Counter event detector:** Used to monitor a specific counter for a particular threshold value and generate an event. After a counter event has been published, the counter monitoring logic can be reset to start monitoring the counter immediately or can be reset when a second threshold is called and an exit value is crossed.

- **IP SLA event detector:** This detector publishes an event when an IP service level agreement (SLA) reaction is triggered.

- **Interface event detector:** This detector monitors interface counters based on a defined threshold value. The threshold can be specified as an absolute value or an incremental value.

- **CLI event detector:** The event detector triggers when a specified command is entered via a console or Telnet/SSH (Secure Shell) session. This detector screens CLI commands that match a regular expression. When a match is found, an event is published and the CLI event detector can perform a logical match before the command is parsed and executed.

- **NetFlow event detector:** When a NetFlow event is triggered, the NetFlow event detector publishes an event.

- **Custom CLI event detector:** This event detector publishes an event that adds and enhances an existing CLI command. The user can define a specific character or any other value when entered in the CLI. The CLI compares this input, and if a match is found, an action is triggered:

  - **Synchronous publishing of CLI events:** The CLI command is not fully executed until the EEM policy exits. Therefore, the EEM policy can control whether the command is executed.

  - **Asynchronous publishing of CLI events:** The CLI policy is published, and then the command is executed.

  - **Asynchronous publishing of CLI events with command skipping:** The CLI event is published, but the command is not executed.

  - **Enhanced object tracking event detector:** This event detector is triggered when a status of the tracked object changes. A unique number identifies each tracked object. This number is specified on the tracking CLI. The detector process uses this number to track a specific object. The tracking process periodically polls the tracked objects and notes any change in value. The changes in the tracked object are communicated to event detector process, either immediately or after a specified delay. The object values are reported as either up or down. Enhanced object tracking is now integrated with EEM to allow EEM to report on the status change of a tracked object. For example, Hot Standby Router Protocol (HSRP) may change because of the loss of a neighbor router or from an interface state change.

- **Routing event detector:** This event detector is invoked when routing information in the Routing Information Base (RIB) has been changed.

- **Resource event detector:** The Embedded Resource Manager (ERM) monitors system resource usage to better understand scalability needs by allowing you to configure threshold values for resources such as the CPU, buffers, and memory.

- **GOLD event detector:** The Generic Online Diagnostics (GOLD) event detector publishes an event when a GOLD failure event is detected. GOLD can detect faults in hardware and provide a trigger to proactively indicate the state of the device. There are two primary tests for GOLD: the Power-On Self Test (POST) and the GOLD test. The POST test runs during the boot process and verifies the CPU subsystem, system memory, and peripherals. GOLD performs packet-switching and ASIC memory tests using runtime drivers. GOLD is available on various Cisco platforms such as the

Catalyst 6500, 4500, and 3750 switches and the 7600 CRS-1 routers.

The GOLD diagnostic capabilities are as follows:

- **Boot diagnostics:** Tests conducted during boot time or online insertion or removal of modules.

- **Health monitoring diagnostics:** Tests that run in the background while the system is in operation.

- **On-demand diagnostics:** This enables you to conduct various tests on demand using the CLI.

- **Scheduled diagnostics:** This enables you to conduct various tests at a scheduled date, time, and frequency using the CLI.

- **Event detector IOS watchdog:** This detector monitors an IOS task for excessive use of the CPU or memory. Thresholds can be specified when these processes are watched.

- **Watchdog System Monitor (WDSysMon) event detector for Cisco IOS software modularity:** This detects infinite loops, dead locks, and memory leaks in the IOS software modularity process.

- **RF event detector:** When one or more redundancy framework (RF) events occur during synchronization in a dual Router Processor (RP) system, an RF event detector publishes the event. The RF detector can also detect when as RP changes the role from active.

- **Remote-procedure call (RPC) event detector:** This event detector enables you to invoke EEM policies from outside the router over an encrypted connection using SSH. RPC event detectors uses Simple Object Access protocol (SOAP) data encoding to exchange Extensible Markup Language (XML)-based messages.

- **System Manager event detector:** This event detector is seen in modular IOS. It generates an event for processes within modular IOS for start, normal, abnormal stop, and restart events.

- **OIR event detector:** This event detector publishes an event when a hardware module insertion or removal occurs.

- **Application event detector:** This event detector can kick start a script based on a user-defined event within a script.

- **Process event detector:** This event detector pertains to IOS with Software Modularity and is used to monitor process starts, restarts and stops.

- **None event detector:** This event detector publishes an event when the Cisco IOS event manager runs a CLI command and executes an EEM policy. This is the "manual" way of running a script, which you may consider using to test the script functionality or creating custom commands.

Software Release Support for EEM

The EEM event detectors have evolved based on IOS releases. The functionality of the event detection and action depends on the specific release. Tables 4-1 through 4-9 provide some insight as to which features are supported on which versions of code.

EEM is available for the Catalyst 6500 series switches, Integrated Services Routers (ISRs), 7200 series routers, 7300 series routers, 7600 series routers, 10000 series routers, Catalyst 4500 series switches, Catalyst 3550, 3560, and 3700 series switches, the ASR-1000 series routers, and the Nexus platform.

The following software release have support for EEM: IOS Software Release 12.2SX, 12.2SR, 12.2SB, 12.4, 12.4T, 12.2SG, 12.2SE, IOS XE and future versions, IOS XR, and NX OS.

Table 4-1   *Embedded Event Manager 1.0*

Software Release	Supported Events	Actions
Support available in Cisco IOS Releases 12.0(26)S and 12.3(4)T and later releases	SNMP event detector allows a standard SNMP MIB object to be monitored. When a specific threshold is crossed, an event is generated. The syslog event detector allows for screening syslog messages.	Generate a Cisco Networking Services (CNS) event for upstream process by a CNS device. Reload the Cisco IOS software. Switch to a secondary processor in a fully redundant hardware configuration. Generate prioritized syslog messages.

Table 4-2   *Embedded Event Manager 2.0*

Software Release	Supported Events	Actions
Support available from Cisco IOS Release 12.2(25)S and later releases	Application-specific event allows the EEM to publish an event. Counter event detector publishes an event when a named counter crosses a specified threshold. The interface counter event detector publishes an event when an interface counter for a specified interface crosses a defined threshold. The timer event detector publishes events for the following four different types of timers: absolute time of day, countdown, watchdog, and CRON. The IOS WDSysMon event detector publishes an event when the CPU or memory utilization of a process crosses a threshold.	Run a Cisco-defined Tcl policy Publish an application-specific event Generate an SNMP trap by EEM

Table 4-3 *Embedded Event Manager 2.1*

Software Release	Supported Events	Actions
Support available from Cisco IOS Release 12.3(14)T, 12.2(18)SXF5, 12.2(28)SB, 12.2(33)SRA, and later releases	None. When the event manager **run** command executes an EEM policy, the None event detector publishes an event. When an insertion or removal of a line card takes place, the OIR event detector publishes an event. When a regular expression match is seen, the CLI event detector publishes an event. GOLD support was added in EEM 2.1.5 for IOS modularity with 12.2(18)SXF4.	Execution of CLI command using a script. Send a short e-mail. Manually run an EEM policy and permit running of multiple concurrent policies using the new event manager schedule script command. Support for SNMP event detector rate-based events.

Table 4-4 *Embedded Event Manager 2.2*

Software Release	Supported Events	Actions
Support available from Cisco IOS Release 12.4(2)T, 12.2(31)SB3, 12.2(33)SRB, and later releases	Enhanced object tracking event detector. Enhanced object tracking provides complete separation between the objects to be tracked and the action to be taken by a client when a tracked object changes. When the ERM reports an event for the specified policy, the resource event detector publishes an event. When more than one event is seen during the synchronization of the dual RP system, the RF event detector publishes an event.	Read the state of a tracked object. Set the state of tracked object.

Table 4-5   *Embedded Event Manager 2.3*

Software Release	Supported Events	Actions
Supported from IOS Release 12.2(33)SXH and later releases for the Cisco Catalyst 6500 series switches and introduces enhancements to the GOLD event detector for that product. EEM 2.3 was integrated into 12.4(11)T and was the first single-source release of EEM.	GOLD diagnostics Added support for the **pattern** keyword to the **action** CLI command, which enables you to run interactive commands using applets	The **event gold** command was enhanced with the addition of the following commands: **action-notify** **testing-type** **test-name** **test-id** **consecutive-failure** **platform-action** **maxrun** GOLD event detector support the following environment variables: **Boot diagnostic level** **Card index, name, serial number** **Port counts** **Test counts** Read-only applet GOLD event detectors, which include the following: **Test name, attribute, total run count** **Test result per test, port, or device** **Total failure count, last fail time** **Error code** **Occurrence of consecutive failures**

Table 4-6   *Embedded Event Manager 2.4*

Software Release	Supported Events	Actions
Supported from Cisco IOS Release 12.4(20)T, 12.2(50)SE, 12.2(33)SXI, and later releases	The SNMP notification event detector enables you to view SNMP traps coming into the router. An SNMP notification event is generated when an incoming SNMP trap message matches specified values or crosses specified thresholds. The RPC event detector enables you to invoke EEM policies from outside the router over an encrypted connection using SSH. EEM 2.4 added enhancements to the following event detectors: Interface counter rate-based trigger: This feature adds the ability for an interface event to be triggered based on a rate of change over a period of time. For entry and exit value, the rate can be specified. SNMP delta value: This publishes the difference between the monitored object identifier (OID) value at the beginning of the monitored period and the actual OID value when the event is published.	Multiple event support The **show event manager** commands were enhanced to show multiple events. The *parameter* argument has been added to the event manager **run** command for a maximum of 15 parameters. The display of job ID and status can be seen using the **show event manager** command. The ability to kill a running policy through the **event manager scheduler clear command** was also added. EEM accepts extensions for byte-code scripts *.tbc on valid EEM policies. Tcl extension support with EEM now include *.tcl for user policies and *tm for system policies. Byte-code extension. Registration substitution enhancement for multiple parameters.

Table 4-7   *Embedded Event Manager 3.0*

Software Release	Supported Events	Actions
Cisco IOS Release 12.4(22)T and later releases	When route entries change in the Routing Information Base (RIB), the routing event detector publishes an event. When a NetFlow event is triggered, a NetFlow event detector publishes an event. When an IP SLA reaction is triggered, the IP SLA event detector publishes an event. The custom CLI event detector publishes an event to add and enhance existing CLI command syntax.	**Class-based scheduling** can be assigned to a class. Three new Tcl commands are introduced: **event_completion** **event_wait** **event_completion_with_wait** Two new IOS commands are supported: **action gets** **action puts** Applet input support via the console. **Variable logic for applets:** Conditional logic can be applied to the applet through the variable logic feature in EEM. A programmable interface that encapsulates **show** commands in an XML interface. Signature verification for a Tcl script. **Support authenticating e-mail servers.** The keyword **source addr** is added in Tcl e-mail templates to specify it is either an IPv6 or IPv4 address. SNMP library extensions for SNMP **getid, inform, trap,** and **set-type** operations included in the EEM applet action info and **Tcl sys_reqinfo_snmp** commands. **SNMP notification IPv6 support:** IPv6 address is supported for the source and destination IP addresses. **CLI library XML-PI support:** Provides a programmable interface that encapsulates CLI **show** commands in an XML format in a consistent way across different Cisco products.

Table 4-8 *Embedded Event Manager 3.1*

Software Release	Supported Events	Actions
Cisco IOS Release 15.0(1)M and later releases	The SNMP object event detector enables you to replace the trap with an OID. SNMP notification and intercept outgoing SNMP messages. The **action syslog** command can now specify the facility.	The **description** command was added. AAA (authentication, authorization, and accounting) bypass is now enabled. The **cli_run** and cli_run_interactive were added.

Table 4-9 *Embedded Event Manager 3.2*

Software Release	Supported Events	Actions
Cisco IOS release 12.2(52)SE and later releases	Cisco Discovery Protocol (CDP) and Link Layer Discovery Protocol (LLDP) neighbor event detector provides notification when a neighbor is added, deleted, or updated Interface link and line status notifications. Identity event detector for AAA. MAC address table event detector that generates an event when new MAC is learned.	The following commands were added: **debug event manager** **event identity** **event mat** **event neighbor-discovery** **show event manager detector**

Platform and IOS Considerations for EEM

The previous tables give you a good idea of what code version will be required to support your specific needs, but you should still review the platform and IOS before deploying EEM. Conduct the following steps before implementation:

Step 1.   Use the feature navigator to verify the support of EEM features in the code train: http://www.cisco.com/go/fn.

Step 2.   For specific features and functionality support, the release notes will provide definitive answers for your specific platform and image.

Step 3.   EEM will consume memory resources. Remember to allocate storage space (flash) for the Tcl scripts.

Step 4.   The operation of EEM will also require some additional CPU cycles. This factor must be considered by verifying the impact of the EEM scripts on the device in a test environment.

Writing an EEM Applet

The process of writing EEM applets is relatively simple, especially if you have any experience using IOS CLI. The following section guides you through the five-step process of creating an applet.

Step 1.   Enter into configuration mode:

```
Router#configure terminal
```

Step 2.   Configure an applet name:

```
event manager applet name of the applet
```

For example, the following statement will create an applet called **TEST**:

```
Router(config)#event manager applet TEST
```

Step 3.   Configure an event that will cause the event manager to take an action. You guessed it, use the **event** command:

```
Router(config-applet)#event ?
  application        Application specific event
  cli                CLI event
  config             Configuration policy event
  counter            Counter event
  env                Environmental event
  interface          Interface event
  ioswdsysmon        IOS WDSysMon event
  ipsla              IPSLA Event
  nf                 NF Event
  none               Manually run policy event
  oir                OIR event
  resource           Resource event
  rf                 Redundancy Facility event
  routing            Routing event
  rpc                Remote Procedure Call event
  snmp               SNMP event
  snmp-notification  SNMP Notification Event
  syslog             Syslog event
```

```
tag                  event tag identifier
timer                Timer event
track                Tracking object event
```

As seen from the output, there are several events that can be used to trigger the event manager.

Step 4.   Define an action or actions to be initiated, with the **action** keyword. Because several actions can be defined, an alphabetic sort is used on the label to determine the order of operation:

```
Router(config-applet)#action WORD  Label
```

As a matter of best practice, using numeric values is a very good way to sort actions. For example, you can label actions starting with 1.0, 2.0, 3.0 and so on. In the event you need to make an addition between event 1.0 and 2.0, you can easily add 1.5 without having to change any labels.

Note   Because actions are interpreted alphabetically, action 10.0 would execute after action 1.0 and before 9.0.

```
Router(config-applet)#action 1.0 ?
  add               Add
  append            Append to a variable
  break             Break out of a conditional loop
  cli               Execute a CLI command
  cns-event         Send a CNS event
  comment           add comment
  context           Save or retrieve context information
  continue          Continue to next loop iteration
  counter           Modify a counter value
  decrement         Decrement a variable
  divide            Divide
  else              else conditional
  elseif            elseif conditional
  end               end conditional block
  exit              Exit from applet run
  force-switchover  Force a software switchover
  foreach           foreach loop
  gets              get line of input from active tty
  handle-error      On error action
  help              Read/Set parser help buffer
```

```
if               if conditional
increment        Increment a variable
info             Obtain system specific information
mail             Send an e-mail
multiply         Multiply
policy           Run a preregistered policy
publish-event    Publish an application specific event
puts             print data to active tty
regexp           regular expression match
reload           Reload system
set              Set a variable
snmp-trap        Send an SNMP trap
string           string commands
subtract         Subtract
syslog           Log a syslog message
track            Read/Set a tracking object
wait             Wait for a specified amount of time
while            while loop
```

Event actions have many alternatives, and so you have tremendous flexibility.

Step 5.   Exit from applet configuration mode and save your configuration. Because applets are part of the configuration, there are no additional steps.

Note   You must exit the applet submode configuration for the applet to get registered. Entering the **do show run** command will not show the newly created applet.

```
Router(config-applet)#end
Router#copy running-config startup-config
```

Practical Example of an Event Trigger

The following example creates an applet that matches a syslog pattern using a regular expression. When the interface GigabitEthernet2/0 changes state to down, an event trigger will be generated. This is one of the most common ways to write an applet:

```
Router(config-applet)#event syslog pattern "Interface GigabitEthernet2/0, changed
  state to down"
```

The regular expression match in this example is extremely rudimentary. You could also create a regular expressing matching or excluding particular characters, and so on.

Using Object Tracking as an Event Trigger

Object tracking offers another powerful way to create event triggers. A unique number is used to track a specific object through a client process. The client process can be HSRP, static routes, SLA, and so on. The tracked objects are polled periodically, and changes in state are monitored. When a change occurs, the interested client process can be notified immediately of after a predefined delay. The object values are reported as either up or down.

A number of features are incorporated into object tracking that warrant some additional clarification, including the following:

- **Unique number:** A unique number can be used to track a specified object.

- **Threshold:** This allows a tracked list to be configured to use a weight or percentage threshold to measure the state of the list. Each object in a tracked list can be assigned a threshold weight. The state of the tracked list is determined by whether the threshold has been met.

- **Boolean AND function:** When a tracked list has been assigned a Boolean AND function, it means that each object defined within a subset must be in an up state before the tracked object is defined as up.

- **Boolean OR function:** When a tracked list has been assigned a Boolean OR function, it means that at least one object defined within a subset must be in an up state before the tracked is defined as up.

The next example explains how to use event tracking. Begin by using the **track** command to track the status of the line-protocol on interface GigabitEthernet 0/1:

```
Router(config)#track 1 interface gigabitEthernet 0/1 line-protocol
```

You can now configure the event to track the state of the object, in this case, object 1:

```
Router(config-applet)#event track 1 state down
```

Based on the status of object tracking, a user-defined action can be triggered. As you can see, this is a powerful tool to have in your network tool bag!

Creating Applet Actions

After the event trigger has been initiated, a single action or multiple actions can be generated. This section provides an example of how to use applet actions. In the following example, the CLI event detector watches for the **configure terminal** command, as follows:

```
Router(config-applet)#event cli pattern "configure terminal" sync no skip no
```

A couple of other parameters that should be addressed are **sync** and **skip**. The **sync** option set to **no** will run the command asynchronously, and if it is set to **yes**, the result will determine whether the command will be run. The **skip** option when set to **no** will execute the command, and set to **yes** the command will not be executed.

Configure the user-defined action that will be taken when the line-protocol of gigabitEthernet 0/1 changes state to down. The event trigger will add the "**ip route 0.0.0.0 0.0.0.0 10.1.1.1**" statement. The configuration is as follows:

```
Router(config)#track 1 interface gigabitEthernet 0/1 line-protocol
Router(config)#event manager applet TEST
Router(config-applet)#event track 1 state down
Router(config-applet)#action 1.0 cli command "enable"
Router(config-applet)#action 2.0 cli command "configure terminal"
Router(config-applet)#action 3.0 cli command "ip route 0.0.0.0 0.0.0.0 10.1.1.1"
```

Other events could include a syslog pattern match, as follows:

```
Router(config-applet)#event syslog pattern "Up->Down"
```

Other actions could be to generate a syslog message, as follows:

```
Router(config-applet)#action 1.0 syslog msg "!!Experiencing Network Slowness to
    10.1.23.2!!"
```

From the preceding configuration examples, the actions can be quite varied, including any user-defined CLI commands. Based on the action, the user can configure a static route, change the Border Gateway Protocol (BGP) neighbor statement, generate a syslog event, and so on.

Note   Certain EEM actions that set internal variables can be accessed within the EEM policy. For example, using the following action command, **action 3.0 cli command "show ver"**, the result of the "**show ver**" command will be stored in the $_cli_result variable. This variable can then be used to generate a user-defined function using syslog, snmp-trap action, and so on.

Examples of EEM Applets

The next example uses an EEM script to monitor network performance between an IP SLA sender and an IP SLA receiver using probe messages. The User Datagram Protocol (UDP) message in this example are used to emulate a specific traffic type. Having the ability to craft probes to match a specific type of traffic, for example voice, allows you to determine how that traffic will behave on the network with all the associated Quality of Service (QoS) policies, Access Control Lists (ACL), and so on. The applet will generate a syslog message indicating that the network is down when the UDP messages are delayed or no longer received.

Two routers are used to accomplish this task. R1 is used as the initiator or sender of the SLA probes, and R2 is configured as the responder. Delay or loss of connectivity to the destination of the UDP message activates the EEM script. The EEM script tracks the syslog message for the **track** command that is used to monitor the response of the IP SLA probes.

The responder, R2, is configured to accept the probes and provide a response. The responder should be configured before the sender; otherwise, the sender will display a down state until the responder is configured:

```
ip sla responder
ip sla responder udp-echo ipaddress 10.1.23.2 port 54321
```

The IP SLA probe is configured to send UDP messages sourced from the IP address of 10.1.13.1 port 54321 to the destination IP address of 10.1.23.2. The frequency of the probe is set to 30 seconds and the threshold to 35 milliseconds. If the probe exceeds 35 milliseconds, the state will be changed to "down". The probe is scheduled to start at the current time and will continue indefinitely. The **track** command initiates the process:

```
ip sla 10
 udp-echo 10.1.23.2 54321 source-ip 10.1.13.1
 threshold 35
 frequency 30
ip sla schedule 10 start-time now recurring
track 10 ip sla 10
```

The following EEM applet monitors the syslog message generated by the track message to create a new user-defined syslog message, slowness in the network.

```
event manager applet IPSLA_Track
 event syslog pattern "10 ip sla 10 state Up->Down"
 action 1.0 syslog msg "!!Experiencing Network Slowness to  10.1.23.2!!"
```

Note   An alternative approach would be to use the track event detector, but it is not available on all code releases.

To view the track status of R1, use the following command:

```
r1#show track 10
Track 10
  IP SLA 10 state
  State is Up
    15 changes, last change 00:16:41
  Latest operation return code: OK
  Latest RTT (millisecs) 29
```

Did you notice the **Latest RTT (millisecs)** parameter is 29 milliseconds? When it crosses the 35-millisecond threshold, the state will be changed to down. The following output shows the tracking state changing to a down. In looking at the track state, you can see that the Latest RTT is now 37 milliseconds, which is over the threshold of 35 milliseconds:

```
%TRACKING-5-STATE: 10 ip sla 10 state Up->Down
r1#show track 10
Track 10
  IP SLA 10 state
  State is Down
    10 changes, last change 00:00:12
  Latest operation return code: Over threshold
  Latest RTT (millisecs) 37
```

An IP SLA has many features that you can incorporate within applets and Tcl scripts. Cisco IP SLA allows users to analyze IP service levels for IP applications and services by using active traffic monitoring. This is achieved by probes that generate traffic in a continuous and predictable manner that is then used to measure network performance. IP SLAs collect a unique subset of these performance metrics:

- Delay (both round trip and one way)

- Jitter (directional)

- Packet loss (directional)

- Packet sequencing (packet ordering)

- Path (per hop)

- Connectivity (directional)

- Server or website download time

To achieve the specified operation, you can configure the IP SLA with specific probes and leverage it in multiple ways:

- Enterprise customers can verify service levels across the service provider (SP) cloud.

- Enables you to understand the network performance at different levels.

- Enables you to understand the application impact before and after applying QoS.

- Assists in network troubleshooting.

- In conjunction with EEM, it can be used to make intelligent Layer 7-based routing decisions.

Configuring the IP SLA Sender and Responder

The following steps walk you through the configuration of the responder and sender:

Step 1.   Enable the IP SLA responder on the receiver end.

Command-line configuration:

```
ip sla Entry Number
```

For example:

```
ip sla 10
```

Step 2. Configure the IP SLA operation type.

The following is a list of the available operation types. The operation types may change based on Cisco IOS code version.

- **dhcp:** DHCP operation
- **dlsw:** DLSW operation
- **dns:** DNS query operation
- **ethernet:** Ethernet operation
- **exit:** Exit operation configuration
- **ftp:** FTP operation
- **http:** HTTP operation
- **icmp-echo:** ICMP echo operation
- **mpls:** MPLS operation
- **path-echo:** Path Discovered ICMP echo operation
- **path-jitter:** Path discovered ICMP jitter operation
- **slm:** SLM operation
- **tcp-connect:** TCP connect operation
- **udp-echo:** UDP echo operation
- **udp-jitter:** UDP jitter operation

The following example uses Internet Control Message Protocol (ICMP) and does not require an additional router configured as a responder. It does require that a device is capable of responding back to ICMP echo request messages:

```
Router(config-ip-sla)#icmp-echo 10.1.1.1 source-ip 10.1.1.2
r2(config-ip-sla-echo)#frequency 10
```

In this example, ICMP probes are configured for destination 10.1.1.1, with a source address of 10.1.1.2. The frequency that the probe are sent is every 10 seconds.

Step 3. Configure threshold conditions, if required. The threshold is a period or hold time for the IP SLA to report an incident and is used to monitor the IP SLA event.

For example:

```
r2(config-ip-sla-echo)#threshold 30
```

In this step, the threshold is defined as 30 milliseconds.

Step 4.   Schedule the IP SLA operation, using the following command syntax:

```
ip sla monitor schedule operation-number [life {forever  seconds}]
[start-time {hh:mm [:ss] [month day  day month]  pending | now | after
hh:mm:ss] [ageout seconds] [recurring]
```

■ **operation-number:** References the IP SLA probe.

■ **life:** An optional field that sets the operation to run forever or for a specific number of seconds. The range is from 0 to 2147483647. The default is 3600 seconds (1 hour).

■ **start-time:** An optional parameter used to configure the time for the operation to begin collecting information. To start at a specific time, enter the hour, minute, second (in 24-hour notation), and day of the month. Enter **now** to start the operation immediately. Set the *hh:mm:ss* to indicate that the operation should start after the entered time has elapsed.

■ **ageout seconds:** An optional field that specifies the number of seconds to keep the data of the probe in memory, when it is not actively collecting information. The range is 0 to 2073600 seconds, the default is 0 seconds (the probe does not timeout).

■ **recurring:** An optional parameter used to set the operation to automatically run every day.

Tip   IP SLA is commonly used with object tracking and EEM scripts. It can be used to generate syslog messages when a specific condition occurs in the network.

Applet and IP SLA Route Failover Example

This applet is used to monitor the delay for remote sites that are connected through a carrier network with an alternate path for backup. The EEM script monitors the delay to a particular address and changes the route based on the response from the destination. This method can be used at remote sites that require only the default route to reach the hub. The IP SLA probe is based on ICMP (note that ICMP probes do not require IP SLA responder configured at the destination); other probes could also be configured based on specific requirement.

As depicted in Figure 4-2, there are two routers in this example, R1 and R2. R1 has a primary path to R2 and is using the E0/0 interface. The backup path between R1 and R2 is using the E1/0 interface. Instead of using a routing protocol, a default and static route is the method used for next-hop reachability. R1 has a static route for the 192.168.1.0/24 subnet toward 10.1.1.2. During failover, the 192.168.1.0/24 subnet will have a new static route toward 172.16.1.2, and the existing static route will be removed. Similarly, R2 has a default route pointing toward 10.1.1.1. During failure of the E0/0 link, a new default route is installed to 172.16.1.1, and the existing static route is removed. The next-hop reachability of the interface is monitored using IP SLA probes. A minor modification can be made to achieve millisecond failover between the two nodes. Object tracking is used to track the IP SLA probes. The object tracking generates a syslog message and in turn activates the EEM script. This script changes the static or the default route and displays a user-defined syslog message that provides the path taken by the packet. In this example, both routers are running Cisco IOS Version 12.4(19.11)T code.

Figure 4-2 *EEM/IPSLA for Static Routing Decision Example*

The commented configurations outlined in Table 4-10 will help you understand the steady or normal state of operation.

R1	R2
The *track-object is* monitoring IP SLA probe 100.	The *track-object is* monitoring IP SLA probe 100.
```R1#show track 100Track 100 IP SLA 100 reachability Reachability is Up 7 changes, last change 00:00:50 Latest operation return code: OK Latest RTT (millisecs) 4```	```R2#show track 100Track 100 IP SLA 100 reachability Reachability is Up 9 changes, last change 00:01:55 Latest operation return code: OK Latest RTT (millisecs) 4```
The **show track** command indicates the status of the IP SLA probes. As shown in the output above, the probes are being received.	The **show track** command indicates the status of the IP SLA probes. As shown in the output above, the probes are being received.
```R1#show ip sla statistics 100Round Trip Time (RTT) for Index 100 Latest RTT: 1 millisecondsLatest operation start time: *08:40:15.663 PST Sun Oct 11 2009Latest operation return code: OKNumber of successes: 72Number of failures: 52Operation time to live: 3353 sec```	```R2#show ip sla statistics 100Round Trip Time (RTT) for Index 100 Latest RTT: 4 millisecondsLatest operation start time: *08:41:19.011 PST Sun Oct 11 2009Latest operation return code: OKNumber of successes: 106Number of failures: 50Operation time to live: 3288 sec```
This command provides the history of the events that have triggered all the applets.	This command provides the history of the events that have triggered all the applets.

continues

Table 4-10 *EEM/IP SLA for Static Routing Configuration Example (Continued)*

R1	R2

```
R1#show event manager history events          R2#show event manager history events
No.    Time of Event        Event Type   Name      No.    Time of Event        Event Type   Name
1   Sun Oct11 08:37:09 2009   syslog    applet: #100   1   Sun Oct11 08:36:33 2009   syslog    applet: #100
2   Sun Oct11 08:37:09 2009   syslog    applet: #101   2   Sun Oct11 08:36:48 2009   syslog    applet: #101
3   Sun Oct11 08:37:14 2009   syslog                   3   Sun Oct11 08:37:13 2009   syslog    applet: #100
4   Sun Oct11 08:39:20 2009   syslog    applet: #101   4   Sun Oct11 08:37:39 2009   syslog    applet: #101
5   Sun Oct11 08:42:45 2009   syslog    applet: #100   5   Sun Oct11 08:37:49 2009   syslog    applet: #100
6   Sun Oct11 08:42:50 2009   syslog    applet: #101   6   Sun Oct11 08:37:54 2009   syslog    applet: #101
R1#                                                    7   Sun Oct11 08:38:49 2009   syslog    applet: #100
                                                       8   Sun Oct11 08:39:19 2009   syslog    applet: #101
```

In the steady-state operation, the route for 192.168.1.0/24 points to 10.1.1.2.	In the steady-state operation, the default route points to 10.1.1.1.

R1	R2
R1#**show ip route**	r2#**show ip route**
Codes: C - connected, S - static, R - RIP, M - mobile, B - BGP	Codes: C - connected, S - static, R - RIP, M - mobile, B - BGP
D - EIGRP, EX - EIGRP external, O - OSPF, IA - OSPF inter area	D - EIGRP, EX - EIGRP external, O - OSPF, IA - OSPF inter area
N1 - OSPF NSSA external type 1, N2 - OSPF NSSA external type 2	N1 - OSPF NSSA external type 1, N2 - OSPF NSSA external type 2
E1 - OSPF external type 1, E2 - OSPF external type 2	E1 - OSPF external type 1, E2 - OSPF external type 2
i - IS-IS, su - IS-IS summary, L1 - IS-IS level-1, L2 - IS-IS level-2	i - IS-IS, su - IS-IS summary, L1 - IS-IS level-1, L2 - IS-IS level-2
ia - IS-IS inter area, * - candidate default, U - per-user static route	ia - IS-IS inter area, * - candidate default, U - per-user static route
o - ODR, P - periodic downloaded static route	o - ODR, P - periodic downloaded static route
Gateway of last resort is not set	Gateway of last resort is 10.1.1.1 to network 0.0.0.0
172.16.0.0/24 is subnetted, 1 subnets	172.16.0.0/24 is subnetted, 1 subnets
C 172.16.1.0 is directly connected, Ethernet1/0	C 172.16.1.0 is directly connected, Ethernet1/0
10.0.0.0/24 is subnetted, 1 subnets	10.0.0.0/24 is subnetted, 1 subnets
C 10.1.1.0 is directly connected, Ethernet0/0	C 10.1.1.0 is directly connected, Ethernet0/0
S 192.168.1.0/24 [1/0] via 10.1.1.2	C 192.168.1.0/24 is directly connected, Loopback0
192.169.2.0/32 is subnetted, 1 subnets	S* 0.0.0.0/0 [1/0] via 10.1.1.1
C 192.169.2.2 is directly connected, Loopback1	R2#
R1#	

Table 4-11 shows the results during the failure of the primary link between R1 and R2.

Table 4-11   *EEM/IP SLA for Static Routing Failure Scenario*

R1	R2
To simulate a failure, the Ethernet interface 0/0 on R1 will be shutdown. We can then observe the results of the simulated failure.	When the e0/0 interface is shut down on R1 router, the *EEM script is triggered and traffic will change to the backup path.*

R1	R2
```R1(config)#int e0/0```	```r```
```R1(config-if)#shut```	
```R1(config-if)#end```	```R2#```
```R1#```	```*Oct 11 09:00:25.343: %TRACKING-5-```
```R1#```	```STATE: 100 ip sla 100 reachability```
```*Oct 11 09:00:22.023: %SYS-5-CON-```	```Up->Down```
```FIG_I: Configured from console by```	```R2#```
```console```	```*Oct 11 09:00:26.607: %HA_EM-6-LOG:```
```*Oct 11 09:00:22.975: %LINK-5-```	```#100: back up route```
```CHANGED: Interface Ethernet0/0,```	```R2#```
```changed state to administratively```	```*Oct 11 09:00:26.611: %SYS-5-CON-```
```down```	```FIG_I: Configured from console by```
```*Oct 11 09:00:23.983: %LINEPROTO-5-```	```vty0```
```UPDOWN: Line protocol on Interface```	
```Ethernet0/0, changed state to down```	
```R1#```	

R1	R2
Object tracking detects the IP SLA probe "down" state.	
```*Oct 11 09:00:24.503: %TRACKING-5-```	
```STATE: 10 ip sla 10 reachability```	
```Up->Down```	
```*Oct 11 09:00:26.503: %TRACKING-5-```	
```STATE: 100 ip sla 100 reachability```	
```Up->Down```	
EEM scripts gets triggered and changes the path to back up. A new syslog message is added by the script to let the admin know the traffic path is passing through back up.	
```*Oct 11 09:00:28.015: %HA_EM-6-LOG:```	
```#100: back up route```	

R1	R2
The **show ip route** displays the new route that is installed in the table and the original route that points to the primary link is removed.	*The* **show ip route** command shows the new default route has been installed in the table and the original default route that points to the primary link has been removed.

R1#**show ip route**	R2#**show ip route**

```
R1#show ip route

*Oct 11 09:00:28.015: %SYS-5-CON-
FIG_I: Configured from console by
vty0
R1#show ip route
Codes: C - connected, S - static,
R - RIP, M - mobile, B - BGP
    D - EIGRP, EX - EIGRP external,
O - OSPF, IA - OSPF inter area
    N1 - OSPF NSSA external type 1,
N2 - OSPF NSSA external type 2
    E1 - OSPF external type 1, E2 -
OSPF external type 2
    i - IS-IS, su - IS-IS summary,
L1 - IS-IS level-1, L2 - IS-IS
level-2
    ia - IS-IS inter area, * - can-
didate default, U - per-user static
route
    o - ODR, P - periodic downloaded
static route


Gateway of last resort is not set


    172.16.0.0/24 is subnetted,
1 subnets
C    172.16.1.0 is directly connect-
ed, Ethernet1/0
S  192.168.1.0/24 [1/0] via
172.16.1.2
    192.169.2.0/32 is subnetted,
1 subnets
C    192.169.2.2 is directly
connected, Loopback1
R1#
```

```
R2#show ip route
Codes: C - connected, S - static,
R - RIP, M - mobile, B - BGP
    D - EIGRP, EX - EIGRP external,
O - OSPF, IA - OSPF inter area
    N1 - OSPF NSSA external type 1,
N2 - OSPF NSSA external type 2
    E1 - OSPF external type 1, E2 -
OSPF external type 2
    i - IS-IS, su - IS-IS summary,
L1 - IS-IS level-1, L2 - IS-IS
level-2
    ia - IS-IS inter area, * - can-
didate default, U - per-user static
route
    o - ODR, P - periodic downloaded
static route


Gateway of last resort is 172.16.1.1
to network 0.0.0.0


    172.16.0.0/24 is subnetted,
1 subnets
C    172.16.1.0 is directly connect-
ed, Ethernet1/0
    10.0.0.0/24 is subnetted,
1 subnets
C    10.1.1.0 is directly connected,
Ethernet0/0
C    192.168.1.0/24 is directly
connected, Loopback0
S* 0.0.0.0/0 [1/0] via 172.16.1.1
R2#
```

Table 4-12 shows the results when the primary link is restored.

Table 4-12   *EEM/IP SLA for Static Routing Restoration Scenario*

R1	R2

In this example, the primary interface is restored and we can observe the behavior.
 	
`R1(config)#interface e0/0`
`R1(config-if)#no shut`
`R1(config-if)#`
 	
`*Oct 11 09:21:25.515: %LINK-3-UPDOWN: Interface Ethernet0/0, changed state to up`
`*Oct 11 09:21:26.515: %LINEPROTO-5-UPDOWN: Line protocol on Interface Ethernet0/0, changed state to up`
`R1(config-if)#end`
`R1#`
	When the e0/0 interface has been restored on R1.

The track object detects the SLA probe and changes from down to an up state.	The track object detects the SLA probe and changes from a down to an up state.

`*Oct 11 09:21:27.887: %TRACKING-5-STATE: 100 ip sla 100 reachability Down->Up`
`*Oct 11 09:21:28.387: %SYS-5-CON-FIG_I: Configured from console by console`
	`R2#`
	`*Oct 11 09:21:26.987: %TRACKING-5-STATE: 100 ip sla 100 reachability Down->Up`
	The EEM applet generates the syslog message "back to primary route."
	
	`*Oct 11 09:21:28.239: %HA_EM-6-LOG: #101: back to primary routeR2#`
	`*Oct 11 09:21:28.255: %SYS-5-CON-FIG_I: Configured from console by vty0`

The EEM applet generates a syslog message, "back to primary route."	The primary route is restored and the back-up route is removed.

R1	R2

*Oct 11 09:21:29.287: %HA_EM-6-LOG: #101: back to primary route
 	
R1#
 	
*Oct 11 09:21:29.287: %SYS-5-CON-FIG_I: Configured from console by vty0
 	
R1#
 	
*Oct 11 09:21:32.899: %TRACKING-5-STATE: 10 ip sla 10 reachability Down->Up
 	
! The primary route is restored and the
! back up route is removed.
 	
R1#
 	
R1#**show ip route**
 	
Codes: C - connected, S - static, R - RIP, M - mobile, B - BGP
 	
   D - EIGRP, EX - EIGRP external, O - OSPF, IA - OSPF inter area
 	
   N1 - OSPF NSSA external type 1, N2 - OSPF NSSA external type 2
 	
   E1 - OSPF external type 1, E2 - OSPF external type 2
 	
   i - IS-IS, su - IS-IS summary, L1 - IS-IS level-1, L2 - IS-IS level-2
 	
   ia - IS-IS inter area, * - candidate default, U - per-user static route
 	
   o - ODR, P - periodic downloaded static route
 	
Gateway of last resort is not set.
 	
   172.16.0.0/24 is subnetted, 1 subnets
C   172.16.1.0 is directly connected, Ethernet1/0
   10.0.0.0/24 is subnetted, 1 subnets
C   10.1.1.0 is directly connected, Ethernet0/0
S   192.168.1.0/24 [1/0] via 10.1.1.2
   192.169.2.0/32 is subnetted, 1 subnets
C   192.169.2.2 is directly connected, Loopback1
	R2#**show ip route**
	
	Codes: C - connected, S - static, R - RIP, M - mobile, B - BGP
	
	   D - EIGRP, EX - EIGRP external, O - OSPF, IA - OSPF inter area
	
	   N1 - OSPF NSSA external type 1, N2 - OSPF NSSA external type 2
	
	   E1 - OSPF external type 1, E2 - OSPF external type 2
	
	   i - IS-IS, su - IS-IS summary, L1 - IS-IS level-1, L2 - IS-IS level-2
	
	   ia - IS-IS inter area, * - candidate default, U - per-user static route
	
	   o - ODR, P - periodic downloaded static route
	
	Gateway of last resort is 10.1.1.1 to network 0.0.0.0
	
	   172.16.0.0/24 is subnetted, 1 subnets
	C 172.16.1.0 is directly connected, Ethernet1/0
	   10.0.0.0/24 is subnetted, 1 subnets
	C 10.1.1.0 is directly connected, Ethernet0/0
	C 192.168.1.0/24 is directly connected, Loopback0
	S* 0.0.0.0/0 [1/0] via 10.1.1.1

Table 4-13 shows the final configuration of R1 and R2.

Table 4-13   *EEM/IP SLA for Static Routing Configuration*

R1	R2

```R1#show run```
 ```Building configuration...```
 	
 ```Current configuration : 2831 bytes```
 ```!```
 ```version 12.4```
 ```!```
 ```hostname R1```
 ```!```
 ```ip cef```
 ```! To track IP SLA 100```
 ```track 100 ip sla 100 reachability```
 ```!```
 ```!```
 ```!```
 ``` interface Ethernet0/0```
 ``` ip address 10.1.1.1 255.255.255.0```
 ```!```
 ```interface Ethernet1/0```
 ``` ip address 172.16.1.1 255.255.255.0```
 ```!```
 ```!```
 ```ip forward-protocol nd```
 ```ip route 192.168.1.0 255.255.255.0```
 ```10.1.1.2```
 ```!```
	```r2#show run```
	 ```Building configuration...```
	
	 ```Current configuration : 2667 bytes```
	 ```!```
	 ```version 12.4```
	 ```!```
	 ```hostname r2```
	 ```!```
	 ```!```
	 ```ip cef```
	 ```!```
	 ```track 100 ip sla 100 reachability```
	 ```!```
	 ```interface Loopback0```
	 ``` ip address 192.168.1.1```
	 ```255.255.255.0```
	 ```!```
	 ```interface Ethernet0/0```
	 ``` ip address 10.1.1.2 255.255.255.0```
	 ```!```
	 ```interface Ethernet1/0```
	 ``` ip address 172.16.1.2 255.255.255.0```
	 ```!```
	 ```ip route 0.0.0.0 0.0.0.0 10.1.1.1```
	 ```!```

! IP SLA 100 is configured using an ICMP-ECHO probe, the timeout and frequency is adjusted for quicker convergence.
 	
 ```ip sla 100```
 ``` icmp-echo 10.1.1.2 source-ip```
 ```10.1.1.1```
 ``` timeout 5```
 ``` frequency 2```
 ```ip sla schedule 100 start-time now```
 ```recurring```
 ```!```
	! IP SLA 100 is configured using an ICMP-ECHO probe, the timeout and frequency is adjusted for quicker convergence.
	
	 ```!```
	 ```ip sla 100```
	 ``` icmp-echo 10.1.1.1 source-ip```
	 ```10.1.1.2```
	 ``` timeout 5```
	 ``` frequency 2```
	 ```ip sla schedule 100 start-time now```
	 ```recurring```
	 ```!```

R1	R2

EEM Applet triggered during failure.

| *EEM Applet triggered during failure.* |

```
event manager applet #100
 event syslog pattern "ip sla 100
reachability
Up->Down"
 action 1.0 cli command "enable"
 action 1.1 cli command "config
terminal"
 action 2.0 cli command "no ip route
192.168.1.0 255.255.255.0 10.1.1.2"
 action 3.0 cli command "ip route
192.168.1.0 255.255.255.0 172.16.1.2"
 action 4.0 syslog msg "back up
route"
```

```
event manager applet #100
 event syslog pattern "ip sla 100
reachability
Up->Down"
 action 1.0 cli command "enable"
 action 1.1 cli command "config
terminal"
 action 2.0 cli command "no ip route
0.0.0.0 0.0.0.0 10.1.1.1"
 action 3.0 cli command "ip route
0.0.0.0 0.0.0.0 172.16.1.1"
 action 4.0 syslog msg "back up
route"
```

When the EEM applet triggered once, the primary link is restored.

When the EEM applet triggered once, the primary link is restored.

```
event manager applet #101
 event syslog pattern "ip sla 100
reachability
Down->Up"
 action 1.0 cli command "enable"
 action 1.1 cli command "config
terminal"
 action 2.0 cli command "no ip route
192.168.1.0 255.255.255.0 172.16.1.2"
 action 3.0 cli command "ip route
192.168.1.0 255.255.255.0 10.1.1.2"
 action 4.0 syslog msg "back to
primary route"
!
end
```

```
event manager applet #101
 event syslog pattern "ip sla 100
reachability
Down->Up"
 action 1.0 cli command "enable"
 action 1.1 cli command "config
terminal"
 action 2.0 cli command "no ip route
0.0.0.0 0.0.0.0 172.16.1.1"
 action 3.0 cli command "ip route
0.0.0.0 0.0.0.0 10.1.1.1"
 action 4.0 syslog msg "back to
primary route"
!
end
```

The preceding example could be applied to any situation where time-sensitive applications are constrained to function appropriately only within certain network conditions. Having the ability to proactively measure the real-time network conditions and alter the behavior of the traffic pattern will ultimately create a better user experience.

Applet That Monitors the Default Route

In this example, a simple EEM applet is used to monitor events in the routing table. This can be useful for overall network management. Figure 4-3 illustrates the network topology for this example.

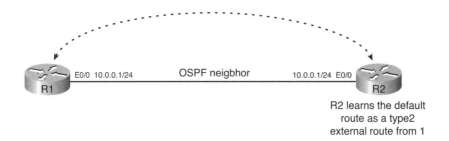

Figure 4-3   *EEM Routing Event Detection Example*

The objective of this applet is to generate probes from one Cisco IOS device to another and monitor the statistics of the probe messages. When a condition in the network occurs such that the probes are no longer received within a specified set of parameters, the applet will change the default route to an alternative path.

The following script is installed on R2 and monitors the availability of the default route in the routing table. When the default route is removed, it generates a user-defined syslog message "Default route is removed." The configuration is as follows:

```
event manager applet ROUTING
 event routing network 0.0.0.0/0 type remove
 action 1.0 syslog msg "Default route removed"
```

The next script detects when the default route has been restored:

```
event manager applet ROUTING#!
 event routing network 0.0.0.0/0 type add
 action 1.0 syslog msg "Default route restored"
```

The routing table during normal activity is as follows:

```
R2#show ip route
Codes: L - local, C - connected, S - static, R - RIP, M - mobile, B - BGP
D - EIGRP, EX - EIGRP external, O - OSPF, IA - OSPF inter area
N1 - OSPF NSSA external type 1, N2 - OSPF NSSA external type 2
E1 - OSPF external type 1, E2 - OSPF external type 2
i - IS-IS, su - IS-IS summary, L1 - IS-IS level-1, L2 - IS-IS level-2
ia - IS-IS inter area, * - candidate default, U - per-user static route
o - ODR, P - periodic downloaded static route, H - NHRP
+ - replicated route, % - next hop override

Gateway of last resort is 10.0.0.1 to network 0.0.0.0

O*E2  0.0.0.0/0 [110/1] via 10.0.0.1, 00:33:22, Ethernet0/0
10.0.0.0/8 is variably subnetted, 2 subnets, 2 masks
```

```
C          10.0.0.0/24 is directly connected, Ethernet0/0
L          10.0.0.2/32 is directly connected, Ethernet0/0
```

When R2 loses connectivity to R1, the following information will be generated.

■   R2 loses its Open Shortest Path First (OSPF) relationship:

```
%OSPF-5-ADJCHG: Process 1, Nbr 10.0.0.1 on Ethernet0/0 from FULL to DOWN,
Neighbor Down: Dead timer expired
```

■   The default route is not seen in the routing table:

```
R2#show ip route
Codes: L - local, C - connected, S - static, R - RIP, M - mobile, B - BGP
       D - EIGRP, EX - EIGRP external, O - OSPF, IA - OSPF inter area
       N1 - OSPF NSSA external type 1, N2 - OSPF NSSA external type 2
       E1 - OSPF external type 1, E2 - OSPF external type 2
       i - IS-IS, su - IS-IS summary, L1 - IS-IS level-1, L2 - IS-IS level-2
       ia - IS-IS inter area, * - candidate default, U - per-user static
  route
       o - ODR, P - periodic downloaded static route, H - NHRP
       + - replicated route, % - next hop override

Gateway of last resort is not set

       10.0.0.0/8 is variably subnetted, 2 subnets, 2 masks
C         10.0.0.0/24 is directly connected, Ethernet0/0
L         10.0.0.2/32 is directly connected, Ethernet0/0
R2#
```

■   The EEM script is triggered once the default route has been removed and the following syslog message is generated:

```
%HA_EM-6-LOG: ROUTING: Default route removed
```

When the connection is restored from R1 to R2, the following information is generated:

■   The OSPF adjacency is established:

```
%OSPF-5-ADJCHG: Process 1, Nbr 10.0.0.1 on Ethernet0/0 from LOADING to FULL,
  Loading Done
```

■   The EEM script is triggered once the default route is restored and a syslog message is generated:

```
%HA_EM-6-LOG: ROUTING#!: Default route restored
```

■   You can use the **show ip route** command to view the routing information:

```
R2#show ip route
Codes: L - local, C - connected, S - static, R - RIP, M - mobile, B - BGP
        D - EIGRP, EX - EIGRP external, O - OSPF, IA - OSPF inter area
        N1 - OSPF NSSA external type 1, N2 - OSPF NSSA external type 2
        E1 - OSPF external type 1, E2 - OSPF external type 2
        i - IS-IS, su - IS-IS summary, L1 - IS-IS level-1, L2 - IS-IS level-2
        ia - IS-IS inter area, * - candidate default, U - per-user static
  route
        o - ODR, P - periodic downloaded static route, H - NHRP
        + - replicated route, % - next hop override

Gateway of last resort is 10.0.0.1 to network 0.0.0.0

O*E2  0.0.0.0/0 [110/1] via 10.0.0.1, 00:00:19, Ethernet0/0
        10.0.0.0/8 is variably subnetted, 2 subnets, 2 masks
C         10.0.0.0/24 is directly connected, Ethernet0/0
L         10.0.0.2/32 is directly connected, Ethernet0/0
```

To view the details of the EEM script, use the **show event manager detector routing detailed** command, as demonstrated here:

```
R2#show event manager detector routing detailed
No.  Name              Version   Node      Type
1    routing           02.00     node0/0   RP

        Tcl Configuration Syntax:
        ::cisco::eem::event_register_routing
                 [tag <tag-val>]
                 network <network>/<length>
                 [ge <ge-length>]
                 [le <le-length>]
                 [ne <ne-length>]
                 [type {add   remove   modify   all}]
      [protocol <protocol-val>]
                 [queue_priority {normal | low | high | last}]
                 [maxrun <sec.msec>] [nice {0   1}]

        Tcl event_reqinfo Array Names:
        event_id
        event_type
        event_type_string
        event_pub_time
        event_pub_sec
        event_pub_msec
        event_severity
```

```
        network
        mask
        protocol
        type
        lastgateway
        distance
        time
        time_sec
        time_msec
        metric
        lastinterface
        Applet Configuration Syntax:
        [ no ] event [tag <tag-val>] routing
                network <network>/<length>
                [ge <ge-length>]
                [le <le-length>]
                [ne <ne-length>]
                [type {add   remove   modify   all}]
                [protocol <protocol-val>]
                [maxrun <sec.msec>]

        Applet Built-in Environment Variables:
        $_event_id
        $_event_type
        $_event_type_string
        $_event_pub_time
        $_event_pub_sec
        $_event_pub_msec
        $_event_severity
        $_routing_network
        $_routing_mask
        $_routing_protocol
        $_routing_type
        $_routing_lastgateway
        $_routing_distance
        $_routing_time
        $_routing_time_sec
        $_routing_time_msec
        $_routing_metric
    $_routing_lastinterface
```

Applets can definitely help you monitor the elements in the routing table. More complex user-defined actions can also be performed for route path selection.

Applet and Application Failover with a Network Address Translation Example

In this example, EEM is used in conjunction with object tracking and Network Address Translation (NAT) to provide high availability for an application.

The objective is to achieve access to a server, whose address is NATed to the IP address 172.16.1.1. Host1 (10.61.1.1) resides in RA, and host2 (10.61.1.2) resides in RB. RA is the primary host that services the application. When RA is down, the traffic for 172.16.1.1 will be sent to RB (that is, host 2). Figure 4-4 provides an overview of the network.

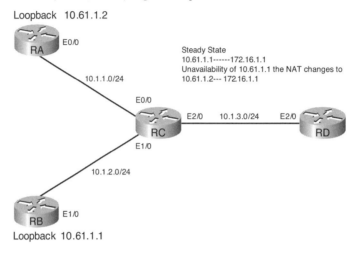

Figure 4-4   *EEM IP SLA and NAT Example*

This example uses four routers: RA, RB, RC, RD. RA and RB represent host1 (10.61.1.1) and host2 (10.61.1.2), respectively. RC is the router that maintains the IP SLA probes, EEM, and the NAT configuration. RD initiates traffic to the primary services address of 172.16.1.1. RA and RB have default route pointing to RC. RC and RD have a routing protocol relationship. The configuration and operation of the script follows.

During normal operation, the following conditions will be exhibited:

■   Ping from RD to the IP address 172.16.1.1:

```
RD#ping 172.16.1.1
Type escape sequence to abort.
Sending 5, 100-byte ICMP Echos to 172.16.1.1, timeout is 2 seconds:
!!!!!
Success rate is 100 percent (5/5), round-trip min/avg/max = 1/6/12 ms
RD#
```

■   The packet flow through RC translates the traffic destined for 172.16.1.1 to host1 (10.61.1.1). RC has a route that sends the packets destined to 172.16.1.1 through E0/0 (outgoing interface to RA). Interface E2/0 facing is configured as the NAT inside.

E0/0 facing RA is configured as the NAT outside. The configuration for NAT on RC is as follows:

```
ip nat inside source static 10.61.1.1 172.16.1.1
```

■ Looking at the NAT translations, you can see the operation of the translation:

```
RC#show ip nat  translations
Pro Inside global      Inside local     Outside local     Outside global
icmp 172.16.1.1:35     10.61.1.1:35     10.1.3.2:35       10.1.3.2:35
--- 172.16.1.1         10.61.1.1        ---               ---
```

■ Any traffic sent from RD will get translated from 172.16.1.1 to 10.61.1.1 when the packet traverses through interface E0/0 (inside NAT interface of RC). The following is the **route** statement added to RC that adds 172.16.1.1 route pointing to interface E0/0:

```
RC#show ip route 172.16.1.1
Routing entry for 172.16.1.1/32
  Known via "static", distance 1, metric 0 (connected)
  Tag 1
  Redistributing via ospf 1
  Advertised by ospf 1 subnets tag 1 route-map TEST
  Routing Descriptor Blocks:
  * directly connected, via Ethernet0/0
      Route metric is 0, traffic share count is 1
      Route tag 1
```

■ RC is configured with IP SLA probes. These probes monitor the availability of 10.61.1.1 and are linked to object tracking. The status of the IP SLA probes will be tracked and a syslog message will be generated. The EEM script uses the syslog message to make a determination of which service to direct traffic toward:

```
RC#show ip sla statistics 1

Round Trip Time (RTT) for       Index 1
        Latest RTT: 4 milliseconds
Latest operation start time: *20:13:57.146 PST Fri Oct 9 2009
Latest operation return code: OK
Number of successes: 358
Number of failures: 0
Operation time to live: Forever
```

■ This following output shows that the IP SLA probe operation is up:

```
RC#show track 3
Track 3
  IP SLA 1 reachability
  Reachability is Up
```

```
     25 changes, last change 01:18:41
  Latest operation return code: OK
  Latest RTT (millisecs) 1
```

The EEM applet is configured on RC. This applet will be be used only during failover. During a failover scenario, when RA is not reachable, the traffic will be directed to RB (host2, 10.61.1.2). The following list shows the configuration required on RC:

Step 1.   Define the name of the applet:

```
event manager applet #3
```

Step 2.   Trigger the applet using the following pattern match **ip sla 1 reachability Down->Up**:

```
event syslog pattern "ip sla 1 reachability Down->Up"
```

Step 3.   Access the enable prompt and clear the translations:

```
action 1.0 cli command "enable"
action 1.1 cli command "  clear ip nat translation *"
```

Step 4.   Change to configuration mode and remove the existing NAT translation:

```
action 2.0 cli command "config terminal"
action 3.0 cli command "no ip nat inside source static 10.61.1.2
  172.16.1.1"
```

Step 5.   Add the new NAT translation that points to host1:

```
action 4.0 cli command "ip nat inside source static 10.61.1.1
  172.16.1.1"
```

Step 6.   The **nat inside** statement is removed from E1/0:

```
action 5.0 cli command "interface E1/0"
action 6.0 cli command "no ip nat inside"
```

Step 7.   The **nat inside** statement is added to E1/0:

```
action 7.0 cli command "int e 0/0"
action 8.0 cli command " ip nat inside"
```

Step 8.   The **route** statement for 172.16.1.1 for the previous NAT inside interface is removed:

```
action 9.0 cli command "no ip route 172.16.1.1 255.255.255.255
  Ethernet1/0 tag 1"
```

Step 9.   The **route** statement for 172.16.1.1 on interface E1/0 is added:

```
action 9.1 cli command "ip route 172.16.1.1 255.255.255.255
  Ethernet0/0 tag 1"
```

Step 10. The operation of the script is as follows:

```
RC#show ip nat translations
Pro Inside global      Inside local      Outside local    Outside global
icmp 172.16.1.1:36     10.61.1.1:36      10.1.3.2:36      10.1.3.2:36
--- 172.16.1.1         10.61.1.1         - - -            - - -
RC#show track
Track 3
  IP SLA 1 reachability
  Reachability is Up
    27 changes, last change 01:20:52
  Latest operation return code: OK
  Latest RTT (millisecs) 4
Note:  Show the traffic is traversing to host1 at RA
```

When a failure happens, the following occurs:

Step 1. The following output from RC shows what happens when the traffic changes from host1 (10.61.1.1) to host2 (10.61.1.2):

```
%SYS-5-CONFIG_I: Configured from console by console
%TRACKING-5-STATE: 3 ip sla 1 reachability Up->Down
```

Step 2. The EEM policy is triggered and the configuration changes is completed based on the script:

```
SYS-5-CONFIG_I: Configured from console by vty0
```

Step 3. After the script is executed, the new translation is moved to 10.61.1.2, as shown:

```
RC#show ip nat translations
Pro Inside global      Inside local      Outside local    Outside global
--- 172.16.1.1         10.61.1.2         - - -            - - -
```

Step 4. The route has now changed:

```
RC#show ip route 172.16.1.1
Routing entry for 172.16.1.1/32
  Known via "static", distance 1, metric 0 (connected)
  Tag 1
  Redistributing via ospf 1
  Advertised by ospf 1 subnets tag 1 route-map TEST
  Routing Descriptor Blocks:
  * directly connected, via Ethernet1/0
      Route metric is 0, traffic share count is 1
      Route tag 1
```

Step 5.   The original **nat inside** statement is removed:

```
RC#show run interface  e0/0
Building configuration...
Current configuration : 64 bytes
!
interface Ethernet0/0
ip address 10.1.1.2 255.255.255.0
end
```

Step 6.   The new **nat inside** statement is now pointing to host2:

```
RC#show run int  e1/0
Building configuration...
Current configuration : 102 bytes
!
interface Ethernet1/0
 ip address 10.1.2.2 255.255.255.0
 ip nat inside
 ip virtual-reassembly
end
```

Step 7.   Traffic from RD is now sent to 172.16.1.1 at RC:

```
RC#show ip nat translations
Pro Inside global      Inside local     Outside local    Outside global
icmp 172.16.1.1:37     10.61.1.2:37     10.1.3.2:37      10.1.3.2:37
--- 172.16.1.1         10.61.1.2        ---              ---
```

On recovery, the following events occur:

```
RC#
%TRACKING-5-STATE: 3 ip sla 1 reachability Down->Up
```

Step 1.   The syslog message shows that the IP SLA probe is in the up state:

```
RC#
%SYS-5-CONFIG_I: Configured from console by vty0
```

Step 2.   The NAT translation is changed from 10.61.1.2 to 10.61.1.1:

```
RC#show ip nat translations
Pro Inside global      Inside local     Outside local    Outside global
--- 172.16.1.1         10.61.1.1        ---              ---
```

Step 3.   The route to 172.16.1.1 is pointing to interface E0/0:

```
RC#show ip route 172.16.1.1
Routing entry for 172.16.1.1/32
  Known via "static", distance 1, metric 0 (connected)
  Tag 1
  Redistributing via ospf 1
  Advertised by ospf 1 subnets tag 1 route-map TEST
  Routing Descriptor Blocks:
  * directly connected, via Ethernet0/0
      Route metric is 0, traffic share count is 1
      Route tag 1
```

Step 4.   The **nat inside** statement is now removed from E1/0:

```
RC#show run int  e1/0
Building configuration...

Current configuration : 64 bytes
!
interface Ethernet1/0
 ip address 10.1.2.2 255.255.255.0
end
```

Step 5.   The **nat inside** statement is added to E0/0:

```
RC#show run int  e0/0
Building configuration...
Current configuration : 102 bytes
!
interface Ethernet0/0
 ip address 10.1.1.2 255.255.255.0
 ip nat inside
 ip virtual-reassembly
end
```

Step 6.   Traffic from RD now traverses RC to reach host1 (10.61.1.1).

The pertinent configuration commands on RC are as follows:

```
RC#show run
track 2 ip sla 2 reachability
track 3 ip sla 1 reachability
interface Ethernet0/0
 ip address 10.1.1.2 255.255.255.0
 ip nat inside
interface Ethernet2/0
 ip address 10.1.3.1 255.255.255.0
 ip nat outside
router ospf 1
redistribute static subnets tag 1 route-map TEST
```

```
 network 0.0.0.0 255.255.255.255 area 0
ip route 10.61.1.1 255.255.255.255 Ethernet0/0
ip route 10.61.1.2 255.255.255.255 Ethernet1/0
ip route 172.16.1.1 255.255.255.255 Ethernet0/0 tag 1
ip nat inside source static 10.61.1.1 172.16.1.1
ip sla 1
 icmp-echo 10.1.1.1
 frequency 5
ip sla schedule 1 life forever start-time now
ip sla 2
 icmp-echo 10.1.2.1
 frequency 5
ip sla schedule 2 life forever start-time now
access-list 1 permit 172.16.1.1
route-map TEST permit 1
 match ip address 1
event manager applet #2
 event syslog pattern "ip sla 1 reachability Up->Down"
 action 1.0 cli command "enable"
 action 1.1 cli command "  clear ip nat translation *"
 action 2.0 cli command "config terminal"
 action 3.0 cli command "no ip nat inside source static 10.61.1.1 172.16.1.1"
 action 4.0 cli command "ip nat inside source static 10.61.1.2 172.16.1.1"
 action 5.0 cli command "int e 0/0"
 action 6.0 cli command "no ip nat inside"
 action 7.0 cli command "int e 1/0"
 action 8.0 cli command "ip nat inside"
 action 9.0 cli command "no ip route 172.16.1.1 255.255.255.255 Ethernet0/0 tag 1"
 action 9.1 cli command "ip route 172.16.1.1 255.255.255.255 Ethernet1/0 tag 1"
event manager applet #3
 event syslog pattern "ip sla 1 reachability Down->Up"
 action 1.0 cli command "enable"
 action 1.1 cli command "  clear ip nat translation *"
 action 2.0 cli command "config terminal"
 action 3.0 cli command "no ip nat inside source static 10.61.1.2 172.16.1.1"
 action 4.0 cli command "ip nat inside source static 10.61.1.1 172.16.1.1"
 action 5.0 cli command "int e 1/0"
 action 6.0 cli command "no ip nat inside"
 action 7.0 cli command "int e 0/0"
 action 8.0 cli command " ip nat inside"
 action 9.0 cli command "no ip route 172.16.1.1 255.255.255.255 Ethernet1/0 tag 1"
 action 9.1 cli command "ip route 172.16.1.1 255.255.255.255 Ethernet0/0 tag 1"
```

This script can be used to achieve dynamic active/standby redirection of traffic. The host could be multiple hops away, and the same principle can be applied with a slight modification to the configuration.

To view all the event detectors, use the following command:

```
Router#show event manager detector all
No.   Name                   Version    Node        Type
1     appl                   01.00      node0/0     RP
2     syslog                 01.00      node0/0     RP
3     routing                02.00      node0/0     RP
4     track                  01.00      node0/0     RP
5     resource               01.00      node0/0     RP
6     cli                    01.00      node0/0     RP
7     counterp9.676          01.00      node0/0     RP
8     interface              01.00      node0/0     RP
9     ioswdsysmon            01.00      node0/0     RP
10    none                   01.00      node0/0     RP
11    oir                    01.00      node0/0     RP
12    snmp                   01.00      node0/0     RP
13    snmp-notification      01.00      node0/0     RP
14    timer                  01.00      node0/0     RP
15    ipsla                  01.00      node0/0     RP
16    nf                     01.00      node0/0     RP
```

The name event describes what can be tracked by using EEM.

To view the details of the events that can be monitored, use the following command:

```
Router#show event manager detector ipsla detailed
No.   Name                   Version    Node        Type
1     ipsla                  01.00      node0/0     RP

      Tcl Configuration Syntax:
      ::cisco::eem::event_register_ipsla
              [tag <tag-val>]
              group_name <group-name value>
              operation_id <operation-id value>
              [reaction_type <reaction_type value>]
              [dest_ip_addr <destination-ip-address>]
              [queue_priority {normal | low | high | last}]
              [maxrun <sec.msec>] [nice {0   1}]

      Tcl event_reqinfo Array Names:
      event_id
      event_type
      event_type_string
      event_pub_time
      event_pub_sec
      event_pub_msec
      event_severity
```

```
            group_name
            oper_id
            condition
            react_type
            dest_ip_addr
            threshold_rising
            threshold_falling
            threshold_count
            threshold_count2
  Applet Built-in Environment Variables:
            $_event_id
            $_event_type
            $_event_type_string
            $_event_pub_time
            $_event_pub_sec
            $_event_pub_msec
            $_event_severity
            $_ipsla_group_name
            $_ipsla_oper_id
            $_ipsla_condition
            $_ipsla_react_type
            $_ipsla_threshold_type
            $_ipsla_dest_ip_addr
            $_ipsla_threshold_rising
            $_ipsla_threshold_falling
            $_ipsla_threshold_count
            $_ipsla_threshold_count2
          $_ipsla_measured_threshold_value
```

Using EEM and Tcl Scripts

EEM policies have two primary components, an event and an action:

- An **event** keyword is used to establish a criteria when the policy is run.

- A user-defined action in the policy provides the response to the detected event.

Within Cisco IOS, system policies are already built and provide a great starting point for writing scripts. You can show the available system policies on the Cisco IOS device using the following command:

```
Router#show event manager policy available system
No.  Type    Time Created              Name
1    system  Wed Feb 6  22:28:15 2036  ap_perf_test_base_cpu.tcl
2    system  Wed Feb 6  22:28:15 2036  cl_show_eem_tech.tcl
3    system  Wed Feb 6  22:28:15 2036  no_perf_test_init.tcl
```

```
4     system  Wed Feb 6  22:28:15 2036  sl_intf_down.tcl
5     system  Wed Feb 6  22:28:15 2036  tm_cli_cmd.tcl
6     system  Wed Feb 6  22:28:15 2036  tm_crash_reporter.tcl
7     system  Wed Feb 6  22:28:15 2036  tm_fsys_usage.tcl
```

Programming Policies with Tcl

Event manager policies consist of one or more EEM detectors combined with a Tcl script. The Tcl script can perform tasks based on a trigger from the EEM detectors. EEM policies consist of required elements and optional elements. The required elements are event register and the Tcl script body. The other optional elements include namespace import, entry status, and exit status. Figure 4-5 describes the EEM policies that are the foundation for the script itself.

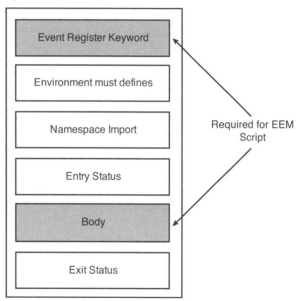

Figure 4-5 *Functional Specifications for Tcl Scripts*

Note   Although namespace import is not mandatory, it requires that you will have to fully qualify all the EEM Tcl procedures.

Figure 4-5 illustrates the basic elements for Tcl scripts, as follows:

■ **Event Register Keyword:** To start any policy, the policy needs to be described and registered. This is done using the event **register** keyword.

■ **Environment Must Define:** The variables that need to be used in the Tcl script need to be defined in the router configuration, using environment variable in the event manager configuration.

- **Namespace Import:** Namespace import refers to all Tcl commands closely related to EEM.

- **Entry Status:** This determines whether an earlier policy has been run for the same event. Based on the result of the previous policy (if executed), the current policy may or may not be executed.

- **Body:** The actual body of the Tcl script that defines the policy.

- **Exit Status:** This provides the criteria used by EEM to determine the exit policy.

Tcl Example Used to Check for Interface Errors

The EEM script in this section checks the interface counters, and if errors are seen, it generates an e-mail to the selected account.

For the script to operate properly, you need to define environment variables. The variables include the following elements:

```
event manager environment _email_server e_mail_server.com
event manager environment _email_to destination_account
event manager environment _email_from source_account
event manager environment _cron_entry 0-59/2 0-23/1 * * 0-7
event manager environment _show_cmd show interface | include errors
event manager directory user policy flash:
```

Note   Variables that begin with an underscore (_) character are reserved for Cisco internal use and could be overwritten by system variables.

```
event manager policy interface_errors_email.tcl
```

Tip   When configuring the source account using authentication to the SMTP server, use the following format:

event manager environment _email_server USERPASSWORD@SERVER_IP_ADDRESS

Step 1.   The beginning of the Tcl script registers the CRON timer with user-defined parameters gleaned from the **event manager** variables:

```
::cisco::eem::event_register_timer cron name crontimer2 cron_entry
$_cron_entry maxrun_sec 240
```

Step 2.   Verify the existence of all the environment variables you need for the script. If any of them are not available, print out an error message and quit.

Step 3.   Validate that the **_email_server** environment variable is set:

```
if {![info exists _email_server]} {
```

Step 4.   If the environment variable **_email_server** has not been detected, save the error and quit:

```
set result \
    "Policy cannot be run: variable _email_server has not been set"
error $result $errorInfo
}
```

Step 5.   The following section checks whether the required environment variable **_email_from** exists:

```
if {![info exists _email_from]} {
```

Step 6.   If an error is detected in the environment variable (**_email_from**), save the reason for the error and exit the script:

```
set result \
    "Policy cannot be run: variable _email_from has not been set"
error $result $errorInfo
}
```

Step 7.   The following section checks whether the required environment variable **_email_to** exists:

```
if {![info exists _email_to]} {
```

Step 8.   If an error is detected in the environment variable (**_email_to**), save the reason for the error and exit the script:

```
set result \
    "Policy cannot be run: variable _email_to has not been set"
error $result $errorInfo
}
```

Step 9.   The following section checks whether the **_email_cc** environment variable exists. Because this is not a required parameter, the variable will be configured as an empty string if nothing has been entered:

```
if {![info exists _email_cc]} {
```

Step 10.   The **_email_cc** is an option, but must set to an empty string if not configured:

```
    set _email_cc ""
}
```

Step 11.   Verify that the **_show_cmd** environment variable is set, because this will be used to collect the IOS **show** command output and send it in the e-mail body:

```
if {![info exists _show_cmd]} {
```

Step 12.   If there is an error, collect the information and exit the script:

```
            set result \
              "Policy cannot be run: variable _show_cmd has not been set"
            error $result $errorInfo
        }
```

Step 13. Load the standard EEM libraries. The procedures **error** and **cli_open** are standard EEM library procedures:

```
namespace import ::cisco::eem::*
namespace import ::cisco::lib::*
```

Step 14. Query the event info and log a message:

```
array set arr_einfo [event_reqinfo]
```

Step 15. If any problems were detected, variable **_cerrno** is set to a nonzero value, and the variable named **_cerr** contains the details of the problem:

```
if {$_cerrno != 0} {
    set result [format "component=%s; subsys err=%s; posix err=%s;\n%s" \
        $_cerr_sub_num $_cerr_sub_err $_cerr_posix_err $_cerr_str]
    error $result
}
```

Step 16. The following variables are used to store the time of the error:

```
global timer_type timer_time_sec
set timer_type $arr_einfo(timer_type)
set timer_time_sec $arr_einfo(timer_time_sec)
```

Step 17. Log a message:

```
set msg [format "timer event: timer type %s, time expired %s" \
        $timer_type [clock format $timer_time_sec]]
```

Step 18. Send the message to the syslog process:

```
action_syslog priority info msg $msg
```

Step 19. If any problems were detected, the variable **_cerrno** is set to a nonzero value and the variable named **_cerr** will contain the details of the problem:

```
if {$_cerrno != 0} {
    set result [format "component=%s; subsys err=%s; posix err=%s;\n%s" \
        $_cerr_sub_num $_cerr_sub_err $_cerr_posix_err $_cerr_str]
    error $result
}
```

Step 20. Execute the **show** command from the environment variable **_show_cmd**:

```
if [catch {cli_open} result] {
```

Step 21. If there is a problem with the **show** command, end the script because of the error:

```
    error $result $errorInfo
} else {
```

Step 22. With a success, save the results to the array **cli1**:

```
    array set cli1 $result
}
```

Step 23. Because the **cli_open** was successful, use the variable **fd** from now on to access the CLI.

Step 24. Enter IOS enable mode for proper display of many **show** commands:

```
if [catch {cli_exec $cli1(fd) "en"} result] {
```

Step 25. In the event of an error, end the script:

```
    error $result $errorInfo
}
```

Step 26. Execute the IOS **show** command, and save the result:

```
if [catch {cli_exec $cli1(fd) $_show_cmd} result] {
```

Step 27. If a problem occurred executing the IOS **show** command, end the script now:

```
    error $result $errorInfo
} else {
```

Step 28. Save the output of the IOS **show** command in variable **cmd_output**:

```
    set cmd_output $result
}
```

Step 29. If a problem occurred closing access to the CLI, end the script now:

```
if [catch {cli_close $cli1(fd) $cli1(tty_id)} result] {
    error $result $errorInfo
}
```

Step 30. Log the success of the CLI command:

```
set msg [format "Command \"%s\" executed successfully" $_show_cmd]
```

Step 31. Send the message to the syslog process:

```
action_syslog priority info msg $msg
```

Step 32. If any problems were detected, the variable **_cerrno** is set to a nonzero value and the variable named **_cerr** will contain the details of the problem:

```
if {$_cerrno != 0} {
    set result [format "component=%s; subsys err=%s; posix err=%s;\n%s" \
        $_cerr_sub_num $_cerr_sub_err $_cerr_posix_err $_cerr_str]
    error $result
}
```

Collect the input and output errors using the IOS **show** command from the environment variable:

Step 1.   Wherever a space appears, save it in the **mylist** variable:

```
set mylist [split $cmd_output " "]
```

Step 2.   Create an identical copy of the variable that will be modified as we work out the results:

```
set newlist [split $cmd_output " "]
```

Step 3.   Create counter variables to keep track of how many interface input and output errors were detected:

```
set inputerror 0
set outputerror 0
```

Step 4.   The **curpos** variable is a pointer to a specific position in the string **newlist**. Look for the first occurrence of the word **input** in **mylist** and save that location as **curpos**:

```
set curpos [lsearch $mylist input]
```

Step 5.   Search through the string **newlist** until there are no longer any instances of the word **input**, at this time **curpos** will be set to 0:

```
while {$curpos > 0} {
```

Step 6.   Set the variable **prev** to the location in the string just prior to the value of **curpos**:

```
set prev [expr $curpos - 1]
```

Step 7.   The **curerror** variable contains the actual number of input errors:

```
set curerror [lindex $mylist $prev]
```

Step 8.   Increment the variable **inputerror** if there were any input errors:

```
if {$curerror > 0} {incr inputerror}
```

Step 9.   Change the word **input** to **junk** in the string **newlist**. This is done to prevent counting the same error multiple times:

```
set newlist [lreplace $newlist $curpos $curpos junk]
```

Step 10.   Search for the word **input** in the string **newlist**:

```
    set curpos [lsearch $newlist input]
}
```

Step 11. Look for the first occurrence of the word **output** in the string **newlist** and set the variable **curpos** to that location:

```
set curpos [lsearch $mylist output]
```

Step 12. Search through the string **newlist** until there are no longer any instances of the word **output**, at this time **curpos** will be set to 0:

```
while {$curpos > 0} {
```

Step 13. Set the variable **prev** to the location in the string just prior to the value of **curpos**:

```
set prev [expr $curpos - 1]
```

Step 14. The **curerror** variable contains the actual number of input errors:

```
set curerror [lindex $mylist $prev]
```

Step 15. Increment the variable **inputerror** if there were any input errors:

```
if {$curerror > 0} {incr outputerror}
```

Step 16. Change the word **input** to **junk** in the string **newlist**. This is done to prevent counting the same error multiple times:

```
set newlist [lreplace $newlist $curpos $curpos junk]
```

Step 17. Search for the word **output** in the string **newlist**:

```
    set curpos [lsearch $newlist output]
}
```

Step 18. Check whether there were any interface errors:

```
if {$inputerror < 1 && $outputerror < 1} {
```

Step 19. If both variables **inputerror** and **outputerror** are 0, this indicates that there were not any errors:

```
set result "no interface errors found"
```

Step 20. Because there were not any errors detected, end the script:

```
 error $result
}
```

Send an e-mail indicating that the interface errors were detected.

Step 1. Collect the name of the Cisco IOS device:

```
set routername [info hostname]
if {[string match "" $routername]} {
```

Step 2.   If the IOS device is missing the **hostname** configuration command, display
the following error message:

```
    error "Host name is not configured"
}
```

Step 3.   Concatenate the **show** command output with a standard e-mail template from
the library and get the e-mail server IP address:

```
if [catch {smtp_subst [file join $tcl_library email_template_cmd.tm]}
  result] {
    error $result $errorInfo
}
```

Step 4.   Send the e-mail message:

```
if [catch {smtp_send_email $result} result] {
    error $result $errorInfo
}
```

Figure 4-6 shows the e-mail received from the IOS device.

> From router TCLRouter: Periodic show interface I i errors Output
>
> ▾ ray.blair@comcast.net <ray.blair@comcast.net>
>
> **To:** Ray Blair <rablalr@cisco.com>

```
    1 input errors, 0 CRC, 1 frame, 0 overrun, 0 ignored
    0 output errors, 0 collisions, 3 interface resets
    0 input errors, 0 CRC, 0 frame, 0 overrun, 0 ignored
    0 output errors, 0 colloisions, 0 interface resets
    0 input errors, 0 CRC, 0 frame, 0 overrun, 0 ignored, 0 abort
    0 output errors, 0 colisions, 6 interface resets
    0 input errors, 0 CRC, 0 frame, 0 overrun, 0 ignored, 0 abort
    0 output errors, 0 collisions, 6 interface resets
TCLRouter#
```

Figure 4-6   *Script Error Results*

Tcl Example Used to Check the CPU Utilization

The sample script in this section checks the CPU, and if it exceeds a 60 percent threshold, generates an e-mail.

Step 1.   The following event manager commands configured on the IOS device are
used to define the environment variables in the Tcl script:

```
event manager environment _email_server e_mail_server.com
event manager environment _email_to destination_account
event manager environment _email_from source_account
event manager environment _cron_entry 0-59/2 0-23/1 * * 0-7
```

```
event manager environment _show_cmd show proc cpu | i five
event manager environment _percent 60
event manager dir user pol flash:
event manager policy cpu_threshold_email.tcl
```

Note   Because of an aspect of implementation (bug) in code prior to EEM Release 2.3, it is recommended to use the IP address of the mail server and not the name.

Step 2.   The beginning of the Tcl script registers the CRON timer with user-defined parameters gleaned from the **event manager** variables:

```
::cisco::eem::event_register_timer cron name crontimer2 cron_entry
$_cron_entry maxrun_sec 240
```

Step 3.   The following section checks whether the required environment variable **_email_server** exists:

```
if {![info exists _email_server]} {
```

Step 4.   If an error is detected in the environment variable (**_email_server**), save the reason for the error and exit the script:

```
set result \
        "Policy cannot be run: variable _email_server has not been set"
error $result $errorInfo
}
```

Step 5.   The following section checks whether the required environment variable **_email_from** exists:

```
if {![info exists _email_from]} {
```

Step 6.   If an error is detected in the environment variable (**_email_from**), save the reason for the error and exit the script:

```
set result \
        "Policy cannot be run: variable _email_from has not been set"
error $result $errorInfo
}
```

Step 7.   The following section checks whether the required environment variable **_email_to** exists:

```
if {![info exists _email_to]} {
```

Step 8.   If an error is detected in the environment variable (**_email_to**), save the reason for the error and exit the script:

```
set result \
        "Policy cannot be run: variable _email_to has not been set"
```

```
error $result $errorInfo
}
```

Step 9. The following section checks whether the **_email_cc** environment variable exists. Because this is not a required parameter, the variable will be configured as an empty string if nothing has been entered:

```
if {![info exists _email_cc]} {
set _email_cc ""
}
```

Step 10. Verify that the **_show_cmd** environment variable is set. This parameter will be used to collect the Cisco IOS **show** command output and send it in the e-mail body:

```
if {![info exists _show_cmd]} {
```

Step 11. If there is an error, collect the information and exit the script:

```
    set result \
        "Policy cannot be run: variable _show_cmd has not been set"
error $result $errorInfo
}
```

Step 12. Load the standard EEM libraries. For example, the **namespace import** statement **error** and **cli_open** are standard EEM library procedures:

```
namespace import ::cisco::eem::*
namespace import ::cisco::lib::*
```

Step 13. Query the event info and log a message:

```
array set arr_einfo [event_reqinfo]
```

Step 14. If any problems were detected, the variable **_cerrno** is set to a nonzero value, and the variable named **_cerr** will contain the details of the problem:

```
if {$_cerrno != 0} {
    set result [format "component=%s; subsys err=%s; posix err=%s;\n%s" \
        $_cerr_sub_num $_cerr_sub_err $_cerr_posix_err $_cerr_str]
    error $result
}
```

Step 15. The following variables are used to store the time of the error:

```
global timer_type timer_time_sec
set timer_type $arr_einfo(timer_type)
set timer_time_sec $arr_einfo(timer_time_sec)
```

Step 16. Log a message:

```
set msg [format "timer event: timer type %s, time expired %s" \
        $timer_type [clock format $timer_time_sec]]
```

Step 17.   Send the message to the syslog process:

```
action_syslog priority info msg $msg
```

Step 18.   If any problems were detected, the variable **_cerrno** is set to a nonzero value, and the variable named **_cerr** will contain the details of the problem:

```
if {$_cerrno != 0} {
    set result [format "component=%s; subsys err=%s; posix err=%s;\n%s" \
        $_cerr_sub_num $_cerr_sub_err $_cerr_posix_err $_cerr_str]
    error $result
}
```

Step 19.   Execute the **show** command from the environment variable **_show_cmd**:

```
if [catch {cli_open} result] {
```

Step 20.   If there is a problem with the **show** command, end the script because of the error:

```
error $result $errorInfo
} else {
```

Step 21.   With a success, save the results to the array **cli1**:

```
    array set cli1 $result
}
```

Step 22.   Because the **cli_open** was successful, use the variable **fd** from now on to access the CLI.

Step 23.   Enter IOS enable mode for proper display of many **show** commands:

```
if [catch {cli_exec $cli1(fd) "en"} result] {
```

Step 24.   In the event of an error, end the script:

```
    error $result $errorInfo
}
if [catch {cli_exec $cli1(fd) $_show_cmd} result] {
```

Step 25.   If a problem occurred executing the IOS **show** command, end the script now:

```
error $result $errorInfo
} else {
```

Step 26.   Save the output of the IOS **show** command in variable **cmd_output**:

```
    set cmd_output $result
}
if [catch {cli_close $cli1(fd) $cli1(tty_id)} result] {
```

Step 27. If a problem occurred closing access to the CLI, end the script now:

```
error $result $errorInfo
}
```

Step 28. Log the success of the CLI command:

```
set msg [format "Command \"%s\" executed successfully" $_show_cmd]
```

Step 29. Send the message to the syslog process:

```
action_syslog priority info msg $msg
```

Step 30. If any problems were detected, the variable **_cerrno** is set to a nonzero value, and the variable named **_cerr** will contain the details of the problem:

```
if {$_cerrno != 0} {
    set result [format "component=%s; subsys err=%s; posix err=%s;\n%s" \
        $_cerr_sub_num $_cerr_sub_err $_cerr_posix_err $_cerr_str]
    error $result
}
```

Step 31. Collect the actual CPU percentage from the **show** command. The variable **foundposition** will point to the beginning of the word "**five**" in the string "**five minutes:**".

```
set foundposition [string first "five minutes: " $cmd_output]
```

Step 32. We get the string length of "**five minutes:**" so that it can be easily removed later:

```
set cutoff [string length "five minutes: "]
```

Step 33. Only process the output if **foundposition** actually found the string "**five minutes: **":

```
if {$foundposition > -1} {
```

Step 34. Set the variable **begin** to the location of the beginning of the number after "**five minutes: **":

```
set begin [expr $foundposition + $cutoff]
```

Step 35. Set the variable **end** to the location of the end of the number after "**five minutes: **". This assumes that the number is no longer than three digits; it could be one, two, or three digits long:

```
set end [expr $begin + 3]
```

Step 36. Save the number variable **realcpu**. This variable might or might not contain the % character, depending on how many digits long it is. For example, if the variable was at 100, the **realcpu** variable will not have the % character present because only three digits were saved. If it were a two-digit number like 50, you would have the % character in the variable **realcpu**:

```
set realcpu [string range $result $begin $end]
```

Step 37.   Check whether the % character was found. If it was, remove it:

```
set foundpercent [string first "%" $realcpu]
if {$foundpercent > -1} {
```

Step 38.   Remove any trailing white space characters:

```
set realcpu [string trimright $realcpu]
```

Step 39.   Remove the % character if it is present:

```
        set realcpu [string trimright $realcpu "%?"]
    }
}
```

Step 40.   Compare the CPU usage to the **%60** value specified. If the CPU usage exceeded the set max, the variable **realcpu** contains the actual number from the **show** command:

```
if {$realcpu < $_percent} {
    set result "CPU did not exceed the set percent"
    error $result
}
```

Step 41.   Collect the name of the Cisco IOS device:

```
set routername [info hostname]
if {[string match "" $routername]} {
```

Step 42.   If the IOS device is missing the **hostname** configuration command, display the following error message:

```
    error "Host name is not configured"
}
```

Step 43.   Send an e-mail indicating that the CPU was above the configured limit. Concatenate the **show** command output with a standard e-mail template from the library and get the e-mail server IP address:

```
if [catch {smtp_subst [file join $tcl_library email_template_cmd.tm]}
result] {
    error $result $errorInfo
}
```

Step 44.   Send the e-mail message:

```
if [catch {smtp_send_email $result} result] {
    error $result $errorInfo
}
```

Summary

The Embedded Event Manager (EEM) includes detectors for notification of a particular event, the event manager that controls the operation of predetermined actions, and the policies that can be either an applet or Tcl script. EEM has continued to evolve, with more feature functionality with each subsequent release.

From the examples in this chapter, you can see the differences in applets and Tcl scripts and the power you have to customize your own applications to automate monitoring and troubleshooting processes.

References

Cisco Beyond (a repository for user-contributed EEM policies):
http://tinyurl.com/yetbqgq

Cisco Embedded Automation Systems: http://www.cisco.com/go/easy

Cisco IOS Embedded Event Manager (EEM): http://www.cisco.com/go/eem

Writing Embedded Event Manager Policies Using Cisco IOS CLI:
http://tinyurl.com/yjveq6q

Cisco IOS IP Service Level Agreements (SLAs): http://www.cisco.com/go/ipsla

Chapter 5

Advanced Tcl Operation in Cisco IOS

This chapter covers the following topics:

- Introduction to the Syslog Protocol
- Configuring Syslog Server Parameters in Cisco IOS
- Syslog Tcl Script Example
- Sending Syslog Messages to a File
- Putting the Syslog Script into Operation
- Introduction to Embedded Syslog Manager
- Using Tcl as a Web Server
- Introduction to IP SLA
- Tcl Script Refresh Policy
- SNMP Proxy Event Detector
- RPC Requests
- Multiple-Event Support for Event Correlation
- Using the **clear** Command

To this point, the examples in this book have been relatively simple. This chapter covers some more complicated Tcl scripts and their use with Cisco IOS. Some examples are more complicated because they involve handling a specific network protocol as a server. Therefore, they may have more work to do to service incoming requests from clients. The first advanced Tcl script presented functions as a syslog daemon.

One important set of Tcl commands that might prove particularly helpful when writing a network server is the socket library. The syslog example demonstrates the use of sockets, which are built directly in to Tcl in Cisco IOS. A socket library simplifies the programmer's job of writing a network server by handling the complexities of the networking protocol. Instead of concentrating on how to handle the incoming network connection, the programmer can focus on the important part, handling the incoming data.

Introduction to the Syslog Protocol

The syslog protocol allows network devices to send small text messages to a central server that can be viewed by network administrators. The main purposes of syslog messages are to document failures, monitor trends, collect pertinent statistics, and send alarm messages to a central location. The central device is typically a syslog server running a software application that collects data and displays it in a format suitable for human consumption. This information will help network administrators with capacity planning, maintaining network security, troubleshooting, and so on. Ultimately, this data provides network administrators with a better overall understanding of what is happening with the network.

The actual syslog messages consist of five parts:

- An optional timestamp.

- The message "facility," or what part of the system the message is coming from, also known as a mnemonic.

- The "severity," or how serious is the issue. Severity ranges from 0, meaning an absolute emergency, to a value of 7, which is used for debugging messages. Table 5-1 shows a list of syslog severities in IOS.

- The message name follows after severity. This is a short abbreviation for the message name that can be used for correlation of many messages.

- The final portion is the text of the syslog message. The message text will vary from message to message. For example, a syslog message printed on the console of a Cisco IOS router might appear as follows:

```
*Dec  6 21:07:05.754: %LDP-5-NBRCHG: LDP Neighbor 10.131.191.252:0 (4) is UP
```

The preceding example is a syslog message that contains the following five fields:

Timestamp: Dec 6 21:07:05.754

Facility Name: LDP

Severity: 5 (Notifications)

Name: NBRCHG

Text: LDP Neighbor 10.131.191.252:0 (4) is UP

Note Cisco IOS has a concept of a subfacility that follows the facility. The subfacility is separated from the facility by a hyphen (-). This is typically seen using the Catalyst 6500 when the switching engine generates a syslog message as follows:

```
%SWITCH-SP-5-NOTICE ...
```

Table 5-1   *IOS Syslog Severity Levels*

Severity	Text Name	Meaning
0	Emergencies	System is unusable.
1	Alerts	Immediate action needed.
2	Critical	Critical conditions.
3	Errors	Error conditions.
4	Warnings	Warning conditions.
5	Notifications	Normal but significant conditions.
6	Informational	Informational messages.
7	Debugging	Debugging messages.

Configuring Syslog Server Parameters in Cisco IOS

By default, Cisco IOS displays these syslog messages on the console, along with the date and time the syslog message occurred (timestamp). If you do not want to see every syslog message printed on the console, but instead only want to be notified of severity 3 messages or lower, configure the following:

```
Router#config terminal
Enter configuration commands, one per line. End with CNTL/Z.
Router(config)#logging console errors
```

Only severity 3 (or worse, meaning severity 0, 1, or 2) syslog messages will appear on the console.

By default, syslog messages will have a timestamp with the date and time, including the millisecond entry, of the message. It is also possible to change the format of the timestamp, which begins each message. For example, to change the timestamp to use the uptime of the Cisco IOS device, enter the following:

```
Router(config)#service timestamps log uptime
```

Note   By default, Cisco IOS uses uptime for service timestamps. To enable a timestamp field with the data and time, you must use the following command in configuration mode:

```
Router(config)#service timestamps log datetime
```

The syslog messages will have a timestamp showing the uptime of the Cisco IOS device, in other words, how much time has elapsed since the device booted up.

It is also possible to completely disable the timestamps from appearing in the syslog messages. To do so, configure the following:

```
syslogSender#configure terminal
Enter configuration commands, one per line. End with CNTL/Z.
syslogSender(config)#no service timestamps log
syslogSender(config)#end
syslogSender#
```

Sequence numbers can be optionally included before the timestamp. To enable this, configure **service sequence-numbers,** as shown here:

```
syslogSender#configure terminal
Enter configuration commands, one per line. End with CNTL/Z.
syslogSender(config)#service sequence-numbers
syslogSender(config)#end
syslogSender#
000039: *Jan  9 21:12:12.751: %SYS-5-CONFIG_I: Configured from console by console
syslogSender#
```

In the preceding example, you can see that the sequence number has been added to the beginning of the syslog message before the timestamp. In this case, the sequence number is 39. Sequence numbers enable you to determine whether messages have been dropped or lost.

Messages can also be saved in a small text buffer. The buffer can save only a certain number of messages before becoming full. Once full, the oldest are removed to make space for the newest messages. To configure the buffer size for the syslog message, change the size of the logging buffer as follows:

```
Router(config)#logging buffered 1000000
```

The number **1000000** represents how many bytes of local memory will be used to save outgoing syslog messages. To review all the setting for the syslog in the Cisco IOS device, enter the following command:

```
Router#show logging
syslog logging: enabled (0 messages dropped, 12 messages rate-limited,
 0 flushes, 0 overruns, xml disabled, filtering disabled)
No Active Message Discriminator.

No Inactive Message Discriminator.

    Console logging: level errors, 46 messages logged, xml disabled,
                     filtering disabled
    Monitor logging: level debugging, 0 messages logged, xml disabled,
                     filtering disabled
```

```
     Buffer logging:   level debugging, 9 messages logged, xml disabled,
                         filtering disabled
     Exception Logging: size (4096 bytes)
     Count and timestamp logging messages: disabled
     Persistent logging: disabled
     Trap logging: level informational, 72 message lines logged
Log Buffer (1000000 bytes):
2d20h: %SYS-5-CONFIG_I: Configured from console by console
2d20h: %LDP-5-CLEAR_NBRS: Clear LDP neighbors (*) by console
2d20h: %LDP-5-NBRCHG: LDP Neighbor 10.131.159.251:0 (3) is DOWN (User cleared
  session manually)
2d20h: %LDP-5-NBRCHG: LDP Neighbor 10.131.191.252:0 (4) is DOWN (User cleared
  session manually)
2d20h: %LDP-5-NBRCHG: LDP Neighbor 10.131.191.252:0 (1) is UP
2d20h: %LDP-5-NBRCHG: LDP Neighbor 10.131.159.251:0 (2) is UP
```

The output of the command will show various settings related to the syslog and the contents of the local buffer, which holds the syslog messages. As you can see, console logging is enabled, and the severity level of messages will be **error** or **severity 3** (or worse). In addition, the size of the internal buffer has been enlarged to 1000000 bytes and will store severity level **debugging** or **severity 7** (or worse).

Now that you have an understanding of the syslog operation in Cisco IOS, you can see how the syslog messages can be sent to a remote host for central correlation.

The syslog protocol allows both User Datagram Protocol (UDP) and Transmission Control Protocol (TCP) to be used to send messages between devices. UDP messages are not acknowledged; they are sent in one direction only. For this reason, TCP support was added to Cisco IOS to provide a small level of guarantee that messages are delivered to the central syslog server. Because it is possible for network interruptions to bring down the TCP connection, a special syslog message is generated every time the TCP connection is established or torn down.

Note   The Berkeley Software Distribution (BSD) syslog protocol, described in RFC 3164, does not mention the use of TCP as a method to transport information.

To see a syslog message being sent to a remote host, you must configure the IOS device to begin sending messages to the host, tell it what protocol to use, and provide the IP address of the remote host. In this example, syslog messages will be generated by an IOS router with the hostname of syslogSender:

```
syslogSender#config terminal
Enter configuration commands, one per line. End with CNTL/Z.
syslogSender(config)#logging host 10.10.10.1 transport tcp port 9500
syslogSender(config)#end
syslogSender#
```

```
*Dec  6 22:09:39.175: %SYS-5-CONFIG_I: Configured from console by console
syslogSender#
*Dec  6 22:10:00.231: %SYS-6-LOGGINGHOST_STARTSTOP: Logging to host 10.10.10.1
port 9500 started - CLI initiated
syslogSender#
```

From the previous configuration, the router has been configured to send logging messages to the host (or syslog daemon) with the IP address of 10.10.10.1. In addition, TCP port 9500 will be used for the connection.

Now that the Cisco IOS router has been configured to send the messages to a specific host, we will use a Tcl script to receive the actual syslog messages.

Note   The most common method of transporting syslog data is over UDP. Using TCP to transport the messages is less common. The default syslog port is UDP port 514.

Syslog Tcl Script Example

The following script opens a TCP socket and listens for incoming connections from the syslog sender. When syslog messages are received on the socket, they are printed on the console of the IOS device. If the socket connection closes, the server continues to listen for additional socket connections. When users are ready to exit the syslog daemon, they can press Esc to exit back to the IOS prompt.

The following is an example of the Tcl syslog daemon script.

To begin, configure the procedures.

Configure all incoming connections to use the variable name **my_sock**:

```
global my_sock
```

Set all incoming data to use the variable name **my_data**:

```
global my_data
```

The next command handles starting and stopping the server, and calling the **on_connect** procedure for incoming socket connections:

```
proc Listener {port action} {
```

The **global** command links the local variable to the global variable:

```
global my_sock
if {$action == "START"} {
```

On startup, open a socket and save the socket handle to the variable **my_sock**. Also, tell the socket to call the **on_connect** procedure for any incoming connections:

```
  set my_sock [socket -server on_connect $port]
} else {
```

If there is a problem, close the socket for cleanup:

```
    if {[info exists my_sock]} {
       puts "Closing my socket"
         close $my_sock
     }
   }
   return $my_sock
}
```

The procedure **on_connect** is called whenever a new socket connection has been established:

```
proc on_connect {newsock clientAddress clientPort} {
    puts "socket is connected now"
```

Configure the socket for nonblocking operation:

```
fconfigure $newsock -blocking 0
```

If the new socket is readable, call the procedure **handleInput**:

```
fileevent  $newsock readable [list handleInput $newsock]
}

proc handleInput {f} {
    global my_data
```

If the socket was closed, delete the handler (for example, the sending device closes the socket). This is important, because we would otherwise try to read data from a closed socket:

```
if {[eof $f]} {
```

When the end of the file is reached, remove the **handleInput** procedure for incoming events on the socket and set it to an empty list.

```
fileevent $f readable {}
```

Close the socket:

```
    close      $f
    return
}
```

Read the incoming text data and save the text data into **my_data**:

```
set my_data [read -nonewline $f]
```

Remove any nonprintable characters using a regular expression:

```
regsub -all  {<[0-9]+>[0-9]+: } $my_data " " output
```

Verify whether there is any data in the string:

```
if {[string length $output]} {
```

With data available, show it to the user:

```
  puts stdout "$output"
}
```

Wait for more data:

```
}
```

Configure the main portion of the Tcl script. So far, we have just defined the procedures above this point.

Set the break key to the Esc key:

```
exec "term esc 27"
```

Call the procedure to listen for an incoming socket, using TCP port 9500:

```
Listener 9500 START
```

Wait for any events on the incoming socket connection:

```
vwait my_sock
```

Syslog Tcl Script Sample Output

The following section demonstrates the use of the Tcl syslog daemon script.

From the command line of the IOS device, initiate the script using the following command:

```
syslogDaemon#tclsh flash:syslogd_book.tcl
```

In this case, the file is located in the root directory of the flash: file system. This IOS device is configured as the syslog server or receiver of the syslog messages.

The syslog daemon will initially wait for any incoming connections. Next, add the **logging host** configuration command to allow the IOS device to connect to the syslog server. This IOS device is configured to send logging information to the syslog server:

```
syslogSender#conf t
Enter configuration commands, one per line. End with CNTL/Z.
syslogSender(config)# logging host 10.10.10.1 transport tcp port 9500
syslogSender(config)#end
syslogSender#
*Dec  8 02:29:25.244: %SYS-5-CONFIG_I: Configured from console by console
syslogSender#
*Dec  8 02:29:26.264: %SYS-6-LOGGINGHOST_STARTSTOP: Logging to host 10.10.10.1
  port 9500 started - CLI initiated
syslogSender#
```

Two different routers must be used for this example, which can connect across the network. One router is named syslogSender, and it generates the syslog messages. The second router is named syslogDaemon, and it collects the syslog messages to be displayed on the console. Note that in production networks, a router will not typically be used as a syslog daemon.

The syslog server built in to Cisco IOS will attempt a TCP connection to the Tcl syslog daemon script. The following is the message displayed on syslogDaemon about the socket connection:

```
socket is connected now
 *Dec  8 02:29:25.244: %SYS-5-CONFIG_I: Configured from console by console
 *Dec  8 02:29:26.264: %SYS-6-LOGGINGHOST_STARTSTOP: Logging to host 10.10.10.1
 port 9500 started - CLI initiated
```

The preceding messages are generated from the user exiting out of configure terminal mode (SYS-5-CONFIG_I), and the syslog server creates a message whenever it successfully connects to any syslog daemon (SYS-6-LOGGINGHOST_STARTSTOP).

To generate additional syslog messages, you clear the Multiprotocol Label Switching (MPLS) Label Distribution Protocol (LDP) neighbor on the IOS device sending syslog messages:

```
syslogSender#clear mpls ldp neighbor *
```

The output from the IOS device acting as the syslog server displays the following messages:

```
*Dec  8 02:36:14.434: %LDP-5-CLEAR_NBRS: Clear LDP neighbors (*) by console
 *Dec  8 02:36:14.446: %LDP-5-NBRCHG: LDP Neighbor 10.131.191.252:0 (1) is DOWN
(User cleared session manually)
 *Dec  8 02:36:14.446: %LDP-5-NBRCHG: LDP Neighbor 10.131.159.251:0 (2) is DOWN
(User cleared session manually)
 *Dec  8 02:36:14.594: %LDP-5-NBRCHG: LDP Neighbor 10.131.159.251:0 (3) is UP
*Dec  8 02:36:14.571: %LDP-5-NBRCHG: LDP Neighbor 10.131.191.251:0 (1) is DOWN
(TCP connection closed by peer) *Dec  8 02:36:17.374: %LDP-5-NBRCHG: LDP
Neighbor 10.131.191.252:0 (4) is UP
*Dec  8 02:36:17.443: %LDP-5-NBRCHG: LDP Neighbor 10.131.191.251:0 (2) is UP
```

To exit from the syslog daemon, press the Esc key.

Here is the complete syslog Tcl script example:

```
# syslog Daemon & socket example


#all incoming connection will be on the socket named "my_sock"
    global my_sock
#all incoming texutal data will be on the socket named "my_sock"
    global my_data
#Listener procedure handles starting and stopping the server
# and calling on_connect procedure for incoming socket connections
proc Listener {port action} {
```

```
    # the global variable is known by the procedure also
        global my_sock
        if {$action == "START"} {
            # we are being told to startup, so open a socket and save the
            # socket handle in my_sock.  Also tell the socket to call
            # on_connect procedure for any incoming connections
            set my_sock [socket -server on_connect $port]
        } else {
            # we are being told to shutdown, so close the socket for
            # cleanup purposes
            if {[info exists my_sock]} {
                #if the socket is really there, close it
                    puts "Closing my socket"

                close $my_sock
            }
        }
        return $my_sock
}


# Procedure on_connect is called whenever a new socket connection is
# made by a syslog server
proc on_connect {newsock clientAddress clientPort} {
    puts "socket is connected now"
    # configure the socket for no blocking operation
    # this is import and because we do not want to block on any read later
    fconfigure $newsock -blocking 0
    # if the new socket is readable, then set the procedure handleInput
    # to be called whenever input arrives
    fileevent  $newsock readable [list handleInput $newsock]
}


# Procedure called whenever input arrives on the readable socket
# connection.
proc handleInput {f} {
    global my_data

    # Delete the handler if the socket was closed for example the
    # other side closes the socket.  This is important because we would
    # otherwise try to read data from a closed socket
    if {[eof $f]} {
        # we got the End of File character: clean up
        # first, remove the handleInput procedure for incoing events
```

```
        # on the socket, set it to an empty list
         fileevent $f readable {}
        # close the socket
         close      $f
        # exit procedure
         return
    }


    # Read and handle the incoming text data

    # set my_file [ open /var/log/router_tcp.log a ]

    # save the text data into my_data
    set my_data [read -nonewline $f]
    # remove any nonprintable characters using a regular expression
    regsub -all  {<[0-9]+>[0-9]+: } $my_data " " output

    # check whether there was text data
    if {[string length $output]} {
        # there was some data to print, show it to the user
        puts stdout "$output"
    }
    # at this point we will wait again for more data
}


# The beginning of the TCL script, so far we have just defined
# procedures above this point

# set the break key to ESC key
exec "term esc 27"
# call the procedure to listen for incoming socket, using tcp port 9500
Listener 9500 START
# wait for any events on the incoming socket connection
vwait my_sock
```

Sending Syslog Messages to a File

The Tcl interpreter provides access to the file system for reading and writing files. Instead of just showing the syslog messages on the console, it is possible to create a file that can be retrieved later. Depending on where the file is placed on the router, it can also be made available for other network devices.

Files can be thought of as *channels*. To get a list of all the current channels in the Tcl interpreter, enter the following in Tcl shell:

```
syslogDaemon(tcl)#file chan
stderr stdout stdin
```

You can see that there are three default channels that Tcl automatically opens when starting up. These so-called *standard* channels are used for getting input and output to the user and for reporting errors. In Chapter 2, "Tcl Interpreter and Language Basics," you learned how to open a file for reading the contents of the file. Now you examine how to open a file and write data into the file.

The next example opens/creates a file called syslog on disk0: for writing only (**WRONLY**). To open the file, enter the following command in the Tcl shell:

```
syslogDaemon(tcl)#open disk0:syslog WRONLY
file0
```

If the file did not exist before opening it, it will be created. If the file already existed, it will be opened to write additional data into it. Many different modes can be used when opening a file. In this case, we have chosen to create file that is write-only, meaning it can only be written to but not read from. Your complete access options are **RDONLY**, **WRONLY, RDWR, APPEND, CREAT EXCL, NOCTTY, NONBLOCK, TRUNC, r, r+, w, w+, a,** and **a+**. However, only some of the modes are supported in Cisco IOS, as described in Table 5-2.

When a file has been successfully opened, it returns a channel name or handle that can be used to access the file as long as the file remains open. To get a list of the channels that are currently open, enter the following command in the Tcl shell:

```
syslogDaemon(tcl)#file chan
file0 stderr stdout stdin
```

The preceding list indicates that **file0** is currently open. Next, add the word **testing** to the opened file, using the following command:

```
syslogDaemon(tcl)#puts file0 testing
```

When you have completed writing information into the file, it should be closed, as follows:

```
syslogDaemon(tcl)#close file0
```

The file is now closed and you can verify by checking the open channels once again:

```
syslogDaemon(tcl)#file chan
stderr stdout stdin
```

You can see that **file0** has been removed from the list of known channels.

To verify that the data put into the file is actually there, you can do a quick check of the length of the file with the **file size** command:

```
syslogDaemon(tcl)#file size disk0:syslog
8
```

Table 5-2 *Supported File Access Modes in Cisco IOS*

Access Mode	Meaning
RDONLY	File may only be read from.
WRONLY	File may only be written to.
RDWR	File may be both read from and written to. However, Cisco IOS cannot read a file opened in this mode, only write to the file.
r	File may only be read from and must exist
r+	File may be read from and written to and must exist. However, Cisco IOS cannot read a file opened in this mode, only write to the file.
w	File may only be written to. If the file exists, it will be truncated; if not, the file will be created.
w+	File may be read from or written to. If the file exists, it will be truncated; if not, the file will be created. However, Cisco IOS cannot read a file opened in this mode, only write to the file.
a	File may be appended to.
a+	File may be read from or appended to. However, Cisco IOS cannot read a file opened in this mode, only write to the file.

The output of the preceding command indicates that there is a total of eight characters in this file. This matches what was entered earlier; the word *testing* is seven characters long plus there is a newline character that is automatically appended to the end, for a total of eight characters. You can also validate the contents of the file by copying the data into a variable.

First, the file needs to be opened. Because you will not be adding or writing information into the file, you can open the file in a read-only mode so that you do not accidentally change the contents:

```
syslogDaemon(tcl)#open disk0:syslog RDONLY
file0
```

Next, the contents of the file is read into a local variable called **incoming_data**, using the following command:

```
syslogDaemon(tcl)#set incoming_data [read -nonewline file0]
testing
```

From the preceding output, you can see that the contents of the file match the information that was originally added.

Now that you have successfully created a new file with the Tcl interpreter, you can modify the syslog example to create a text file containing the incoming syslog messages. This example uses the TCP port number and filename to write the data as parameters to the script. The **argc** and **argv** will be used to access the incoming parameters provided in **tclsh scriptname arg1, arg2, arg3**.

The main body of the script is used to examine the incoming arguments provided to the Tcl shell. If the number of parameters does not match what the script is expecting, we immediately exit the script. The port and filename are required parameters. It is always a good idea to perform some error checking on the variables passed to the script to prevent any unexpected problems.

Syslog Server Script Procedures

The following script is the complete example of the syslog server that will write to a text file:

Step 1.   All incoming connection will be on the socket named **my_sock**:

```
global my_sock
```

Step 2.   All incoming data will be directed to the socket named **my_sock**:

```
global my_data
```

Step 3.   Create the **my_mode** variable to save the mode of operation. **1** is for writing to the console, and **2** is for writing to the console and the file and will be configured later:

```
global my_mode
```

Step 4.   Set the file handle to **my_file**:

```
global my_file
```

Step 5.   The **Listener** procedure handles starting and stopping the server, and calling the **on_connect** procedure for incoming socket connections:

```
proc Listener {port action filename} {
```

Step 6.   Set the variables as global:

```
global my_sock
global my_file
global my_mode
set my_mode 0
if {$action == "START"} {
```

Step 7. Open a socket and save the socket handle in **my_sock**. Initiate the **on_connect** procedure for any incoming connections:

```
set my_sock [socket -server on_connect $port]
```

Step 8. Set **my_mode** to **1**, which will write to the console only:

```
    set my_mode 1
} elseif {$action == "STARTWriting"} {
    set my_sock [socket -server on_connect $port]
    set my_file [open $filename WRONLY]
```

Step 9. Set **my_mode** to **2**, which will write to the console and file:

```
    set my_mode 2
} else {
```

Step 10. Close the socket for cleanup purposes:

```
        if {[info exists my_sock]} {
                puts "Closing my socket"
            close $my_sock
      }
    }
    return $my_sock
}
```

Step 11. Close the file:

```
if {[info exists my_file]} {
  #if the socket is really there, close it
    puts "Closing my file"

    close $my_file
}
```

Step 12. The procedure **on_connect** is called whenever a new socket connection is initiated by a syslog server:

```
proc on_connect {newsock clientAddress clientPort} {
    puts "socket is connected now"
```

Step 13. Configure the socket for noblocking operation. This is important because you do not want to block on a read function later in the script:

```
fconfigure $newsock -blocking 0
```

Step 14.   If the new socket is readable, set the procedure **handleInput** to be called whenever input arrives:

```
fileevent  $newsock readable [list handleInput $newsock]
}
```

Step 15.   Call the following procedure whenever input arrives on the readable socket connection:

```
proc handleInput {f} {
```

Step 16.   Provide access to global variables inside the procedures, by declaring them as global:

```
global my_data
global my_file
global my_mode
```

Step 17.   Delete the handler if the socket was closed. For example, the syslog sender closes the socket. If the socket is left open, the script would continue to try and read data from a closed socket:

```
if {[eof $f]} {
```

Step 18.   On an End of File (EoF) character, clean up by removing the **handleInput** procedure for incoming events on the socket and set it to an empty list:

```
fileevent $f readable {}
```

Step 19.   Close the socket:

```
close     $f
```

Step 20.   Exit the procedure:

```
    return
}
```

Step 21.   Read and handle the incoming text data and save the text data to the variable **my_data**:

```
set my_data [read -nonewline $f]
```

Step 22.   Remove any nonprintable characters using the following regular expression:

```
regsub -all  {<[0-9]+>[0-9]+: } $my_data " " output
```

Step 23.   Check whether there was text data:

```
if {[string length $output]} {
```

Step 24.   If there is data, show it to the user:

```
puts stdout "$output"
```

Step 25.   If the variable **my_mode** is set to **2**, write to the file and the console:

```
if {[expr ($my_mode == 2)]} {
```

Step 26.   Write the data to the file:

```
        puts $my_file $output
    }
  }
}
```

The body of the script is defined in the section that follows.

Syslog Server Script Body

The usage guidelines for the script are as follows:

syslogd *port* [*filename*]

Where

- *port* is the TCP port to listing for incoming connection.

- *filename* is optional to write the syslog data.

Check the incoming variable arguments. If the user forgot to provide any, display an informative help message:

```
if {$argc == 0} {
    puts "Usage: syslogd port filename"
    puts "port is the TCP port to listing for incoming connection"
    puts "filename is optional parameter to use for writing the syslog data"
    return
}
set port [lindex $argv 0]
```

Verify that the user provided port is a number. Check whether the port is a digit using the **string is ...** command, which returns a value of **1**. Compare the value to **1** and terminate the script if it does not match:

```
if {[expr (1 != [string is digit $port])]} {
    puts "must provide a numeric port number"
    return
}
```

Check that the port is in the acceptable range (for example, the ephemeral port range, or at least greater than 0, and less than 65536). If the user entered an out-of-range port number, provide a warning message and terminate the script:

```
#verify port is in the valid range
if ([expr (1 != (0 < $port))]) {
    puts "port number too low"
    return
}
#verify port is in the valid range
if ([expr (1 != ($port < 65536))]) {
    puts "port number too high"
    return
}
if {$argc == 1} {
```

The user only provides the **port** input parameter:

```
Listener $port START 0
} elseif {$argc == 2} {
```

The user provides two input parameters, the port and filename. Save the filename the user provided in **my_filename**:

```
set my_filename [lindex $argv 1]
```

Call the procedure to listen for incoming syslog connections and configure the procedure to write messages to a file:

```
    Listener $port STARTWriting $my_filename
} else {
```

If the user provided more than two input parameters and there is at least one additional **arg** that is not understandable, we remind the user of the correct usage and end the script:

```
    puts "Usage: syslogd port filename"
    puts "port is the TCP port to listing for incoming connection"
    puts "filename is optional parameter to use for writing the syslog data"
    return
}
```

Set the break key to the Esc key:

```
exec "term esc 27"
```

Call the procedure to listen for incoming sockets, using TCP port provided by user input. Wait for any events on the incoming socket connection:

```
vwait my_sock
```

Putting the Syslog Script into Operation

From the enable prompt of the IOS device configured as the syslog server, put the script into operation with incorrect parameters to validate the functionality of the script:

```
syslogDaemon#tclsh disk0:syslogd_book2.tcl
Usage: syslogd port filename
port is the TCP port to listing for incoming connection
filename is optional parameter to use for writing the syslog data
syslogDaemon#$syslogd_book2.tcl 9500 flash:syslog.txt extra-parameter
Usage: syslogd port filename
port is the TCP port to listing for incoming connection
filename is optional parameter to use for writing the syslog data
syslogDaemon#
```

Now input the correct parameters:

```
syslogDaemon#tclsh flash:syslogd_book2.tcl 9500 flash:syslog.txt
```

Now, the syslog daemon is waiting for incoming messages. By disabling and enabling logging on the syslog sender, syslog messages will be generated:

```
syslogSender(config)#no logging host 10.10.10.1 transport tcp port 9500
syslogSender(config)#
*Dec 13 00:20:34: %SYS-6-LOGGINGHOST_STARTSTOP: Logging to host 10.10.10.1 port
  9500 stopped - CLI initiated
*Dec 13 00:20:35: %SYS-6-LOGGINGHOST_STARTSTOP: Logging to host 10.10.10.1 port
  9500 stopped - disconnection
syslogSender(config)#logging host 10.10.10.1 transport tcp port 9500
syslogSender(config)#end
syslogSender#
*Dec 13 00:20:40: %SYS-5-CONFIG_I: Configured from console by console
syslogSender#
*Dec 13 00:20:41: %SYS-6-LOGGINGHOST_STARTSTOP: Logging to host 10.10.10.1 port
9500 started - CLI initiated
syslogSender#
```

From the following messages, you can see that the syslog daemon has correctly displayed the incoming syslog messages on the console:

```
syslogDaemon#
socket is connected now
 *Dec 13 00:20:40: %SYS-5-CONFIG_I: Configured from console by console
 *Dec 13 00:20:41: %SYS-6-LOGGINGHOST_STARTSTOP: Logging to host 10.10.10.1 port
  9500 started - CLI initiated
```

The operation of the script can be verified by checking whether the file was written correctly. Exit the syslog daemon by pressing the **Esc** key and use the **more** command to display the contents of any file on a Cisco IOS device:

```
syslogDaemon#more flash:syslog.txt
 *Dec 13 00:20:40: %SYS-5-CONFIG_I: Configured from console by console
 *Dec 13 00:20:41: %SYS-6-LOGGINGHOST_STARTSTOP: Logging to host 10.10.10.1 port
 9500 started - CLI initiated
syslogDaemon#
```

You can use the syslog daemon script application to collect and store information locally on an IOS device. This information, as you will see later, will be used to create a graphical display of the collected information.

Introduction to Embedded Syslog Manager

The Embedded Syslog Manager (ESM) is a Tcl script-based processing tool for syslog messages that runs on Cisco IOS devices. ESM can take incoming syslog messages and make changes to them before they are sent to their destination. Recall that syslog messages can be sent to the console, remote terminal sessions connected to the router, a local buffer, or specific hosts running a syslog daemon. ESM can make changes to the syslog messages before they arrive at any of these destinations. Other main purposes of ESM include advanced message filtering and severity escalation.

ESM can act as a filter to block particular syslog messages from being sent. A regular expression can be used to match particular syslog messages that are not needed. Entire message facility names can be filtered out. For example, if the user wants to block all the mnemonic SYS messages, it can easily be done with an ESM filter.

Another common application is severity escalation of particular syslog messages. If you write an appropriate ESM script, it can easily change the severity of particular syslog messages to higher or lower. The ESM script looks for syslog messages matching a regular expression and can change the severity of any message matching the pattern.

ESM was first introduced in Cisco IOS Software Release 12.3(2)T and was integrated into Cisco IOS Software Releases 12.3(2)XE and 12.2(25)S.

Filtering Syslog Messages

ESM uses a Tcl script as a filter to drop the incoming syslog messages before sending them out. One or more filters may be applied in a chain to process the incoming syslog messages and sends them on to the next filter for further processing. Each type of syslog destination can have a filter chain applied or not, depending on the IOS device configuration.

For example, the following commands enable ESM and apply a Tcl script filter to all sys-log messages on the console. The filter would not be applied to the other syslog destina-tions, such as the local buffer or syslog hosts:

```
syslogSender#show running-config | include logging
logging console filtered
logging filter disk0:filter.tcl
logging host 10.10.10.1 transport tcp port 9500
```

The **logging console filtered** command applies the ESM Tcl script to all syslog messages on the IOS device console. The **logging filter flash:filter.tcl** command specifies the one and only Tcl script we want to perform the syslog message processing. Finally, there is a command for sending syslog messages to a host, but it receives the original, unfiltered syslog messages.

The string value that the Tcl script returns is the replacement for the original syslog mes-sage. If you want to replace all syslog messages with your own message, you can use the following one-line Tcl script:

```
return "All syslog messages changed to this."
```

To apply the filter, copy the Tcl script to the local storage of the Cisco IOS device and apply the following commands to the IOS device:

```
syslogSender#configure terminal
Enter configuration commands, one per line. End with CNTL/Z.
syslogSender(config)#logging console filtered
syslogSender(config)#logging filter flash:filter.tcl
syslogSender(config)#end
syslogSender#
```

Note Filters can also be located on remote devices. Filters can also be loaded across the network on FTP, HTTP, NVRAM, RCP, and TFTP file systems.

All syslog messages are changed. For example, the typical syslog message that is generat-ed when exiting configuration mode is as follows:

```
%SYS-5-CONFIG_I: Configured from console by console
```

Because you applied the new ESM filter, the output changes to the following message:

```
All syslog messages changed to this.
```

To write a more useful filter, you could create a script that either decides to allow the sys-log message through or not. For example, if you are connected to the Cisco IOS device console, it is not that useful to know you have just exited configuration mode. Therefore, it is not helpful to have SYS-5-CONFIG_I display on the console if the console user is the one making changes. However, you might want to know whether someone has modi-fied the configuration coming in through a remote terminal session. You can write an

ESM filter that only lets the SYS-5-CONFIG_I syslog message through if it does not match the string **console**.

To write this filter, you need to understand how to access the global variables that are provided by ESM in the Tcl filter script. One of the global variables ESM provides is **::orig_msg**, which is used as follows:

```
return $::orig_msg
```

This global variable consists of the original, unmodified syslog message.

In the following example, the filter is named **filter2.tcl** and copied to the local storage of the router. Remove the old **filter.tcl** and add the new **filter2.tcl** command so that only one ESM filter is active. If you make the following configuration change to the router, the filter in action is not very useful either:

```
syslogSender#configure terminal
Enter configuration commands, one per line. End with CNTL/Z.
syslogSender(config)#no logging filter flash:filter.tcl
syslogSender(config)# logging filter flash:filter2.tcl
syslogSender(config)#end
syslogSender#
*Jan 10 00:40:17.671: %SYS-5-CONFIG_I: Configured from console by console
syslogSender#
```

The SYS-5-CONFIG_I syslog message is being displayed, completely unchanged from its original form. Now you can put the two filters together to write a new and more powerful one.

The form of the syslog messages from users exiting on the console is as follows:

```
*Jan 10 01:14:37.418: %SYS-5-CONFIG_I: Configured from console by console
```

The form of syslog messages from users exiting on incoming telnet sessions is as follows:

```
*Jan 10 01:15:20.230: %SYS-5-CONFIG_I: Configured from console by cisco on vty0
(10.10.10.1)
```

The difference in the syslog message text is that the console session configuration always ends in the words **by console**, and the Telnet session configuration always ends with **on vty**, and a number representing which incoming remote terminal session is being used, followed by the IP address of the remote device. You can use this difference in the text to write a new ESM Tcl filter script.

If the user exits out of configuration mode on the console, the string **by console** will be present at the end the original syslog message. For this reason, you can do a global search for the words **by console** and reject the syslog message if it is found. Because you want to display the syslog message only if it does not end in the words **by console**, you can write the following Tcl script and name it **filter3.tcl**:

```
if [string match "*by console" $::orig_msg] {
    return ""
```

```
} else {
    return $::orig_msg
}
```

Copy this new filter to the local storage of the router and remove the old **filter2.tcl** and
add the newly created **filter3.tcl**:

```
syslogSender#configure terminal
Enter configuration commands, one per line. End with CNTL/Z.
syslogSender(config)#no logging filter flash:filter2.tcl
syslogSender(config)#logging filter flash:filter3.tcl
syslogSender(config)#end
syslogSender#
```

On exiting configuration mode, a syslog message was not generated on the Cisco IOS
device console. However, you will be notified with a syslog message when a user modi-
fies the configuration that comes in through a remote terminal session.

Enable Telnet users to connect to the Cisco IOS device by using local authentication with
the following commands:

```
syslogSender(config)#line vty 0 4
syslogSender(config-line)#login local
syslogSender(config-line)#exit
syslogSender(config)#username cisco password cisco
syslogSender(config)#enable password cisco
syslogSender(config)#end
syslogSender#
```

The **line vty 0 4** command enters the configuration submode for virtual terminal sessions
such as Telnet. The **login local** allows the IOS device to use local usernames and passwords for user authentication. The **username** command creates a local user and local
password. The **enable password cisco** command is also needed so that the incoming
Telnet user can access full privilege mode to enter configuration mode. Preferably, use
something other than cisco for your password.

Connect to the router through a Telnet session and exit configuration mode. Syslog messages are generated on the console as follows:

```
syslogDaemon#telnet 10.10.10.2
Trying 10.10.10.2 ... Open

User Access Verification
Username: cisco
Password:
syslogSender>en
Password:
syslogSender#config
```

```
syslogSender#configure terminal
Enter configuration commands, one per line. End with CNTL/Z.
syslogSender(config)#end
syslogSender#
```

From the console connection on the IOS device, the following is displayed:

```
syslogSender#
*Jan 10 01:15:20.230: %SYS-5-CONFIG_I: Configured from console by cisco on vty0
(10.10.10.1)
syslogSender#
```

The ESM Tcl script filter has worked correctly, and you are still being notified of any configuration changes coming from incoming Telnet sessions.

ESM Global Variables

In addition to the global variable **::orig_msg**, many other global variables are available in ESM Tcl scripts, as outlined in Table 5-3. The original syslog message is also broken down into its component parts for convenience. Instead of operating on **::orig_msg**, it is also possible to reconstruct the original syslog message by concatenating the individual parts. Why would this be done? It is used if the Tcl script just needs to change one part of the syslog message and leave the other parts unchanged. That way, the original message can be concatenated with the changed variable.

Table 5-3 *Frequently Used Global ESM Variables with Meanings*

Global Variable	Meaning	Example
::buginfseq	Sequence number of the syslog message (if enabled with "**service sequence-numbers**").	000074:
::timestamp	The timestamp of the syslog message.	*Jan 10 02:01:34.454
::facility	Syslog message facility.	SYS
::severity	Syslog message severity.	5
::mnemonic	Syslog message name.	CONFIG_I
::format	Syslog message text format.	Configured from %s by %s
::msg_args	Syslog message text variables.	console console
::orig_msg	The original, full unmodified syslog message.	000041: *Mar 23 07:08:01.023: %SYS-5-CONFIG_I: Configured from console by console

Global Variable	Meaning	Example
::hostname	The actual hostname in use by the router.	syslogSender
::syslog_facility	A number, which is used for syslog messages. This was traditionally used to determine what process generated the syslog message in a UNIX host. It can be changed globally with the configuration command: **logging facility** *name*.	23
::module_position	This filter's position in the list of filters that can be applied. Multiple filters may be used together to create a "chain." The first one begins at 1 and proceeds higher.	1
::stream	If there are many logging destinations defined, the **stream** variable can be used to direct the output of the filter. Changing the value of the stream will redirect where the syslog message will be directed after processing (see Table 5-4). It can be used to send the syslog messages to certain syslog hosts. For example, configure the following configuration command to restrict the stream for that particular host: **logging host 1.2.3.4 filtered stream 10**.	2
::traceback (Optional. Only some syslog messages will contain this variable.)	A list of hexadecimal values, intended for Cisco development to help understand the syslog message.	
::process (Optional. Only some syslog messages will contain this variable.)	The name of the process generating the syslog message.	
::pid (Optional. Only some syslog messages will contain this variable.)	The process ID of the process generating the syslog message.	

Table 5-4   *ESM Stream Destinations to Use When Setting the* ::stream *Variable*

Number	Destination
0	The standard syslog stream
1	XML-tagged syslog stream
2	Default filtered syslog stream (the default value if unmodified by the filter)
3–9	Reserved
10–65536	User defined

Rebuilding a Syslog Message from Its Components

To write an ESM Tcl script filter that returns the original message made out of its component parts, we write the following Tcl script:

Step 1.   Copy the original format into variable called **text**:

```
set text $::format
```

Step 2.   Create a pointer to the first **msg_arg** in the list we created:

```
set listp 0
```

Step 3.   Loop until you are past the last item in the list you created:

```
while {$listp < [llength $::msg_args]} {
```

Step 4.   Set the variable **beg** to the beginning of the first item:

```
set beg [string first %s $text]
```

Step 5.   Set the variable **end** to the end of the first occurrence of **%s** in text:

```
set end $beg
incr end
```

Step 6.   Replace the **%s** with the actual **msg_arg** it should be, and save this back into the variable **text**:

```
set text [string replace $text $beg $end [lindex $msg_args $listp]]
```

Step 7.   Increment the variable **listp** and point to the next item in the list:

```
    incr listp
}
```

Step 8.   Return the original syslog message from the number of its' component parts:

```
return "$buginfseq$timestamp: %$facility-$severity-$mnemonic: $text"
```

Step 9.   Save the script to a file named **filter7.tcl** and copy it to the local storage of the Cisco IOS device. Remove the old filter **filter3.tcl** and add the newly created filter **filter7.tcl**, as shown:

```
syslogSender#configure terminal
Enter configuration commands, one per line. End with CNTL/Z.
syslogSender(config)#no logging filter flash:filter3.tcl
syslogSender(config)#logging filter flash:filter7.tcl
syslogSender(config)#end
syslogSender#
000079: *Jan 10 23:48:59.519: %SYS-5-CONFIG_I: Configured from console
  by console
syslogSender#
```

You have successfully created a new ESM Tcl filter that can process all the component parts back into the original syslog message. You can verify that the filter is working correctly by signing on through a Telnet session and entering and exiting configuration mode to generate a syslog message:

```
syslogDaemon#telnet 10.10.10.2
Trying 10.10.10.2 ... Open

User Access Verification
Username: cisco
Password:
syslogSender>en
Password:
syslogSender#configure terminal
Enter configuration commands, one per line. End with CNTL/Z.
syslogSender(config)#end
syslogSender#
```

From the IOS device console, you can see the ESM Tcl script filter is working correctly:

```
syslogSender#
000080: *Jan 10 23:50:19.347: %SYS-5-CONFIG_I: Configured from console by cisco
  on vty0 (10.10.10.1)
syslogSender#
```

Displaying/Adding ESM Tcl Script Filters

Now that you have written a few ESM Tcl script filters, you can see how they can be chained together to process syslog messages in turn. The **show logging** command displays information about which ESM filters are currently active:

```
syslogSender#show logging
syslog logging: enabled (1 messages dropped, 11 messages rate-limited,
                    0 flushes, 0 overruns, xml disabled, filtering enabled)
No Active Message Discriminator.

No Inactive Message Discriminator.

    Console logging: level debugging, 54 messages logged, xml disabled,
                        filtering enabled
    Monitor logging: level debugging, 0 messages logged, xml disabled,
                        filtering disabled
    Buffer logging:  level debugging, 93 messages logged, xml disabled,
                        filtering disabled
    Logging Exception size (4096 bytes)
    Count and timestamp logging messages: disabled
    Persistent logging: disabled
Filter modules:
    flash:filter7.tcl
```

Filtering is currently enabled for the console, in which the script **flash:filter7.tcl** is applied. To apply an additional ESM filter in the chain, you can add it to the end of the list. Filter **filter3.tcl** was used to filter the SYS-5-CONFIG_I messages from appearing when the console exits out of configuration mode, but still allows the message to appear when a Telnet session exits out of configuration mode. You can add the filter **filter3.tcl** into the chain of filters:

```
syslogSender#configure terminal
Enter configuration commands, one per line. End with CNTL/Z.
syslogSender(config)#logging filter flash:filter3.tcl
syslogSender(config)#end
```

Use the **show logging** command to view the changes:

```
syslogSender#show logging
syslog logging: enabled (1 messages dropped, 11 messages rate-limited,
                    0 flushes, 0 overruns, xml disabled, filtering enabled)
No Active Message Discriminator.

No Inactive Message Discriminator.

    Console logging: level debugging, 54 messages logged, xml disabled,b
                        filtering enabled
    Monitor logging: level debugging, 0 messages logged, xml disabled,
                        filtering disabled
```

```
    Buffer logging:  level debugging, 94 messages logged, xml disabled,
                     filtering disabled
    Logging Exception size (4096 bytes)
    Count and timestamp logging messages: disabled
    Persistent logging: disabled
Filter modules:
    flash:filter7.tcl
    flash:filter3.tcl
```

Now there are two active filter modules loaded: **filter7.tcl** and **filter3.tcl**. The script **filter3.tcl** filtered out the SYS-5-CONFIG_I message from appearing on the console. If you again exit from configuration mode on an incoming Telnet session, the following syslog message is generated on the console:

```
000087: *Jan 11 00:18:56.095: %SYS-5-CONFIG_I: Configured from console by cisco
  on vty0 (10.10.10.1)
```

Another powerful tool is to use separate streams to send particular syslog messages to different hosts. Suppose that three different remote hosts are listening for syslog messages and are configured as follows:

```
logging 192.168.1.1
logging host 192.168.1.2 filtered stream 10
logging host 192.168.1.3 filtered stream 11
```

In this example, the host 192.168.1.1 will receive all syslog messages. Host 192.168.1.2 will receive only syslog messages redirected to stream 10. This will occur only if the ESM filter sets the **::stream** value to **10**. Similarly, host 192.168.1.3 will receive only syslog messages redirected to stream 11. Again, this will only occur if the ESM filter sets the **::stream** value to **11**.

As you can see, this affords a great deal of flexibility in processing the syslog messages that are sent to different hosts. Using Tcl to decide which syslog messages are sent to which syslog hosts, provides the ability to scale syslog servers and differentiate messages to specific hosts.

Introduction to Embedded Menu Manager

Another feature in Cisco IOS that makes use of Tcl scripting is the Embedded Menu Manager (EMM). EMM was first introduced into Cisco IOS Software Release 12.4(20)T. It enables you to create text-based menus written in XML that present Cisco IOS device users a simplified user interface. As part of the menu, you can use Tcl script language commands.

You can find the XML schema at the following site:

http://www.cisco.com/en/US/prod/iosswrel/ps6537/ps6555/ps9424/cisco_ios_
service_diagnostics_scripts.html

In XML, you need to *tag* every object with a start tag and end tag. The start tag is simply
the element name, surrounded by **<** and **>** characters:

```
<name>
```

Closing the element requires a similar format, but with **</** characters before the name and
> after the name:

```
</name>
```

The first required element in the schema is called *menu*. This must be present in the XML
document, which defines the EMM menu.

You can begin by writing your own menu using the EMM XML schema document as a
guide. The menu will be written in a Menu Definition File (MDF). First you must format
the menu, as follows:

```
<Menu MenuName="My First Menu" schemaVersion="1.1">
      <MenuTitle>
      </MenuTitle>
      <Item>
        <ItemTitle>
            <Constant String="This is the first item"/>
        </ItemTitle>
      </Item>
</Menu>
```

This is the simplest menu we could write. It is called My First Menu and has only one
item called **"This is the first item"**. Save this in a text editor and call it **my.mdf**.

To test the menu, copy the file my.mdf to the Cisco IOS device, and then load the menu
by telling EMM to try to read the MDF file, as follows:

```
Router#emm mdf flash:my.mdf
1. This is the first item
Enter selection:
```

Note   MDF files can also be located on remote devices. MDF files can be loaded across the network on FTP, HTTP, NVRAM, RCP, and TFTP file systems.

The Cisco IOS device has read the menu definition file and immediately started the menu. You can enter the only available choice, by typing number **1**. After selecting **1**, the menu immediately exits.

You can easily make a small change to the menu to show the current time as part of the menu display. To do this, you modify the first item to execute the Cisco IOS command **show clock**. There is an XML tag you can use called **IOSExecCommand**, which allows any Cisco IOS command to be run. One more XML tag needs to be added to **Item**, which is the **ContinuePrompt**. Without the **ContinuePrompt**, you would not see the results of the **show** command. In addition, you must add a second item to the menu, the ability to exit.

Edit the MDF script to contain the new item:

```
<Menu MenuName="My First Menu" schemaVersion="1.1">
      <MenuTitle>
      </MenuTitle>
      <Item ContinuePrompt="true">
              <ItemTitle>
                      <Constant String="This is the first item"/>
              </ItemTitle>
              <IOSExecCommand>"show clock"</IOSExecCommand>
      </Item>
      <Item>
              <ItemTitle>
                      <Constant String="Exit"/>
              </ItemTitle>
      </Item>
</Menu>
```

Copy the MDF script to the Cisco IOS device and use the following command to initiate the menu:

```
Router#emm mdf flash:my2.mdf
1. This is the first item
2. Exit
```

Press **1**:

```
Enter selection:1
*19:04:01.003 PST Sun Jan 17 2010
Press any key to continue...
```

Select **2** to exit the script.

With basics covered, we will continue creating an EMM menu by adding a Tcl script command to the menu.

One Tcl script command previously used is **string length**, which tells you how many characters are in the given string. Another Tcl command you can use is **hostname**. If entered alone, it returns the hostname of the Cisco IOS device. You will use these two commands to count how many characters are in the hostname. To perform that function, you can enter the following command in a Tcl shell and view the length of the hostname string:

```
Router(tcl)#hostname
Router
Router(tcl)#string length [hostname]
6
Router(tcl)#
```

To configure the menu to perform the same Tcl script function to count the hostname length, edit the MDF to contain the new items that will perform the counting.

You must add one new item, which uses the XML tags **EmbeddedTCL** and **TCLCommand**:

```
<Item ContinuePrompt="true">
        <ItemTitle>
                <Constant String="Count Hostname Length"/>
        </ItemTitle>
        <EmbeddedTCL>
                <TCLCommand>return [string length [hostname]]</TCLCommand>
        </EmbeddedTCL>
</Item>
```

After you add the new item to the MDF file, the complete file contains the following:

```
<Menu MenuName="My First Menu" schemaVersion="1.1">
     <MenuTitle>
     </MenuTitle>
     <Item ContinuePrompt="true">
             <ItemTitle>
                     <Constant String="This is the first item"/>
             </ItemTitle>
             <IOSExecCommand>"show clock"</IOSExecCommand>
     </Item>
     <Item ContinuePrompt="true">
             <ItemTitle>
                     <Constant String="Count Hostname Length"/>
             </ItemTitle>
             <EmbeddedTCL>
```

```
                             <TCLCommand>return [string length
  [hostname]]</TCLCommand>
                    </EmbeddedTCL>
        </Item>
        <Item>
                    <ItemTitle>
                            <Constant String="Exit"/>
                    </ItemTitle>
        </Item>
</Menu>
```

Copy the new MDF to the Cisco IOS device and monitor the results:

```
Router#emm mdf flash:my3.mdf
1. This is the first item
2. Count Hostname Length
3. Exit
Enter selection:2
9
Press any key to continue...
```

The menu was able to provide the correct number for the hostname string length.

One of the strengths of EMM is the capability to configure and preload the menus for partic-ular user accounts, by using the **autocommand** option. For example, configure the following:

```
Router(config)#emm mdf flash:my3.mdf
Router(config)#user cisco password cisco
Router(config)#user cisco autocommand emm My First Menu
Router(config)#end
Router#
*Mar 23 22:23:10.575: %SYS-5-CONFIG_I: Configured from console by console
Router#conf t
Enter configuration commands, one per line.  End with CNTL/Z.
Router(config)#line con 0
Router(config-line)#login local
Router(config-line)#end
```

After configuring the preceding, try to log in and see the menu being displayed:

```
Username: cisco
Password: 1. This is the first item
2. Count Hostname Length
3. Exit

Enter selection:
```

> **Caution**   Use caution when enabling **login local** on the console. It is possible to lock yourself out from the router! Instead, consider enabling on **login local** on **line vty 0 4** instead. That way, incoming Telnet sessions will be authenticated with a username and password.

We have demonstrated the ability to use Tcl script commands within the menu. The EMM feature is a powerful tool you can use to build simple user interfaces that allow nearly anything to be done on the Cisco IOS device. It is a great help in writing a customized application to be run on a Cisco IOS device that requires user input.

Using Tcl as a Web Server

One exciting area that exemplifies the value of a Tcl script is the capability to run a web server. This section examines a web server running under the Tcl interpreter. It is freely available, and you can modify it to suit your needs. This Tcl-based web server is easily customizable and is suitable for rapid deployment of small web-based applications running on a Cisco IOS device. A typical application would be to allow a network administrator to modify a device configuration through a web-based interface. Other applications include troubleshooting, network monitoring, and so on.

Cisco IOS does include a small embedded web server already. It enables you to show the diagnostic log, discussed in the previous section. All the messages in the logging buffer are viewable from within the embedded web server. All the Cisco IOS commands can be used from the embedded web server, and the output of the commands will display as a web page presented to the user. An additional command available is the **show technical support** command. This is useful when communicating with Cisco technical support, to rapidly collect the information they may request to troubleshoot problems. A small utility also included that allows the user to initiate ping requests from the Cisco IOS device.

To access the embedded web server, verify the following is configured on the IOS device:

```
Router#show running-config | include http
ip http server
ip http authentication local
no ip http secureserver
```

The command **ip http server** enables the built-in embedded web server. The next command, **ip http authentication local**, is used to query for usernames and passwords when the web server is accessed. Finally, **no ip http secureserver** disables the internal web server that is used when the user tries to connect to the Cisco IOS device using HTTPS.

To determine what IP addresses are configured in the Cisco IOS device, use the command **show ip interface brief**. After examining the output, choose a suitable IP address to use.

Using a web browser, enter the IP address of the Cisco IOS device as the website to browse, as shown in Figure 5-1.

Figure 5-1   *IOS Device Web Interface*

After you enter the IP address of the router, the web browser attempts to communicate with the Cisco IOS router. The response asks for a username and password, as shown in Figure 5-2.

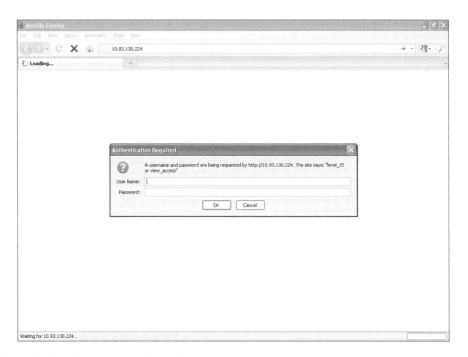

Figure 5-2   *IOS Device Web Authentication*

In this case, you have not yet configured a username or password on the Cisco IOS device. You must cancel this connection and configure the following in the Cisco IOS device in configuration mode:

```
Router#configure terminal
Enter configuration commands, one per line. End with CNTL/Z.
```

```
Router(config)#username cisco privilege 15 password 0 cisco
Router(config)#end
Router#
```

You have now created a user with the name cisco and password cisco that can be used to access the web page. This username will be used in conjunction with the **ip http authentication local** configuration command, which was entered earlier. Typing individual usernames and passwords into the configuration manually is one of the simplest ways to authenticate web page users. Because this configuration is device specific, scalability is a major concern. Another method that offers extensive scalability is to centralize user information about RADIUS or TACACS server. Now that a user has been added to the local database, you can reattempt the connection from a web browser and enter the correct username and password, as shown in Figure 5-3.

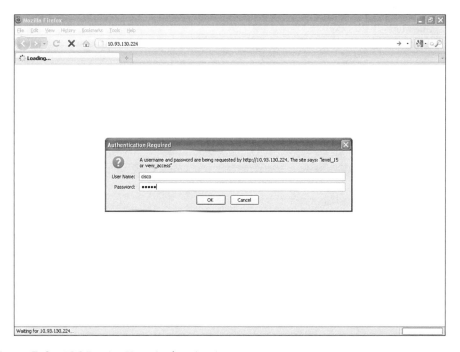

Figure 5-3   *IOS Device User Authentication*

After clicking OK, you are presented with the home page for the Cisco IOS device, as shown in Figure 5-4.

From this page, you can

■   Access the syslog buffer with **show diagnostic log**

■   Execute selected commands with **monitor the router**

■   Collect tech-support information with **show tech-support**

■   Perform ping requests with **extended ping**

■   Access the QoS Device Manager (if this optional component has been installed)

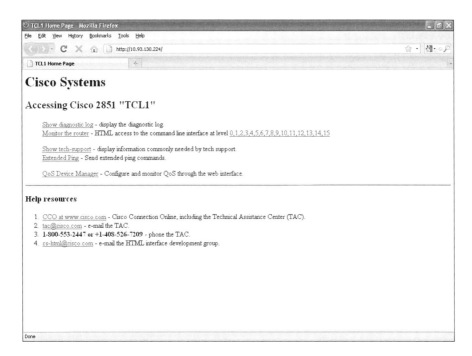

Figure 5-4   *IOS Device HTTP Server Page*

You can see the embedded web server provides valuable information and functions. Any command that you can run from the IOS device console can now be applied through the web interface. The web server, however, is not customizable to a specific application. If you are interested in creating a user interface specific to an application, you must write one. The web server application will provide the foundation for web-based services. Fortunately, the Tcl web-server program has been made freely available for modification.

Obtaining a Free Web Server Application

The Cisco Beyond application repository contains many user-contributed scripts usable on Cisco IOS devices. These applications might work with the Tcl interpreter, EEM, or other scripting done on Cisco IOS. You can access these applications at the following site:

http://www.cisco.com/go/ciscobeyond

Using the Cisco Beyond search engine, you can easily locate the HTTP server application. Enter **http** in the search box and find the HTTP Server with CGI Support script.

This script uses EEM and Tcl to create a web server running on Cisco IOS. After downloading and extracting the HTTP Server with CGI Support package, you have the following files:

- Application_1.tcl

- Application_2.tcl

- Application_3.tcl

- Application_4.tcl

- Instructions.txt

- Mihyar.tcl

- StaticPage.html

- Favicon.ico

- Http_server.tcl

- Index.html

- Logo.gif

- Runcli.tcl

- Sendemail.tcl

- Sitearea-nav.jpg

You learn from the Instructions.txt file that you must place these files on the local storage of your Cisco IOS router. It also mentions that http_server.tcl is hard-coded to use disk2: for the web server files. You can change this by using any text editor. Search for disk2: and replace with an appropriate path for the device that you are using. For example, flash:, disk0, slot0 are possible alternatives. A subdirectory can also be used below the root directory. For example, you can choose to place all the files in a subdirectory named WEB and then alternatively change the word disk2: to flash:/WEB/.

The IOS **copy** command is used to copy the files one by one to your local storage. The following example uses a TFTP server:

```
Router#copy tftp: flash:
Address or name of remote host []? 171.69.1.129
Source filename []? jlautman/http/Application_1.tcl
Destination filename [Application_1.tcl]?
Accessing tftp://10.69.1.129/jlautman/http/Application_1.tcl...
Loading jlautman/http/Application_1.tcl from 10.69.17.19 (via
  GigabitEthernet0/0): !
[OK - 7316 bytes]
7316 bytes copied in 0.980 secs (7465 bytes/sec)
Router#
```

After all the files have been copied to the local storage, such as the flash: directory, the web server can be started. The Instructions.txt file mentions that you need to disable the embedded IOS HTTP web server. You can do so with the following configuration commands:

```
Router#configure terminal
Enter configuration commands, one per line. End with CNTL/Z.
Router(config)#no ip http server
Router(config)#end
Router#
```

The Instructions.txt file describes how to start the web server:

```
Router#configure terminal
Enter configuration commands, one per line. End with CNTL/Z.
Router(config)#event manager directory user policy "flash:/"
Router(config)#event manager policy http_server.tcl
Router(config)#end
Router#event manager run http_server.tcl
```

The **event manager directory** command enables you to specify the file system in which all the *user*-created policies are located. This is in contrast to the included system policies, which are internal and always available.

The **event manager policy** configuration command enables you to specify user policies to be available to run.

Finally, the **event manager run** command enables you to begin the execution of a specific user policy.

After a brief pause, the Cisco IOS router starts up the http_server.tcl script, and you can open the web page in your browser, as shown in Figure 5-5. The web browser will initially load index.html first, which redirects the web browser to display this page.

Reverse Engineering the Web Server

Now that you have seen the web server in operation, you need to know how it operates internally. First of all, note that the following messages are being displayed on the console of the router:

```
Router#GET / HTTP/1.1
file name:
Parameters:
GET /Mihyar.tcl HTTP/1.1
file name:  Mihyar.tcl
Parameters:
GET /logo.gif HTTP/1.1
file name:  logo.gif
```

```
Parameters:
GET /sitearea-nav.jpg HTTP/1.1
file name:  sitearea-nav.jpg
Parameters:
```

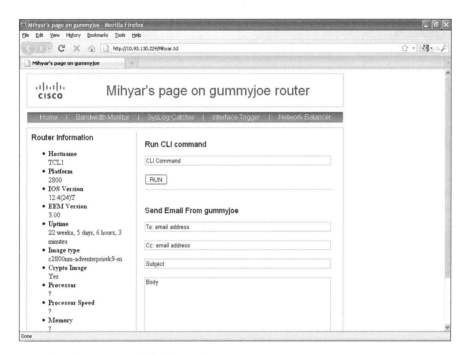

Figure 5-5   *IOS Device HTTP Server Page gummyjoe router*

The first message displayed is a **get**, but the filename is empty. Looking at the code of the http_server.tcl script, you find that it opens a socket on TCP port 80, which is the port that web servers generally use, as shown here:

```
set svcPort 80
...many lines cut ...
# Create a server socket on port $svcPort.
# Call proc accept when a client attempts a connection.
set srvrsock [socket -server accept $svcPort]
while {1} {
```

Inside the **while** loop, which runs forever unless it is interrupted with the **break** statement, you see some lines which reference index.html:

```
} elseif {[regexp "GET /(.*) HTTP/1.1" $l temp request] != 0} {
    puts "$l"
    if {[regexp "(.*)\\?(.*)" $request temp filename param] == 0} {
        set param ""
        set filename $request
```

```
}
set ::parameters $param
puts "file name:  $filename"
puts "Parameters: $::parameters"
if {$filename == ""} {set filename "index.html"}
```

From the preceding code block, it is clear that if no filename is passed to this part of the code, it will be changed to index.html.

You can verify this by entering the filename explicitly in the browser, as shown in Figure 5-6.

Figure 5-6 *IOS Device HTTP index.html Page*

When this page is opened, you see that the same home page appears as before. However, a different set of debug messages are printed on the Cisco IOS device console:

```
Router#GET /index.html HTTP/1.1
file name:  index.html
Parameters:
GET /Mihyar.tcl HTTP/1.1
file name:  Mihyar.tcl
Parameters:
GET /logo.gif HTTP/1.1
file name:  logo.gif
Parameters:
GET /sitearea-nav.jpg HTTP/1.1
file name:  sitearea-nav.jpg
Parameters:
```

This time, the index.html filename is being displayed, indicating that you are correct in your understanding of the Tcl script http_server.tcl. The same home page and the debug messages are nearly identical with the exception of the index.html filename. The first time you opened the web server home page, the code of http_server.tcl replaced the blank filename with index.html. To change the "home page" of the web server for your own specific applications, you can modify the index.html file and save it to the IOS device.

The current contents of index.html is the following:

```
<script type="text/javascript">
document.location = "Mihyar.tcl";
</script>
```

What does this web page tell the web browser to do? It simply tells it to open a web page called Mihyar.tcl. The web browser executes the JavaScript code contained between the **<script>** and **</script>** tags. Note that is the final web page displayed after the web browser loads the index.html file.

Toward the end of the Mihyar.tcl file, you see that there are many lines of code, as shown here:

```
set httpheader "HTTP/1.1 200 OK
Content-Type: text/html; charset=UTF-8
Content-Transfer-Encoding: binary
"
puts $httpsock $httpheader$header$middle$footer
```

The Tcl script code concatenates the header, middle, and footer with **httpheader**, and then it is sent on the **httpsock** channel. Cumulatively, these three components make up the complete web page, which will then be displayed to the user on the web browser.

In the next section, you will create your own example script, chap4e1.tcl. The same format will be maintained, using header, middle, and footer, and combining them all together with **httpheader**.

Creating Your Own Simple Web Page

The goal here is to modify the web server to display your own custom-created web page instead of the default. Begin by modifying the index.html file and associating a script that you write, as follows:

```
<script type="text/javascript">
document.location = "chap4e1.tcl";
</script>
```

Next, create a simple script called chap4e1.tcl. This script will be used to learn about how the web server functions. In this example, the following script will be implemented:

```
set header ""
set middle "<html><body>This web page may be easily customized. Nearly anything
  available to the TCL Interpreter running on Cisco IOS may be easily displayed.
</body>
</html>
"
set footer ""

set httpheader "HTTP/1.1 200 OK
Content-Type: text/html; charset=UTF-8
```

```
Content-Transfer-Encoding: binary
"

puts $httpsock $httpheader$header$middle$footer
```

This script simply creates an empty header and an empty footer. The contents of the web page are entirely within the variable **middle**. It uses the simplest form of HTML tagging. The text begins with **<html><body>** and concludes with **</body></html>**.

To facilitate the operation, both files must be copied to the IOS device. Using a TFTP server to copy the files, the following is an example:

```
Router#copy tftp: flash:
Address or name of remote host []? 10.69.1.129
Source filename []? jlautman/http/index.html
Destination filename [index.html]?
%Warning:There is a file already existing with this name
Do you want to over write? [confirm]
Accessing tftp://10.69.1.129/jlautman/http/index.html...
Loading jlautman/http/index.html from 10.69.17.19 (via GigabitEthernet0/0): !
[OK - 80 bytes]
80 bytes copied in 0.396 secs (202 bytes/sec)
Router#copy tftp: flash:
Address or name of remote host [10.69.1.129]?
Source filename [jlautman/http/index.html]? jlautman/http/chap4e1.tcl
Destination filename [chap4e1.tcl]?
Accessing tftp://10.69.1.129/jlautman/http/chap4e1.tcl...
Loading jlautman/http/chap4e1.tcl from 10.69.17.19 (via GigabitEthernet0/0): !
[OK - 386 bytes]
386 bytes copied in 0.484 secs (798 bytes/sec)
Router#
```

Type the URL **http://10.93.130.224/index.html** to display the web page shown in Figure 5-7.

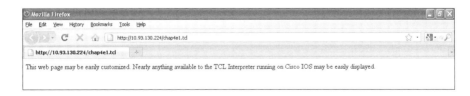

Figure 5-7 *IOS Device HTTP Customized Page*

Note   It might be necessary to reload the page, because certain web browsers might cache the results.

As an alternative method to access the page previously created, you can direct navigate to that specific page. You can get direct access if you type in the full URL of your script. For example, use the following address:

http://10.93.130.224/chap4e1.tcl

Creating a Web Page Using IOS show Commands

This section takes the output from a **show** command and retrieves the current time from the Cisco IOS device. This information will provide the content for our page.

You can start with the previous example and modify it to store the **show** command output and current time. In this example, the file will be saved as chap4e2.tcl.

The following lines prepare to run the specific **show** command:

```
if {[catch {cli_open} output]} {
    error $output $errorInfo
} else {
    array set cli_fd $output
}
```

Step 1.   Enter enable mode on the IOS device:

```
if {[catch {cli_exec $cli_fd(fd) "enable"} output]} {
error $output $errorInfo
}
```

Step 2.   Issue the **show clock** command and capture the current time in variable clock_output:

```
if {[catch {cli_exec $cli_fd(fd) "show clock"} clock_output]} {
error $output $errorInfo
}
```

Step 3.   Close the file handle used for CLI commands:

```
if {[catch {cli_close $cli_fd(fd) $cli_fd(tty_id)} output]} {
    error $output $errorInfo
}
```

Step 4.   Define the HTTP header to show **The time is now:** and include the variable clock_output, which represents the previous **show clock** command:

```
set header "<html><body>The time is now: $clock_output<br>
</body>
</html>
"
```

```
set middle "<html><body>This web page may be easily customized. Nearly
  anything available to the TCL
Interpreter running on Cisco IOS may be easily
displayed.<br>
</body>
</html>
"
set footer ""

set httpheader "HTTP/1.1 200 OK
Content-Type: text/html; charset=UTF-8
Content-Transfer-Encoding: binary
"
puts $httpsock $httpheader$header$middle$footer
```

Step 5.   You also need to modify index.html to reflect the new filename you are using:

```
<script type="text/javascript">
document.location = "chap4e2.tcl";
</script>
```

Step 6.   Copy the files to the IOS device:

```
Router#copy tftp flash:
Address or name of remote host []? 10.69.1.129
Source filename []? jlautman/http/index.html
Destination filename [index.html]?
%Warning:There is a file already existing with this name
Do you want to over write? [confirm]
Accessing tftp://10.69.1.129/jlautman/http/index.html...
Loading jlautman/http/index.html from 10.69.1.129 (via
  GigabitEthernet0/0): !
[OK - 80 bytes]
80 bytes copied in 0.380 secs (211 bytes/sec)
Router#copy tftp flash:
Address or name of remote host [10.69.1.129]?
Source filename [jlautman/http/index.html]? jlautman/http/chap4e2.tcl
Destination filename [chap4e2.tcl]?
Accessing tftp://10.69.1.129/jlautman/http/chap4e2.tcl...
Loading jlautman/http/chap4e2.tcl from 10.69.1.129 (via
  GigabitEthernet0/0): !
[OK - 851 bytes]
851 bytes copied in 0.532 secs (1600 bytes/sec)
Router#
```

Step 7.   From your browser, load the web page. The results will look like Figure 5-8.

How were you able to get the clock output? There are some EEM Tcl library commands that are used. A "handle" is created to interact with the Cisco IOS device, as shown here:

```
if {[catch {cli_open} output]} {
    error $output $errorInfo
} else {
    array set cli_fd $output
}
```

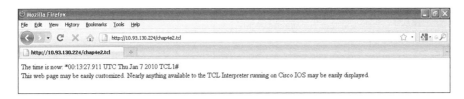

Figure 5-8   *IOS Device HTTP Clock Page*

The handle is stored in the Tcl variable array called **cli_fd**, short for command-line inter-face file descriptor. It is simply a channel on which the Cisco IOS commands will be sent and data will be returned. The **cli_open** could fail if, for example, too many users were connected by Telnet. Only a finite number of connections can be made to the Cisco IOS device, and as such, there are a finite number of resources. If **cli_open** fails, you **catch** the result and send it to the user interface. Otherwise, it would silently fail without display-ing any information about the fault.

Commands are sent one at a time to this **cli_fd** using the EEM Tcl library command **cli_exec**. The **cli_exec** command needs to know what channel will be used to send the command, for example:

```
if {[catch {cli_exec $cli_fd(fd) "enable"} output]} {
error $output $errorInfo
}
```

The results are captured in the **catch** variable as the result of the **cli_exec** in case there is a failure. If it fails, the user will be notified that there is a problem with the Tcl script. The parameters within the quotes, are the actual commands that will be initiated on the Cisco IOS device. In this case, it is the **enable** keyword. This is done to enter privileged mode, which offers many more command options.

The **cli_exec** command is performed again, but this time it is used to save the **show clock** output:

```
if {[catch {cli_exec $cli_fd(fd) "show clock"} clock_output]} {
error $clock_output $errorInfo
}
```

Finally, the file handle is closed to properly clean up:

```
if {[catch {cli_close $cli_fd(fd) $cli_fd(tty_id)} output]} {
    error $output $errorInfo
}
```

Adding User Input to the Web Page

Now that you understand how to use Cisco IOS commands with the web server script, you will investigate how to add user input to the web page. The original web page used the script Mihyar.tcl, which allowed user input (downloaded from the Cisco Beyond site). The original web page contains a Run CLI command box and has a Run button. After you enter a CLI command and click the Run button, the web server application will attempt to run the command, save the output, and present that as a web page to the user.

To view the code used in the Tcl script Mihyar.tcl, you can search for the text "Run CLI command," from which you will find the following block of code:

```
<p><font face='arial' size='4' color='black'>Run CLI command</font></p>
  <form name='runcli' action='runcli.tcl' method='GET' target='_blank'>
  <div align='left'>
  <input type='text' name='CLIcommand' value='CLI Command'
onblur='init_field(this,\"CLI Command\");' onFocus='clear_field(this,\"CLI
  Command\");' style='WIDTH: 440px; color:#000000; font-family: arial; font-size:
  10pt'>
  <br><br>
  <input type='submit' value='RUN'>
  </div>
  </form>
```

This block of code creates an HTML form where user input can be entered. The user information is entered into a text box, and the input is sent as a parameter to the Tcl script named runcli.tcl. The text box is initially populated with the words CLI Command. As soon as the text box is clicked, the words disappear. The initial population of the input box is accomplished with a combination of HTML and JavaScript:

```
onblur='init_field(this,\"CLI Command\");
```

The clearing of the text box when clicked is accomplished with the following command:

```
onFocus='clear_field(this,\"CLI Command\");'
```

The JavaScript that accomplishes this task is as follows:

```
<script>
// clear default value from field when selected
function clear_field(field, value) {if(field.value == value) field.value = '';}
function init_field(field, value) {if(field.value == '') field.value = value;}
</script>
```

The JavaScript code that runs on the web browser will be called to populate the text box. When the text box is selected, it will be called to clear the box.

Using this method, you can modify the sample web page to include a text box for user input. Modify the Tcl script as follows:

```
if {[catch {cli_open} output]} {
    error $output $errorInfo
} else {
    array set cli_fd $output
}
```

Enter enable or privileged mode:

```
if {[catch {cli_exec $cli_fd(fd) "enable"} output]} {
error $output $errorInfo
}
```

Issue the **show clock** command to get the current time and record the output in the **clock_output** variable:

```
if {[catch {cli_exec $cli_fd(fd) "show clock"} clock_output]} {
error $clock_output $errorInfo
}
```

Close the handle used for CLI commands:

```
if {[catch {cli_close $cli_fd(fd) $cli_fd(tty_id)} output]} {
    error $output $errorInfo
}
```

Configure the output to show the clock:

```
set header "<html><body>The time is now: $clock_output<br>
</body>
</html>
"
```

Display the following custom text:

```
set middle "<html><body>This web page may be easily customized. Nearly anything
  available to the TCL
Interpreter running on Cisco IOS may be easily
displayed.<br>
</body>
</html>
"
set footer "
<script>
```

Clear the default value from field when selected:

```
function clear_field(field, value) {if(field.value == value) field.value = '';}
function init_field(field, value) {if(field.value == '') field.value = value;}
</script>
  <input type='text' name='CLIcommand' value='CLI Command'
  onblur='init_field(this,\"CLI Command\");' onFocus='clear_field(this,\"CLI
  Command\");' style='WIDTH: 440px; color:#000000; font-family: arial; font-size:
  10pt'>
  <br><br>
  <input type='submit' value='RUN'>
  </form>
"
set httpheader "HTTP/1.1 200 OK
Content-Type: text/html; charset=UTF-8
Content-Transfer-Encoding: binary
"
puts $httpsock $httpheader$header$middle$footer
```

After you copy the script to the Cisco IOS device and reload the web page in your web browser, you see the results shown in Figure 5-9.

In Figure 5-10, you can verify that clicking the text box clears the text that is in the box.

There is, however, one limitation in the current example. When you enter some text in the box and click the Run button, no action is taken yet. Why is this? After carefully examining the code in the script named Mihyar.tcl, you find that it is connected to another Tcl script with the following code:

```
<form name='runcli' action='runcli.tcl' method='GET' target='_blank'>
```

That line of code was omitted from the sample script. Once you modify the footer section of the script to contain the action to take, the Run button will invoke another Tcl script!

Now that you have seen how to add a text box and button for user input, the next thing to do is modify the web page into a more useful monitoring application.

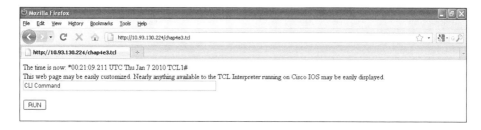

Figure 5-9 *IOS Device HTTP Clock and Command Input*

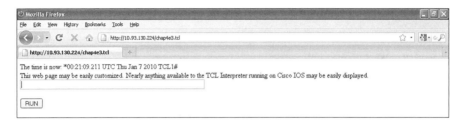

Figure 5-10   *IOS Device HTTP Clock and Command Input Clear Text Box*

Suppose you are getting network performance complaints from users at a remote office. You can create a customized web page to monitor the remote IOS device. In this hypothetical scenario, a network administrator in Hawaii has alerted you that the IP telephones are working but performing poorly. You suspect the network connection between Hawaii and the central IP telephone server.

To quickly get to the root cause of this, you can deploy a Tcl script on the IOS device in Hawaii. The local network administrator can monitor the performance of the circuit through a web browser. The administrator must open the web page on the router, enter in the IP address of the IP telephone server, and click Monitor. The idea is that the network administrator can go to this web page and start monitoring when he or she is having a problem and additional information will be available.

The web page will use a Tcl script in conjunction with the Cisco IOS feature called IP service level agreement (SLA).

Introduction to IP SLA

IP service level agreement (IP SLA) is a feature within Cisco IOS that allows the device to periodically measure the performance of the network. Many customers want to purchase a network connection with a contractual guarantee that their Internet connection will have minimal downtime per year. As a result of this contract, both the Internet service provider (ISP) and the customer purchasing the service might want to monitor their network connection to verify the network is meeting the contractual guarantee. This is where the IP SLA feature becomes useful. It allows the IOS device measure various network conditions.

In its simplest form, you can use IP SLA to initiate an ICMP ping echo request on a periodic basis. This is the same type of ping packet we have all used before. For example, using the command prompt within Windows, you can ping an IP address:

```
C:\>ping 10.93.130.224
Pinging 10.93.130.224 with 32 bytes of data:
Reply from 10.93.130.224: bytes=32 time=43ms TTL=245
Reply from 10.93.130.224: bytes=32 time=43ms TTL=245
Reply from 10.93.130.224: bytes=32 time=43ms TTL=245
Reply from 10.93.130.224: bytes=32 time=44ms TTL=245
Ping statistics for 10.93.130.224:
    Packets: Sent = 4, Received = 4, Lost = 0 (0% loss),
Approximate round trip times in milli-seconds:
    Minimum = 43ms, Maximum = 44ms, Average = 43ms
C:\>
```

You can also perform the same type of ping from within IP SLA on the Cisco IOS device. To configure this, an IP SLA entry must be defined and then scheduled, as follows:

```
Router#configure terminal
Enter configuration commands, one per line. End with CNTL/Z.
Router(config)#ip sla 1
TCL1(config-ip-sla)#icmp-echo 10.21.69.186
TCL1(config-ip-sla-echo)#ip sla schedule 1 start-time now
Router(config)#
```

Note   This syntax assumes 12.4T or higher. 12.4 mainline uses **ip sla monitor**, and earlier releases use **rtr**. Devices supporting EEM and tclsh could support all three syntax variations.

In the preceding example, a new IP SLA entry has been defined with an ID number of 1, using the **ip sla 1** configuration command. The ID number is arbitrary and is just a unique identifier that must be assigned for every entry.

The next configuration command, **icmp-echo 10.21.69.186**, is used to define what type of measurement to perform and the target IP address that you want to measure. In this case, you are doing **icmp-echo**, one of the simplest types of measurement. Other more elaborate measurements can also be conducted, but this requires an IP SLA-capable device as the source and one as the destination.

Finally, the new entry must be scheduled to run using the **ip sla schedule 1 start-time now** configuration command. This command will start the IP SLA process and start collecting data. The default measurement will occur every 60 seconds. This works well for the example. Consequently, the default value will remain unchanged. In this case, the length of time to perform the measurement has not been specified. The default value is 1 hour. This also fits well into the example, so this default value will remain unchanged.

To see the results of the ongoing measurement, enter the following command at the Cisco IOS device console:

```
Router#show ip sla statistics
IPSLAs Latest Operation Statistics
IPSLA operation id: 1
Type of operation: icmp-echo
        Latest RTT: 44 milliseconds
Latest operation start time: *22:06:51.207 UTC Sun Dec 27 2009
Latest operation return code: OK
Number of successes: 7
Number of failures: 0
Operation time to live: 3189 sec
Router#
```

From the previous output, the **IPSLA operation id** you are interested in is **1**. It could have many entries running at the same time. However, you are only interested in **1**. The type of operation entered is displayed as **icmp-echo**. The latest measured round-trip time (RTT) measured by the Cisco IOS device was 44 milliseconds. The time that the measurement was attempted is displayed next. The latest return code or result is displayed as **OK**, which indicates that a response was received. It could also be **timeout** if the Cisco IOS device sent an ICMP echo request but no response was received. Additional information is shown, such as how many successes have occurred (the return code of **OK** is considered a success and a return code of **timeout** to be a failure). Finally, you see the operation will continue for another 3189 seconds.

For more information about IP SLA, see the following web page:

http://www.cisco.com/go/ipsla

Adding the IP SLA Measurement to the Web Page

You can now modify the sample web page script to receive the user input for the IP SLA parameters. When the user enters an IP address, you will use it to configure a new IP SLA measurement entry.

Modifying the Button and Label for User Input

To start, change the name of the text box and the button for entering the data. In this case, change the text box to be called IP Address to Monitor. You can do so by changing the user input section of the Tcl script within the footer section:

```
set footer "
<script>
function clear_field(field, value) {if(field.value == value) field.value = '';}
```

```
function init_field(field, value) {if(field.value == '') field.value = value;}
</script>
  <form name='ipsla' action='ipsla.tcl' method='GET' target='_blank'>
  <input type='text' name='IPSLAmonitor' value='IP address to monitor'
  onblur='init_field(this,\"IP address to monitor\");'
onFocus='clear_field(this,\"IP address to monitor\");' style='WIDTH: 440px;
  color:#000000; font-family: arial; font-size: 10pt'>
  <br><br>
  <input type='submit' value='Begin Monitor'>
  </form>
"
```

Notice the change in the help text? This will make it clear that IP SLA measurements will be initiated. Another item of interest is that the user input data is directed to a different Tcl script, using the **action** command. Previously, the runcli.tcl was executed and now it was replaced with ipsla.tcl. You will now need to create the ipsla.tcl script to begin the measurement, based on the user-provided IP address.

Creating a Tcl Script to Display IP SLA Measurement Results

Start with a simple version of the Tcl script, named ipsla.tcl. The function of this script will be to display the user-provided IP address, as described in the code and descriptions that follow.

The first line of code receives the IP address from the user input and assigns it to the variable **ipaddr**:

```
set ipaddr [lindex $parmlist 1]
set header "<html>
<head>
<title>IP SLA Measurment Results Page</title>
<script>
function clear_field(field, value) {if(field.value == value) field.value = '';}
function init_field(field, value) {if(field.value == '') field.value = value;}
</script>
</head>
<body>
IP SLA Measurment Results Page<br><br>
We are monitoring : <br>
$ipaddr
</body>
</html>"
set middle ""
set footer ""
set httpheader "HTTP/1.1 200 OK
Content-Type: text/html; charset=UTF-8
Content-Transfer-Encoding: binary
"
puts $httpsock $httpheader$header$middle$footer
```

Modifications to the example web page will be used to clarify the user input text box. This new Tcl script will be saved as chap4e4.tcl:

```
if {[catch {cli_open} output]} {
    error $output $errorInfo
} else {
    array set cli_fd $output
}
if {[catch {cli_exec $cli_fd(fd) "enable"} output]} {
error $output $errorInfo
}
```

Issue the **show clock** command and store the information in the **clock_output** variable:

```
if {[catch {cli_exec $cli_fd(fd) "show clock"} clock_output]} {
error $output $errorInfo
}
```

Close the handle used for CLI commands:

```
if {[catch {cli_close $cli_fd(fd) $cli_fd(tty_id)} output]} {
    error $output $errorInfo
}
set header "<html><body>The time is now: $clock_output<br>
</body>
</html>
"
```

The middle section of the HTML output displays information about the operation of the script:

```
set middle "<html><body>This web page will help to monitor any network device
that needs to be measured. An IP SLA Monitoring operation will be automatically
started. Please enter the IP address of the device you want to monitor.<br>
</body>
</html>
"
set footer "
<script>
```

Clear the default value from field when selected:

```
function clear_field(field, value) {if(field.value == value) field.value = '';}
function init_field(field, value) {if(field.value == '') field.value = value;}
</script>
  <form name='ipsla' action='ipsla.tcl' method='GET' target='_blank'>
  <input type='text' name='IPSLAmonitor' value='IP address to monitor'
  onblur='init_field(this,\"IP address to monitor\");'
```

```
onFocus='clear_field(this,\"IP address to monitor\");' style='WIDTH: 440px;
  color:#000000; font-family: arial; font-size: 10pt'>
  <br><br>
  <input type='submit' value='Begin Monitor'>
  </form>
"


set httpheader "HTTP/1.1 200 OK
Content-Type: text/html; charset=UTF-8
Content-Transfer-Encoding: binary
"
puts $httpsock $httpheader$header$middle$footer
```

Putting the New Tcl Scripts into Operation

Copy the two scripts chap4e4.tcl and ipsla.tcl to the Cisco IOS device and you will be ready to try it out!

In the web browser, you can directly open chap4e4.tcl by typing the following URL:

http://10.93.130.224/chap4e4.tcl

After opening the web page, you will see the results in Figure 5-11.

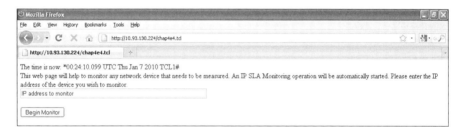

Figure 5-11   *IOS Device HTTP IP SLA*

Enter an IP address in the IP Address to Monitor field and select Begin Monitor. As shown in Figure 5-12, you are now presented with the new web page, which runs ipsla.tcl.

Figure 5-12   *IOS Device HTTP IP SLA Monitoring*

The user-supplied IP address has been correctly saved. You can now begin to modify iplsa.tcl so that it displays the results of IP SLA measurement operation:

```
set ipaddr [lindex $parmlist 1]
if {[catch {cli_open} output]} {
        error $output $errorInfo
} else {
        array set cli_fd $output
}
if {[catch {cli_exec $cli_fd(fd) "enable"} output]} {
        error $output $errorInfo
}
if {[catch {cli_exec $cli_fd(fd) "show ip sla statistics"} ipslaoutput]} {
        error $ipslaoutput $errorInfo
}
if {[catch {cli_close $cli_fd(fd) $cli_fd(tty_id)} output]} {
        error $output $errorInfo
}

set header "<html>
<head>
<title>IP SLA Measurment Results Page</title>
<script>
function clear_field(field, value) {if(field.value == value) field.value = '';}
function init_field(field, value) {if(field.value == '') field.value = value;}
</script>
</head>
<body>
IP SLA Measurment Results Page<br><br>
We are monitoring : <br>
$ipaddr<br><br>
The latest results:<br>
$ipslaoutput
</body>
</html>"
set middle ""
set footer ""
set httpheader "HTTP/1.1 200 OK
Content-Type: text/html; charset=UTF-8
Content-Transfer-Encoding: binary
"
puts $httpsock $httpheader$header$middle$footer
```

When you use the EEM Tcl library commands **cli_open**, **cli_exec**, and **cli_close**, the output of the **show ip sla statistics** command is stored in the variable named **ipslaoutput**.

Now that the output has been collected and stored in the **ipslaoutput** variable, it will be added to the web page with the inclusion of the following commands:

```
The latest results:<br>
$ipslaoutput
```

This allows the new web page to include the current results. Because you have already configured an IP SLA operation, you will now see the results in the web page. After copying ipsla.tcl to the router, you open the web page, enter the IP address, select Begin Monitor, and see the results in Figure 5-13.

Figure 5-13   *IOS Device HTTP IP SLA Monitoring Example*

From the output, you are getting closer to the customized web page that you want to create for the remote network administrator!

Reformatting the IP SLA Output for Readability

The web page displays the text output from the **show ip sla statistics** command, but it is not formatted exactly like it is shown on the console. For example, the following is the display from the console:

```
Router#sh ip sla statistics
IPSLAs Latest Operation Statistics
IPSLA operation id: 1
Type of operation: icmp-echo
        Latest RTT: 231 milliseconds
Latest operation start time: *22:59:51.202 UTC Sun Dec 27 2009
Latest operation return code: OK
Number of successes: 60
Number of failures: 0
Operation time to live: 0
```

Reviewing the web page, the line breaks are missing. Some extra formatting needs to be done to present the **show** command output correctly. Looking back at the runcli.tcl script, you see the following block of code:

```
set commandoutput [string map {"\r\n" "\n" "\"" "&#148;" "<" "&#060;" ">"
  "&#062;" "'" "&#146;"} $commandoutput]
```

Later in the script, the **show** command output is printed with the following parameters:

```
<textarea name='body' style='WIDTH: 710px; HEIGHT: 465px; color:#000000; font-
##family: courier; font-size: 8pt'>$commandoutput</textarea>
```

The first block of Tcl code with the **string map** command replaces \r\n, which represent newlines in the original output, with the \n character, which represents a newline in the web page. Similarly, Table 5-5 shows which characters from the **show** command output are replaced with HTML characters in the web page.

Table 5-5 *Character Replacement from the* **show** *Command Output*

Original Character from show Output	Replacement HTML Character	Displayed Character
\r\n	\n	Line feed
\	&#148;	"
<	&#60;	<
>	&#62;	>
"	&146;	'

The **textarea name** creates an HTML box where the **show** command output will display in a fixed font. The effect of these two changes is to make the **show** command output look identical to the console output.

Now, update ipsla.tcl to properly display the **show** command output:

```
set ipaddr [lindex $parmlist 1]
```

Configure the IP SLA entry:

```
if {[catch {cli_open} output]} {
      error $output $errorInfo
} else {
      array set cli_fd $output
}
if {[catch {cli_exec $cli_fd(fd) "enable"} output]} {
      error $output $errorInfo
}
```

```
if {[catch {cli_exec $cli_fd(fd) "show ip sla statistics"} ipslashowcmd]} {
        error $iplashowcmd $errorInfo
}
if {[catch {cli_close $cli_fd(fd) $cli_fd(tty_id)} output]} {
        error $output $errorInfo
}
set ipslaoutput [string map {"\r\n" "\n" "\"" "&#148;"  "<" "&#060;" ">"
  "&#062;" "'" "&#146;"} $ipslashowcmd]

set header "<html>
<head>
<title>IP SLA Measurment Results Page</title>
<script>
function clear_field(field, value) {if(field.value == value) field.value = '';}
function init_field(field, value) {if(field.value == '') field.value = value;}
</script>
</head>
<body>
IP SLA Measurment Results Page<br><br>
We are monitoring : <br>
$ipaddr<br><br>
The latest results:<br>
<textarea name='body' style='WIDTH: 710px; HEIGHT: 465px; color:#000000; font-
  family: courier; font-size: 8pt'>$ipslaoutput</textarea>
</body>
</html>"
set middle ""
set footer ""
set httpheader "HTTP/1.1 200 OK
Content-Type: text/html; charset=UTF-8
Content-Transfer-Encoding: binary
"
puts $httpsock $httpheader$header$middle$footer
```

Copy ipsla.tcl to the Cisco IOS device and verify that the **show** output is presented correctly. It should appear as shown in Figure 5-14.

Now that the output is presented correctly on the web page, modify the ipsla.tcl script so that it creates the IP SLA automatically. You are currently displaying the results from the IP SLA entry that was created manually. Instead of entering the command manually, modify the Tcl script to enter the IOS device configuration commands that will create the IP SLA entry.

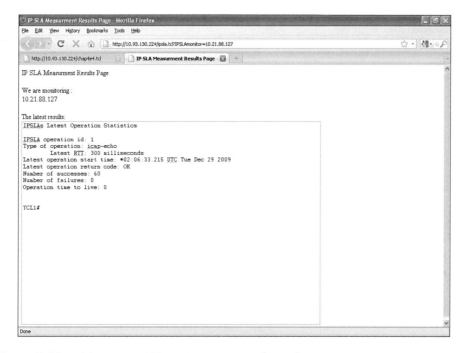

Figure 5-14   *IOS Device HTTP IP SLA Formatted Display*

Automatic Removal and Creation of IP SLA Entries

The first configuration command entered was **ip sla 1**. In this example, you want to first remove entry number 1, if it exists in the configuration. To do so, you must enter the following configuration commands:

```
no ip sla 1
ip sla 1
icmp-echo <put in the ip address from user input in chap4e4.tcl web page>
ip sla schedule 1 start-time now
```

To accomplish these configuration commands, you must make the following changes to the ipsla.tcl script:

```
if {[catch {cli_open} output]} {
      error $output $errorInfo
} else {
      array set cli_fd $output
}
```

Enter "enable" mode:

```
if {[catch {cli_exec $cli_fd(fd) "enable"} output]} {
      error $output $errorInfo
}
```

Enter configuration mode:

```
if {[catch {cli_exec $cli_fd(fd) "config terminal"} output]} {
        error $output $errorInfo
}
```

Delete the IP SLA entry if it exists:

```
if {[catch {cli_exec $cli_fd(fd) "no ip sla 1"} output]} {
        error $output $errorInfo
}
```

Configure the IP SLA entry:

```
if {[catch {cli_exec $cli_fd(fd) "ip sla 1"} output]} {
        error $output $errorInfo
}
```

Set the type of measurement to **icmp-echo** and use the input IP address:

```
if {[catch {cli_exec $cli_fd(fd) "icmp-echo $ipaddr"} output]} {
        error $output $errorInfo
}
```

Begin measuring IP SLA information now:

```
if {[catch {cli_exec $cli_fd(fd) "ip sla schedule 1 start-time now"} output]} {
        error $output $errorInfo
}
```

Exit out of configuration mode:

```
if {[catch {cli_exec $cli_fd(fd) "end"} output]} {
        error $output $errorInfo
}
```

Verify that the entry was created for later display on the web page:

```
if {[catch {cli_exec $cli_fd(fd) "show ip sla configuration 1"} showconfigcmd]} {
        error $showconfigcmd $errorInfo
}
```

Close the handle:

```
if {[catch {cli_close $cli_fd(fd) $cli_fd(tty_id)} output]} {
        error $output $errorInfo
}
```

This new script will take the following steps:

Step 1.   Enter enable mode to be allowed to enter **config terminal** later.

Step 2.   Enter the **config terminal** command to modify the device's running-configuration.

Step 3.   Remove any existing IP SLA entry 1 with **no ip sla 1** command.

Step 4.   Create a new IP SLA entry 1 with **ip sla 1** command.

Step 5.   Specify what type of measurement to take (in this case, **icmp-echo**) and configure the user-provided IP address from the incoming parameter to this web page Tcl script with the **$ipaddr** variable.

Step 6.   Starting the measurement right away with **ip sla schedule 1 start-time now**.

Step 7.   Exit out of configuration mode with **end**.

Step 8.   Use the **show ip sla configuration 1** to verify that the IP SLA entry was created. Save the output of this **show** command in a Tcl variable called **showconfigcmd**. The contents will display later in the web page.

Step 9.   Close the handle **cli_fd** in which you have entered the above commands to properly clean up.

The final change to make is to separate the web page that configures the IP SLA entry from the web page that displays the actual results. You can do so by creating an additional button to display the results.

To add the button, use the following lines of code:

```
<form name='ipslaresult' action='ipslaresult.tcl' method='GET' target='_blank'>
<input type='submit' value='Get IP Sla Result'>
</form>
```

You need to write a new Tcl script to display the results, which will be called ipslaresult.tcl. The title and body of the web page will be changed to IP SLA Measurement Configuration Page.

Putting it all together, this is the new ipsla.tcl script:

```
set ipaddr [lindex $parmlist 1]
if {[catch {cli_open} output]} {
        error $output $errorInfo
} else {
        array set cli_fd $output
}
if {[catch {cli_exec $cli_fd(fd) "enable"} output]} {
        error $output $errorInfo
}
if {[catch {cli_exec $cli_fd(fd) "config terminal"} output]} {
        error $output $errorInfo
}
```

```
if {[catch {cli_exec $cli_fd(fd) "no ip sla 1"} output]} {
        error $output $errorInfo
}
if {[catch {cli_exec $cli_fd(fd) "ip sla 1"} output]} {
        error $output $errorInfo
}
if {[catch {cli_exec $cli_fd(fd) "icmp-echo $ipaddr"} output]} {
        error $output $errorInfo
}
if {[catch {cli_exec $cli_fd(fd) "ip sla schedule 1 start-time now"} output]} {
        error $output $errorInfo
}
if {[catch {cli_exec $cli_fd(fd) "end"} output]} {
        error $output $errorInfo
}
if {[catch {cli_exec $cli_fd(fd) "show ip sla configuration 1"} showconfigcmd]} {
        error $showconfigcmd $errorInfo
}
if {[catch {cli_close $cli_fd(fd) $cli_fd(tty_id)} output]} {
        error $output $errorInfo
}
set ipslaoutput [string map {"\r\n" "\n" "\"" "&#148;"  "<" "&#060;" ">"
  "&#062;" "'" "&#146;"} $showconfigcmd]
set header "<html>
<head>
<title>IP SLA Measurment Configuration Page</title>
<script>
function clear_field(field, value) {if(field.value == value) field.value = '';}
function init_field(field, value) {if(field.value == '') field.value = value;}
</script>
</head>
<body>
IP SLA Measurment Configuration Page<br><br>
We are monitoring : <br>
$ipaddr<br><br>
  <form name='ipslaresult' action='ipslaresult.tcl' method='GET' target='_blank'>
  <input type='submit' value='Get IP Sla Result'>
  </form>
Configuration of IP Sla entry:<br>
<textarea name='body' style='WIDTH: 710px; HEIGHT: 465px; color:#000000; font-
  family: courier; font-size: 8pt'>$ipslaoutput</textarea>
</body>
</html>"
set middle ""
set footer ""
set httpheader "HTTP/1.1 200 OK
Content-Type: text/html; charset=UTF-8
```

```
Content-Transfer-Encoding: binary
"

puts $httpsock $httpheader$header$middle$footer
```

After you have copied the new iplsla.tcl to the Cisco IOS device, the web page appears, as shown in Figure 5-15.

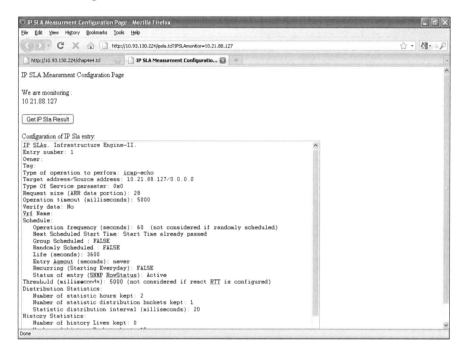

Figure 5-15 *IOS Device HTTP with IP SLA Automatically Configured*

Everything looks great so far!

Displaying the Results of the IP SLA Measurement with Auto-Refresh

There is one final page to write. You need to display the results in a new web page. The results will display using a new Tcl script called ipslaresult.tcl. As an additional enhancement to implement, you want the results page to automatically refresh. You will have the page refresh every minute so that the output will always show the latest ping echo request time displayed.

To accomplish this, add the following JavaScript code into the Tcl script:

```
<script type='text/javascript'>
<!--
  var timer = setInterval('autoRefresh()', 1000 * 60);
  function autoRefresh(){self.location.reload(true);}
//-->
</script>
```

This JavaScript code tells the browser to automatically refresh every minute. The timer expires every 60,000 milliseconds. When the timer expires, it calls **autoRefresh**, which causes the web page to reload.

Putting it all together, the new ipslaresult.tcl script contains the following:

```
if {[catch {cli_open} output]} {
        error $output $errorInfo
} else {
        array set cli_fd $output
}
if {[catch {cli_exec $cli_fd(fd) "enable"} output]} {
        error $output $errorInfo
}
if {[catch {cli_exec $cli_fd(fd) "show ip sla statistics 1"} ipslacmd]} {
        error $ipslacmd $errorInfo
}
if {[catch {cli_close $cli_fd(fd) $cli_fd(tty_id)} output]} {
        error $output $errorInfo
}
set ipslaoutput [string map {"\r\n" "\n" "\"" "&#148;"  "<" "&#060;" ">"
  "&#062;" "'" "&#146;"} $ipslacmd]
set header "<html>
<head>
<title>IP SLA Measurment Result Page with AutoReload</title>
</head>
<script type='text/javascript'>
<!--
  var timer = setInterval('autoRefresh()', 1000 * 60);
  function autoRefresh(){self.location.reload(true);}
//-->
</script>
<body>
IP SLA Measurment Result Page with AutoReload<br><br>
Results of the Latest IP Sla entry:<br>
<textarea name='body' style='WIDTH: 710px; HEIGHT: 465px; color:#000000; font-
  family: courier; font-size: 8pt'>$ipslaoutput</textarea>
</body>
</html>"
set middle ""
set footer ""
set httpheader "HTTP/1.1 200 OK
Content-Type: text/html; charset=UTF-8
Content-Transfer-Encoding: binary
"
puts $httpsock $httpheader$header$middle$footer
```

Verify that the results are correctly presented within the web page, which should appear as shown in Figure 5-16.

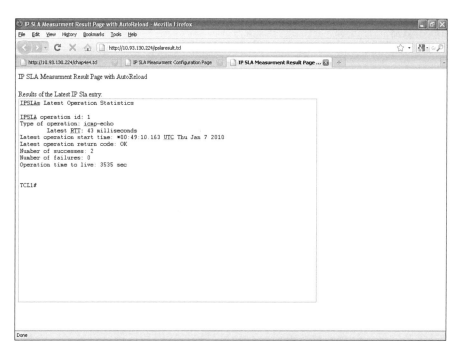

Figure 5-16   *IOS Device HTTP with IP SLA Auto-Refresh*

After 1 minute, the page automatically reloads and presents the latest results, as shown in Figure 5-17.

This completes writing the customized web page for the remote network administrator. Whenever a problem occurs on the network, the web page will be called into action to help troubleshoot the problem. As you have seen, there are nearly limitless possibilities in the type of web application that you can create.

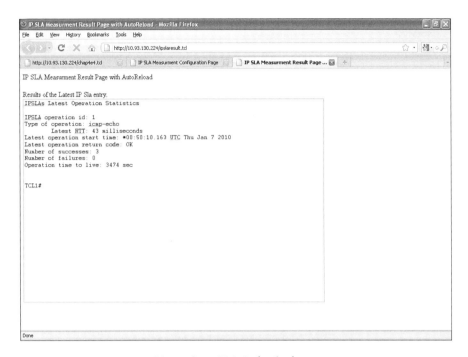

Figure 5-17   *IOS Device HTTP with IP SLA Refreshed*

Tcl Script Refresh Policy

Managing EEM policies in a large network environment can be an administrative burden. You can help reduce required management of scripts on individual IOS devices by using the Tcl script refresh policy.

Script policy refresh includes the following features:

■   Automatic update of the Tcl code from a predetermined location.

■   It can be used to selectively update a specific script or can be used to update all the scripts registered on the IOS device.

■   Figure 5-18 shows the Tcl refresh policy feature in a network. The centralized EEM server updates the Tcl script to all the routers using this feature.

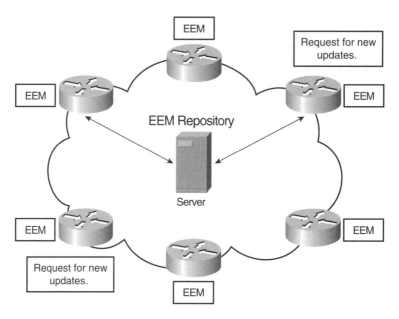

Figure 5-18 *Tcl Refresh Policy Diagram*

The following command is configured on the IOS device in configuration mode and specifies the default location from where the policies are updated:

```
event manager directory user repository url location
```

The following command enables you to update specific scripts or select the group name using a regular expression for the policy to be downloaded. The repository is the location from which the policies can be copied:

```
event manager update user policy [ name policy name | group group name
  expression] repository url location
```

SNMP Proxy Event Detector

The SNMP event detector is initiated when an IOS device sends an SNMP trap. When the event detector is triggered, it can be configured to perform a user-defined action. For example, the IOS device receives an SNMP trap if the uninterruptible power supply (UPS) is on backup. The script can then shut down all noncritical ports.

The proxy event detector functions as listed:

Step 1.   EEM registers with the SNMP proxy server to receive SNMP traps for the user-specified IP address.

Step 2.   The specific IP address sends the protocol data unit (PDU), and the device will queue it on the EEM proxy event detector's receive queue.

Step 3.   The SNMP proxy event detector will review the information based on the criteria from the registered policy.

Step 4.   If a match of the data is detected, the SNMP proxy event detector triggers the EEM script to run an action associated with the registered policy.

Remote-Procedure Call Requests

Remote-procedure call (RPC) requests allow an outside entity to make an XML RPC request, which will invoke an EEM policy or script. The Simple Object Access Protocol (SOAP) message is used to communicate with a server via Secure Shell (SSH) Version 2.

The following is an example of an RPC request:

```
<?xml version="1.0"?>
<SOAP:Envelope xmlns:SOAP="http://www.cisco.com/eem.xsd">
<SOAP:Body>
  <run_emscript>
    <script_name> name of script </script_name>
    <argc> argc value </argc>
    <arglist>
    <l> argv1 value </l>
    <l> argv2 value </l>
          ...
    <l> argvn value </l>
    </arglist>
  </run_Eemscript>
</SOAP:Body>
</SOAP:Envelope>
```

The reply syntax is configured as follows:

```
<?xml version="1.0"?>
<SOAP:Envelope xmlns:SOAP="http://www.cisco.com/eem.xsd">
<SOAP:Body>
    <run_Eemscript_response>
        <return_code> rc </return_code>
        <output> output string </output>
    </run_eemscript_response>
</SOAP:Body>
</SOAP:Envelope>
Configurations tasks:
```

EEM RPC events will also need to be registered and can be run from a Tcl script using the following commands:

```
::cisco::eem::event_register_rpc
namespace import ::cisco::eem::*
puts -nonewline "This is a test"
```

SSH provides an encrypted session for executing server programs. SSH must be configured on the IOS device to allow access to a remote SSH server, as follows:

```
TCL(config)#aaa new-model
TCL(config)#crypto key generate rsa  usage-keys label sshkeys modulus 768
TCL(config)#ip ssh version 2
```

The domain name needs to be configured with **ip domain-name** for SSH to work.

Multiple-Event Support for Event Correlation

A trigger initiates an EEM applet or script. The event detector facilitates multiple triggers that can be used to start a policy. Multiple events can be used to trigger an EEM policy, which can be grouped in a time window and also support Boolean policies. Support of multiple-event correlation provides the ability to trigger a policy given specific events occurring within a window of time. For example, you may not be concerned if a serial interface changes state within a 24 hour period, but if the interface changes state several time within a 1 minute interval (bouncing interface) this may be a reason for alarm. Grouping within a time window offers an additional method to correlate events.

The syntax that defines multiple-event correlation is as follows:

■ Add a new optional **tag** keyword:

```
event tag n1 cli pattern "write mem.*" sync yes
```

The following syntax contains the event statements. This event statement is referenced in the applet. Each of the statements will have a **tag** keyword that is unique to each applet. In the preceding example, **n1** is the **tag** keyword that is referenced in the applet.

■ **trigger**: Use the **trigger** applet configuration command in applet configuration mode to specify complex event configuration parameters. Through this, one or more events can be tracked and the time period specified:

```
[no] trigger [occurs occurs-val] [period period-val] [period-start period-
    start-val] [delay delay-val]
```

■ *occurs-val*: (Optional) Number of times the total correlation is repeated before raising an event. If this field is not specified, an event is raised after the first occurrence.

■ *period-val*: (Optional) The time interval which the number of occurrences in the **trigger** statement should occur. If this is not provided in the CLI, no time period is applied.

■ *period-start-val*: (Optional) This CRON specification field selects the beginning of an event "correlation window." If no period is specified, event monitoring is enabled after the first CRON period occurs and remains enabled.

The following example uses multiple tracking events with an EEM applet. In this example, the EEM applet is triggered by two CLI events, n1 and n2. The event n1 is the **write memory** command, and n2 is the **copy running** * command. The **trigger** for the script to execute is based on either n1 or n2 events occurring. The action for the syslog policy is a syslog message displaying **CONFIG SAVED**. The example follows:

```
event manager applet test1
 event tag n1 cli pattern "write mem.*" sync yes
 event tag n2 cli pattern "copy run.* start.*" sync yes
 trigger occurs 1
  correlate event n1 or event n2
 action 1.0 syslog msg "CONFIG SAVED"
 set 2.0 _exit_status 1
```

Execution of the script is as follows:

```
2811-2#wr mem
Building configuration...
[OK]
*Dec 22 02:23:33.463: %HA_EM-6-LOG: test1: CONFIG SAVED
2811-2#
2811-2#copy running-configs startup-config
Destination filename [startup-config]?
%Error opening flash:running-configs (No such file or directory)
2811-2#
*Dec 22 02:23:44.167: %HA_EM-6-LOG: test1: CONFIG SAVED
2811-2#
```

Using the clear Command

Tcl policy execution waits for user-defined triggers. After the trigger, the system waits for actions to be executed. Occasionally, the script may be in a pending state for a long time, perhaps because of the commands that need to be executed, the trigger criteria, or the logic of the script. In such cases, the **show event manager policy pending** command will display which script is pending. In addition, as of Cisco IOS Software Release 15.0 (which supports EEM 3.1), a new **show event manager policy active** command shows the EEM policies currently running. To clear a pending script, you just issue a **clear** command.

Note   Before executing the **clear** command, you must see the policies that are pending to make sure active scripts are not impacted. Use the **show event manager policy active** command to verify the pending policies, as follows:

```
Router#show event manager policy active
Key: p - Priority   :L - Low, H - High, N - Normal, Z - Last
   s - Scheduling node :A - Active, S - Standby


default class - 1 script event
 no. job id  p s status   time of event    event type     name
  1  1    N A running Wed Jan 6 22:38:34 2010   none Web_Server.tcl
```

To clear the event, use the following command to clear the specified policy or all policies:

```
Router#event manager scheduler clear {policy job-id | all}
```

You can clear a single policy by adding the policy number after the **policy** keyword. If all policies need to be cleared, use the **all** keyword, as follows:

```
Router#event manager scheduler clear all
```

Clearing policies with the **event manager scheduler clear** command is a great alternative to rebooting the router.

Note   The **clear** command was not introduced until EEM Version 2.4.

Summary

This chapter really showed the power of Tcl in IOS, specifically how to program an IOS device to be an SNMP server, how to save information to a file, and how to configure the device to be an HTTP server. In addition, you can provide event correlation and clear events. To scale to a large deployment of EEM, you can use a central server to maintain a repository of scripts that can automatically downloaded to the IOS device.

References

RFC 3164: http://www.ietf.org/rfc/rfc3164.txt

Chapter 6

Tcl Script Examples

This chapter covers the following topics:

- Creating an Application from Start to Finish

- Using Tcl to Troubleshoot Network Problems

- Creating a Web Application for Remote SNMP Graphing

This chapter focuses on how to create your own Tcl application from start to finish. It includes information about creating a flowchart, how to format your code, adding comments, and so on. This chapter also contains three examples to help you get started writing your own applications.

Creating an Application from Start to Finish

The process of writing your own application might be a bit daunting at first glance, especially if you have not had extensive programming experience. However, taking a systematic approach and following the steps outlined in this chapter will have you off and running in no time.

The sections that follow describe how to create the Multiprotocol Label Switching (MPLS) virtual private network (VPN) application that is used as the sample code.

Determine What You Want to Accomplish

The first step in writing any application is to determine what you want to accomplish, or what needs could be met by creating an application.

This chapter demonstrates how to write an application to simplify the MPLS VPN configuration of a "standalone" device through the use of a web front end. This application should provide enough detail to allow a user to easily add or remove configuration parameters without an in-depth understanding of the intricacies of the command-line interface (CLI).

This particular application will be more complex because the code will be written using Tcl and HTML.

Creating a Flowchart

After deciding on the application, the next step is to create a flowchart. The flowchart provides a general overview on how the application should function and will act as the foundation from which to begin.

Figure 6-1 shows a few standard symbols that are used when creating a flowchart, including the following:

- **Direction of flow:** This indicates which way information will flow in the program.

- **Start and end of program:** Self-explanatory.

- **Input or output:** This symbol represents information either being input or output. For example, it could be information received from the keyboard (input) or displayed to the screen (output).

- **Process function:** The process function corresponds to the manipulation of information.

- **Decision:** This symbol indicates a location in the program where a decision needs to be made. It generally represents an answer to a question such as a yes/no, true/false, or potentially might have numerous responses.

- **Connector:** The connector is used to associate specific locations within a flowchart and is commonly used when a flowchart is represented over multiple pages.

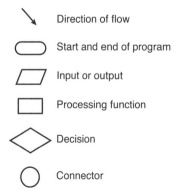

Figure 6-1 *Flowchart Symbols*

The flowchart representing the MPLS VPN application is relatively simple. After the application starts, pertinent information is collected from the router's running-configuration.

This information is then processed along with user input dialog boxes and displayed. After the user enters information, those changes are applied to the device and then displayed.

Figure 6-2 shows the flowchart for the MPLS VPN application.

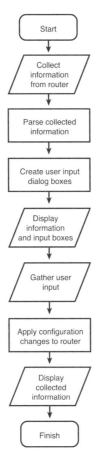

Figure 6-2   *Flowchart for MPLS VPN Application*

Deciding What the User Interface Should Look Like

Now that you have a general idea of what the application is supposed to do, you need to decide what the output should look like and what user information should be collected. This requires the most thoughtful consideration, because making changes to the display generally requires a significant amount of work.

Begin by listing the information that needs to be present in the output. Because this is an MPLS VPN application, the following parameters would be beneficial:

■   Virtual Routing and Forwarding / Route Distinguisher (VRF/RD) information, name, and number

■   Import/export numbers

■   VRF interface status

■   Label interface and status

■   Border Gateway Protocol (BGP) neighbors and status

■   BGP configuration

Next, list the information that you need to gather from the user:

■   VRF name

■   RD

■   Import and export information

■   Interface, IP address, and mask

■   BGP autonomous system number

■   Neighbor IP address

■   Whether the neighbor should be a route reflector client and the source interface

■   Whether the VRF interface should be redistributed in BGP

■   Label Distribution Protocol (LDP) interface, IP address, and mask

■   Whether this information should be added or removed from the configuration

Because this is a web-based application, the output is almost limitless. If you organize the information in sections, by function, this will be the most helpful for the user. Consider the data that needs to be displayed and collected. Which requires the most space? How can it be sectioned and arranged?

One method is to create an object for each one of the related items. This can be accomplished using your favorite graphics program or even using paper and pencil. Manipulate each object until you are satisfied with the output. Remember, this is just a template to follow. As you begin writing code, it might be easier to change the way the information is displayed instead of spending hours trying to make your program fit the template.

Figure 6-3 is the graphic representing what you *initially* wanted the output to look like. Yes, this was created before the application was written!

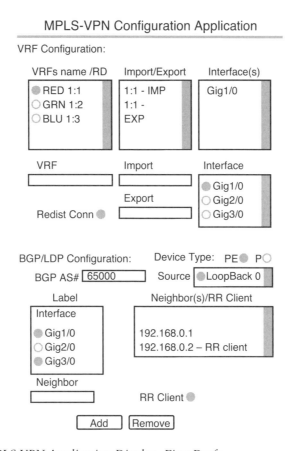

Figure 6-3 *MPLS VPN Application Display: First Draft*

Write the Code in Pseudo-Code

Performing this step is not always necessary, especially if you have experience creating applications, but if you are newer to programming, this will help you tremendously by keeping you on track!

Logically consider the steps required to complete the entire task. Using the flowchart and the user interface will provide the foundation for the program.

Step 1.   Start the program.

Step 2.   Start the web interface.

Step 3.   Display the application title: MPLS-VPN Configuration Application.

Step 4.   Collect the VRF/RD information and display it in a scrolling window at the top left portion of the screen.

Step 5.   Gather the associated import and export information per VRF and display it in a scrolling window at the top center of the screen.

Step 6.   Acquire the VRF interface configuration and display it in a scrolling window at the top right portion of the screen.

Step 7.   Create a user input dialog box for adding a VRF, import, and export information.

Step 8.   Display a scrolling window for interface selection.

Step 9.   Generate a radio button for the selection of redistributing connected routes.

Step 10.   Present an Add and Remove button.

Step 11.   Display the section title BGP/LDP Configuration.

Step 12.   Create radio buttons for Provider Edge/Provider (PE/P) device types.

Step 13.   Collect the BGP autonomous system number (ASN) from the configuration and display it.

Step 14.   Allow the user to select the source interface for the BGP neighbor association.

Step 15.   Generate a scrolling window with the label interfaces highlighted with a radio button.

Step 16.   Display the BGP neighbor information and whether it is a route-reflector client.

Step 17.   Present a selection for the user to input a BGP neighbor IP address.

Step 18.   Display a radio button selection for route-reflector client.

Step 19.   Present an Add and Remove button.

Step 20.   When the user selects Add or Remove, transfer the user input variables to another Tcl program.

Step 21.   Correlate the transferred variables.

The second Tcl program, which performs the processing function "apply configuration changes to router," will require its own flowchart. Before beginning that step, it would be prudent to start your first program to make sure you have all the variables. As you will see, it will be easier to change the program to accommodate the information that needs to be transferred.

Before You Begin

As you begin to create your program, it is imperative that you perform testing in a lab environment. During the creation of the MPLS VPN application, no animals were harmed, but because of infinite programming loops, the router had to be rebooted more times than we are willing to admit.

Caution   It is imperative that you perform testing in a lab environment.

Every program should begin with the brief description, the author, licensing information, and other pertinent facts:

```
# MPLS-VPN Configuration Application written by Ray Blair
# This application is used to configure and individual device as an MPLS-VPN
  P/PE device.
# Copyright 2010 Ray Blair. All rights reserved.
# Redistribution and use in source and binary forms, with or without
  modification, are
# permitted provided that the following conditions are met:
#   1. Redistributions of source code must retain the above copyright notice,
  this list of
#      conditions and the following disclaimer.
#   2. Redistributions in binary form must reproduce the above copyright notice,
  this list
#      of conditions and the following disclaimer in the documentation and/or
  other materials
#      provided with the distribution.
# THIS SOFTWARE IS PROVIDED BY RAY BLAIR ``AS IS'' AND ANY EXPRESS OR IMPLIED
# WARRANTIES, INCLUDING, BUT NOT LIMITED TO, THE IMPLIED WARRANTIES OF
  MERCHANTABILITY AND
# FITNESS FOR A PARTICULAR PURPOSE ARE DISCLAIMED. IN NO EVENT SHALL RAY BLAIR OR
# CONTRIBUTORS BE LIABLE FOR ANY DIRECT, INDIRECT, INCIDENTAL, SPECIAL,
  EXEMPLARY, OR
# CONSEQUENTIAL DAMAGES (INCLUDING, BUT NOT LIMITED TO, PROCUREMENT OF
  SUBSTITUTE GOODS OR
# SERVICES; LOSS OF USE, DATA, OR PROFITS; OR BUSINESS INTERRUPTION) HOWEVER
  CAUSED AND ON
# ANY THEORY OF LIABILITY, WHETHER IN CONTRACT, STRICT LIABILITY, OR TORT
  (INCLUDING
# NEGLIGENCE OR OTHERWISE) ARISING IN ANY WAY OUT OF THE USE OF THIS SOFTWARE,
  EVEN IF
# ADVISED OF THE POSSIBILITY OF SUCH DAMAGE.


# The views and conclusions contained in the software and documentation are
  those of the
# authors and should not be interpreted as representing official policies,
  either expressed
# or implied, of Ray Blair.
# For comments or suggestions please contact the author at rablair@cisco.com
```

To make the program easier to read and understand, you need to follow three primary rules:

Step 1.   Use tabs and spacing to facilitate readability. For example, when using control statements such as **if, while, for,** and so on, indent the commands within the control statement as follows:

```
if {[$VAR1] != 0 && [$VAR2] == 0} {
    if [catch {cli_open} RESULT] {
        error $RESULT $errorInfo
        } else {
        action_syslog msg "This is the result \n $RESULT "
    }
}
```

Vertically aligning the control statement with the associated } makes the program much easier to follow.

Step 2.   Using capital/uppercase letters or a combination for user-defined variables makes the program much easier to read. In the example in the preceding step, you can quickly see that the actual commands are lowercase and the variables are uppercase or a combination of upper- and lowercase. Bottom line: This is what I prefer, but use what you are comfortable with.

Step 3.   Finally, and most important, include lots of comments within the application. If you add comments while you are writing your code, you will not forget to go back and add comments later. I have written programs in the past and was in too much of a hurry to add comments. Attempting to modify the code, months or even days later can be an arduous process without comments.

Starting to Program the Application

The next section steps through configuring the web server and writing the code. You can always use the cut-and-paste method, but examining each line of code will not only help you write your own applications, it will provide you with practice reading someone else's code.

Configuring the Web Server

Using the web server script from Chapter 5, "Advanced Tcl Operation in Cisco IOS," you will modify two parameters. The first being the port and the second the file location or directory. Modifying the port will obfuscate the location of the service, and creating a directory for the files will aid in organizing the files on the IOS device. Make the following changes to the web server Tcl script:

```
set svcPort 8082
```

```
catch {open [file join flash:/TCL/ $filename] r} output
```

Do not forget to start the service on the device:

```
Router#event manager run Web_Server.tcl
```

Be patient, it will take some time to start.

Tip   Opening Tcl server sockets takes precedence over other ports that might be open on the IOS device. For example, if you open a server socket on port 23 (Telnet), the Telnet service on the IOS device will be unavailable and you will not be able to gain access via Telnet.

Writing Code for the MPLS VPN Script

The beginning should contain comments indicating who is to blame, what the application does, licensing restrictions, and liability:

```
# MPLS-VPN Configuration Application written by Ray Blair
# This application is used to configure and individual device as an MPLS-VPN
  P/PE device.
# Copyright 2010 Ray Blair. All rights reserved.
# Redistribution and use in source and binary forms, with or without
  modification, are
# permitted provided that the following conditions are met:
#   1. Redistributions of source code must retain the above copyright notice,
  this list of
#      conditions and the following disclaimer.
#   2. Redistributions in binary form must reproduce the above copyright notice,
  this list
#      of conditions and the following disclaimer in the documentation and/or
  other materials
#      provided with the distribution.
# THIS SOFTWARE IS PROVIDED BY RAY BLAIR ``AS IS'' AND ANY EXPRESS OR IMPLIED
# WARRANTIES, INCLUDING, BUT NOT LIMITED TO, THE IMPLIED WARRANTIES OF
  MERCHANTABILITY AND
# FITNESS FOR A PARTICULAR PURPOSE ARE DISCLAIMED. IN NO EVENT SHALL RAY BLAIR OR
# CONTRIBUTORS BE LIABLE FOR ANY DIRECT, INDIRECT, INCIDENTAL, SPECIAL,
  EXEMPLARY, OR
# CONSEQUENTIAL DAMAGES (INCLUDING, BUT NOT LIMITED TO, PROCUREMENT OF
  SUBSTITUTE GOODS OR
# SERVICES; LOSS OF USE, DATA, OR PROFITS; OR BUSINESS INTERRUPTION) HOWEVER
  CAUSED AND ON
# ANY THEORY OF LIABILITY, WHETHER IN CONTRACT, STRICT LIABILITY, OR TORT
  (INCLUDING
# NEGLIGENCE OR OTHERWISE) ARISING IN ANY WAY OUT OF THE USE OF THIS SOFTWARE,
  EVEN IF
# ADVISED OF THE POSSIBILITY OF SUCH DAMAGE.
```

```
# The views and conclusions contained in the software and documentation are
  those of the
# authors and should not be interpreted as representing official policies,
  either expressed
# or implied, of Ray Blair.
# For comments or suggestions please contact the author at rablair<indexterm
  startref="inddle01063" class="endofrange" significance="normal"/>:}]
```

As you read in the section "Write the Code in Pseudo-Code," earlier in this chapter, you need to display the application title. You will be do so in the HTML section. Step 4 is where you need to collect information from the IOS device. You must experiment to determine the best way to capture the information. You could do so via the **show running-config** command, the **show ip vrf** command, or several others. You obviously want to make this as easy as possible. The one used here is **show ip vrf detail | include ;**.

Another decision you must make is whether to write a Tcl script to implement the application or an Embedded Event Manager (EEM) policy. For this particular application, you can leverage the existing web server introduced in Chapter 5, which is implemented as an EEM policy. Thus, the application itself will be an EEM policy.

The next commands prepare the IOS device to gather information using a **show** command:

```
if [catch {cli_open} RESULT] {
      error $RESULT $errorInfo
        } else {
        array set cli1 $RESULT
}

if [catch {cli_exec $cli1(fd) "en"} RESULT] {
        cli_close $cli1(fd)
        error $RESULT $errorInfo
}
```

Note   The commands within the Cisco IOS CLI are used to determine the best method to gather information.

Using the **show ip vrf detail | include ;** command, collect and store the output in the variable **VRFs**.

For example:

```
Router#show ip vrf detail | include ;
VRF BLU; default RD 1:4; default VPNID <not set>
VRF GRN; default RD 1:2; default VPNID <not set>
VRF Orange; default RD 1:3; default VPNID <not set>
VRF PURPLE; default RD 1:1992; default VPNID <not set>
VRF RED; default RD 1:1; default VPNID <not set>
```

```
if [catch {cli_exec $cli1(fd) "show ip vrf detail | include ;" } RESULT] {
        error $RESULT $errorInfo
    } else {
        set VRFs $RESULT
}
if [catch {cli_close $cli1(fd) $cli1(tty_id)} RESULT] {
        error $RESULT $errorInfo
}
```

To determine how many VRFs are configured on the IOS device, you will use the variable named **COUNT** and set the value to **1**:

```
set COUNT 1
```

The variable **ALL_VRF_INFO** is cleared:

```
set ALL_VRF_INFO ""
```

You need to determine whether there is enough information in the output to continue. In this case, if the length of the string is greater than 10, you can be confident that there is valid information to gather:

```
while {[string length $VRFs]  > 10} {
```

The next statement is relatively complex because there are nested commands. The object is to collect only the information that you need and throw away the rest. This will require some trial and error, and a good way to create the appropriate code is using the Tcl shell on the IOS device. Set the **VRFs** variable as follows:

```
Router(tcl)#set VRFs [exec "show ip vrf detail | include ;"]
VRF BLU; default RD 1:4; default VPNID <not set>
VRF GRN; default RD 1:2; default VPNID <not set>
VRF Orange; default RD 1:3; default VPNID <not set>
VRF PURPLE; default RD 1:1992; default VPNID <not set>
VRF RED; default RD 1:1; default VPNID <not set>
```

Starting in the middle and working outward, the command **string first** looks for the first occurrence of an element in a string. Using the Tcl shell, enter the following command:

```
Router(tcl)#string first "VRF " $VRFs
0
```

The result is 0, indicating the first element in the string, remember that the count starts at 0 and not 1.

Next, use the **expr** command to evaluate the statement, as follows:

```
Router(tcl)#expr [string first "VRF " $VRFs] + 4
4
```

This is entire statement defines the start value for the **string range** command. Now, define the end value using the following combined command:

```
Router(tcl)#expr [string first "; default RD" $VRFs] - 1
6
```

In the following line, the *string range* will assemble elements 4 through 6, which contain the value **BLU**:

```
VRF BLU; default RD 1:4; default VPNID <not set>
```

The results are as follows:

```
Router(tcl)#string range $VRFs [expr [string first "VRF " $VRFs] + 4] [expr
[string first "; default RD" $VRFs] - 1]
BLU
```

Finally, you want to set the variable **VRF($COUNT)** or **VRF(1)** to the VRF name of **BLU**. The variable **COUNT** is used to minimize the number of lines of code. Because it is a variable, it will be used for every VRF, as follows:

```
Router(tcl)#set VRF($COUNT) [string range $VRFs [expr [string first "VRF " $VRFs]
 + 4] [expr
[string first "; default RD" $VRFs] - 1]]
BLU
```

As you can see, using the Tcl shell of the IOS device makes writing the program much easier:

```
    set VRF($COUNT) [string range $VRFs [expr [string first "VRF " $VRFs] + 4]
[expr [string
first "; default RD" $VRFs] - 1]]
```

> **Tip** Using the Tcl shell on the IOS device will expedite the programming and troubleshooting process.

The result of the next command is as follows:

```
Router(tcl)#set RD($COUNT)  [string range $VRFs [expr [string first "; default RD
 " $VRFs] + 12] [expr [string first "; default VPNID" $VRFs] -1]]
 1:4
set RD($COUNT)  [string range $VRFs [expr [string first "; default RD " $VRFs] +
 12] [expr [string first "; default VPNID" $VRFs] -1]]
```

A temporary variable named **ITEM** is used to store the results **BLU 1:4**:

```
set ITEM "<b>$VRF($COUNT)</b><br /> $RD($COUNT)<br />"
```

Did you notice the additions? The **<b>**, **</b>**, and the **
** are HTML commands. This book was not written to go into the detail of HTML programming, because there are many other resources available. However, we will cover some of the basics. The **<b>**

and **</b>** indicate the start and end of text that is to appear in bold, and the **
** is a line break.

The **concat** command concatenates the variable **ITEM** to the variable **ALL_VRF_INFO**, and stores it in the variable **ALL_VRF_INFO**:

```
set ALL_VRF_INFO [concat $ALL_VRF_INFO $ITEM]
```

Because you've collected all the information that you need from the first line of the **show ip vrf detail | include ;** command, you have to clear that line or the **while** statement will result in an endless loop and you will have to reboot your IOS device. By replacing the **VRFs** variable using the **string range** command starting with the first newline statement (**\n**) to the end of the string (**string length**), you can successfully remove the first line, as follows:

```
Router(tcl)#set VRFs [string range $VRFs [expr [string first "\n" $VRFs] +1]
  [string length $VRFs]]
VRF GRN; default RD 1:2; default VPNID <not set>
VRF Orange; default RD 1:3; default VPNID <not set>
VRF PURPLE; default RD 1:1992; default VPNID <not set>
VRF RED; default RD 1:1; default VPNID <not set>
```

The result has removed the line **VRF BLU; default RD 1:4; default VPNID <not set>**:

```
set VRFs [string range $VRFs [expr [string first "\n" $VRFs] +1] [string length
  $VRFs]]
```

The variable **COUNT** is incremented in the next step. As a result, the previous code can be reused:

```
    incr COUNT
}
```

When the **while** loop completes, you must keep track of the number of virtual routing and forwarding instances to be used throughout the program:

```
set NUM_OF_VRFS $COUNT
```

> **Note** Commands that have been previously been commented on will not contain a detailed explanation.

```
if [catch {cli_open} RESULT] {
    error $RESULT $errorInfo
} else {
    array set cli1 $RESULT
}
if [catch {cli_exec $cli1(fd) "en"} RESULT] {
    error $RESULT $errorInfo
}
```

Store the **show running-config** output in a variable called **CONFIG.** You can replicate this process from the Tcl shell using the following command (only the first portion of the configuration is shown):

```
Router(tcl)#set CONFIG [exec "show running-config"]



Building configuration...


Current configuration : 5546 bytes
!
version 12.4
service timestamps debug datetime msec
service timestamps log datetime msec
!
hostname Router
!
boot-start-marker
boot system ftp Public/FTP/c2800nm-adventerprisek9-mz.124-24.T1.bin 192.168.1.50
boot-end-marker
!
logging message-counter syslog
!
aaa new-model
!
!
!
!
aaa session-id common
clock timezone PST -8
!
!
ip cef
!
!
no ip domain lookup
ip vrf BLU
 rd 1:4
 route-target export 1:4
 route-target import 1:4
!
ip vrf GRN
 rd 1:2
 route-target export 1:2
 route-target import 1:2
```

```
!
ip vrf Orange
 rd 1:3
 route-target export 1:3
 route-target import 1:3
!
ip vrf PURPLE
 rd 1:1992
 route-target export 1:1992
 route-target import 1:1992
!
ip vrf RED
 rd 1:1
 route-target export 1:1
 route-target export 1:2
 route-target export 1:3
 route-target import 1:1
 route-target import 1:2
 route-target import 1:3
!
no ipv6 cef
!
multilink bundle-name authenticated
!
!
```

The **show running-config** command is executed, and the result is stored in the variable **CONFIG:**

```
if [catch {cli_exec $cli1(fd) "show running-config" } RESULT] {
    error $RESULT $errorInfo
} else {
    set CONFIG $RESULT
}
if [catch {cli_close $cli1(fd) $cli1(tty_id)} RESULT] {
    error $RESULT $errorInfo
}
```

Initialize the variable **COUNT** to 1 and the clear **IMPORT_EXPORT** variable:

```
set COUNT 1
set IMPORT_EXPORT ""
```

You might have noticed that many of the variables contain an underscore (_). This is done strictly for convenience, so that when you select the text using a double-click, the entire variable is selected. Many applications treat a hyphen (-) similar to a space, requiring you to highlight the entire variable.

In the next section, you need to gather the appropriate information to populate the import/export table. Although there are several ways to collect the data, using the running-configuration is relatively simple.

Comparing the variable **COUNT** with the number of VRFs saved previously, you have a way to retrieve the information from the running-configuration:

```
while {$COUNT < $NUM_OF_VRFS} {
```

The next statement uses the **string first** command, but uses an additional parameter called *startIndex*. The *startIndex* parameter indicates at what position in the string to start the search. It might appear confusing because the **string first** command is used two times within the same statement. In English, this command would read "set the variable **BEGIN** to the first new line element in the string **CONFIG** using the starting position of **ip vrf $VRF($COUNT)** or **ip vrf BLU**." By entering the command in the Tcl shell, you can see that the variable **BEGIN** is set to 619:

```
Router(tcl)#set BEGIN [string first "\n" $CONFIG [string first "ip vrf
  $VRF($COUNT)" $CONFIG]]
619
    set BEGIN [string first "\n" $CONFIG [string first "ip vrf $VRF($COUNT)"
  $CONFIG]]
```

The next command is rudimentary. The variable **END** is set to the first **!** found in the **CONFIG** string beginning at the variable **BEGIN**. The output from the Tcl shell shows that the variable **END** is set to 681:

```
Router(tcl)#set END [string first "!" $CONFIG $BEGIN]
681
    set END [string first "!" $CONFIG $BEGIN]
```

The string **IMP_EXP_STRING** is set to the range of characters in the **CONFIG** variable from the value of **BEGIN + 1** and **END − 1**, as follows:

```
Router(tcl)#set IMP_EXP_STRING [string range $CONFIG [expr $BEGIN +1] [expr $END
  -1]]
 rd 1:4
 route-target export 1:4
 route-target import 1:4

    set IMP_EXP_STRING [string range $CONFIG [expr $BEGIN +1] [expr $END -1]]
```

The next statement verifies the existence of **route-target** within the string **IMP_EXP_STRING**. If the variable exists, the subsequent commands will be initiated:

```
if {[string first "route-target " $IMP_EXP_STRING]} {
```

The following two commands could be combined into a single statement. Sometimes, having several lines makes the program easier to understand.

This statement sets the variable **BEGIN** to the first occurrence of "**route-target**":

```
Router(tcl)#set BEGIN [string first "route-target " $IMP_EXP_STRING]
10
```

```
        set BEGIN [string first "route-target " $IMP_EXP_STRING]
```

To glean the correct information to display, you need to remove the **rd** identifier. You can do so using the following statement:

```
Router(tcl)#set IMP_EXP_STRING [string range $IMP_EXP_STRING [expr $BEGIN -1]
  [expr $END -1]]
 route-target export 1:4
 route-target import 1:4
```

```
        set IMP_EXP_STRING [string range $IMP_EXP_STRING [expr $BEGIN -1] [expr
  $END -1]]
```

It would be redundant to show **route-target** in every line. You can easily remove these with the **regsub** command, as shown:

```
Router(tcl)#regsub -all {route-target } $IMP_EXP_STRING "<br />" IMP_EXP_STRING
2
```

After the command is entered, the output is 2. This indicates the number of occurrences that were changed. You also added the HTML commands to create bold text and add a line break:

```
regsub -all {route-target } $IMP_EXP_STRING "</b><br />" IMP_EXP_STRING
```

The variable **ITEM** is configured to display the VRF name and import and export information, as shown here:

```
Router(tcl)#set ITEM "<b> $VRF($COUNT) $IMP_EXP_STRING <br />"
<b> BLU   </b><br />export 1:4
 </b><br />import 1:4
 <br />
        set ITEM "<b> $VRF($COUNT) $IMP_EXP_STRING <br />"
```

The **concat** command concatenates the variable **ITEM** to the variable **IMPORT_EXPORT**, and stores it in the variable **IMPORT_EXPORT**:

```
    set IMPORT_EXPORT [concat $IMPORT_EXPORT $ITEM]
}
```

Increment the variable **COUNT**:

```
    incr COUNT
}
```

The next portion of code collects the VRF interface status:

```
if [catch {cli_open} RESULT] {
    error $RESULT $errorInfo
```

```
} else {
    array set cli1 $RESULT
}
if [catch {cli_exec $cli1(fd) "en"} RESULT] {
    error $RESULT $errorInfo
}
```

To verify the output and manipulate the variables in the Tcl shell, use the following command:

```
Router(tcl)#set VRF_INTERFACE_CONFIG [exec "show ip vrf interfaces"]
Interface              IP-Address      VRF
Protocol
Lo4                    10.4.4.1        BLU                              up
Lo1007                 192.168.92.38   GRN                              up
Lo1018                 172.17.123.9    GRN                              up
Lo3                    10.3.3.1        Orange                           up
Lo1004                 unassigned      PURPLE                           up
Se0/0/0                10.55.55.5      PURPLE                           down
Lo1001                 172.18.134.3    RED                              up

if [catch {cli_exec $cli1(fd) "show ip vrf interfaces" } RESULT] {
    error $RESULT $errorInfo
} else {
    set VRF_INTERFACE_CONFIG $RESULT
}
if [catch {cli close $cli1(fd) $cli1(tty_id)} RESULT] {
    error $RESULT $errorInfo
}
```

Set and clear variables:

```
set VRF_INTERFACE_OUTPUT ""
set COUNT 1
```

Use the number of VRFs as a counter:

```
while {$COUNT < $NUM_OF_VRFS} {
```

Perform the subsequent functions as long as the variable **VRF_INTERFACE_CONFIG** contains information for the selected VRF. Using the Tcl shell shows that there is pertinent information in the string:

```
Router(tcl)#regexp -all $VRF($COUNT) $VRF_INTERFACE_CONFIG
1
    while {[regexp -all $VRF($COUNT) $VRF_INTERFACE_CONFIG] > 0} {
```

Search through the string **VRF_INTERFACE_CONFIG** for the first location of the name "**Protocol**", add 10 to that value, and set the result to the variable **BEGIN.** In this example, the value is 82, as shown here:

```
Router(tcl)#set BEGIN [expr [string first "Protocol" $VRF_INTERFACE_CONFIG] + 10]
82
        set BEGIN [expr [string first "Protocol" $VRF_INTERFACE_CONFIG] + 10]
```

Set the variable **END** to the expression of the location of the first new line in string **VRF_INTERFACE_CONFIG** starting with the location of the first occurrence of **VRF(COUNT)** or **BLU** in string **VRF_INTERFACE_CONFIG,** as follows:

```
Router(tcl)#set END [expr [string first "\n" $VRF_INTERFACE_CONFIG [expr [string
  first $VRF($COUNT) $VRF_INTERFACE_CONFIG $BEGIN]]]]
163


        set END [expr [string first "\n" $VRF_INTERFACE_CONFIG [expr [string
  first $VRF($COUNT) $VRF_INTERFACE_CONFIG $BEGIN]]]]
```

Set the variable **VRF_INTERFACES** to the range of characters from **BEGIN** − 1 or 82 to **END** or 183, as shown:

```
Router(tcl)#set VRF_INTERFACES [string range $VRF_INTERFACE_CONFIG [expr $BEGIN
  -1] $END]


Lo4                    10.4.4.1        BLU                                up


        set VRF_INTERFACES [string range $VRF_INTERFACE_CONFIG [expr $BEGIN -1]
$END]
```

Remove the **VRF** name from the string, as shown:

```
Router(tcl)#regsub -all $VRF($COUNT) $VRF_INTERFACES " " VRF_INTERFACES
1
```

The **puts** command indicates how the variable **VRF_INTERFACES** was changed:

```
Router(tcl)#puts $VRF_INTERFACES
Lo4                    10.4.4.1                                        up


          regsub -all $VRF($COUNT) $VRF_INTERFACES " " VRF_INTERFACES
```

Remove the spaces, as follows:

```
Router(tcl)#regsub -all {  } $VRF_INTERFACES " " VRF_INTERFACES
32
Router(tcl)#puts $VRF_INTERFACES
Lo4        10.4.4.1                    up


          regsub -all {  } $VRF_INTERFACES " " VRF_INTERFACES
```

Using the variable **ITEM**, add the VRF name, interface parameters, and HTML commands:

```
set ITEM "<b> $VRF($COUNT)</b><br /> $VRF_INTERFACES </b><br />"
```

Concatenate the gathered information into the variable **VRF_INTERFACE_OUTPUT**:

```
set VRF_INTERFACE_OUTPUT [concat $VRF_INTERFACE_OUTPUT $ITEM]
```

Remove the current line so the next line can be processed, as shown:

```
Router(tcl)#set VRF_INTERFACE_CONFIG [string replace $VRF_INTERFACE_CONFIG [expr
  $BEGIN -1] [expr $END]]
Interface              IP-Address      VRF                         Protocol
Lo1007                 192.168.92.38   GRN                         up
Lo1018                 172.17.123.9    GRN                         up
Lo3                    10.3.3.1        Orange                      up
Lo1004                 unassigned      PURPLE                      up
Se0/0/0                10.55.55.5      PURPLE                      down
Lo1001                 172.18.134.3    RED                         up


            set VRF_INTERFACE_CONFIG [string replace $VRF_INTERFACE_CONFIG [expr
    $BEGIN -1] [expr $END]]
      }
```

If there is no additional information to retrieve for the VRF, increment the count to check the next VRF:

```
incr COUNT
}
```

This section of code assembles information to display the status label interface, using the **show mpls interfaces | exc Operational** command, as follows:

```
Router(tcl)#set LDP_INTERFACE_CONFIG  [exec "show mpls interfaces | exc
Operational"]
GigabitEthernet0/0     Yes (ldp)     No        No  No      Yes
GigabitEthernet0/1     Yes           No        No  No      No

if [catch {cli_open} RESULT] {
    error $RESULT $errorInfo
} else {
    array set cli1 $RESULT
}
if [catch {cli_exec $cli1(fd) "en"} RESULT] {
    error $RESULT $errorInfo
}
if [catch {cli_exec $cli1(fd) "show mpls interfaces | exc Operational" } RESULT]
{
    error $RESULT $errorInfo
```

```
} else {
    set LDP_INTERFACE_CONFIG $RESULT
}
if [catch {cli_close $cli1(fd) $cli1(tty_id)} RESULT] {
    error $RESULT $errorInfo
}
```

Clear the variable **LDP_INTERFACES**:

```
set LDP_INTERFACES ""
```

To confirm that there is valid data in the variable, you will look though the string for either a **Yes** or a **No**. The following output reveals that there are 10 occurrences:

```
Router(tcl)#regexp -all {Yes | No} $LDP_INTERFACE_CONFIG
10
while {[regexp -all {Yes | No} $LDP_INTERFACE_CONFIG] > 0} {
```

Set the variable **END** to the first newline in the string **LDP_INTERFACE_CONFIG** starting at character 12, as shown here:

```
Router(tcl)#set END [string first "\n" $LDP_INTERFACE_CONFIG 12]
72
    set END [string first "\n" $LDP_INTERFACE_CONFIG 12]
```

Set the variable **ITEM** to the string range of variable **LDP_INTERFACE_CONFIG** starting a 0 to the value of **END** or 72, as shown:

```
Router(tcl)#set ITEM [string range $LDP_INTERFACE_CONFIG 0 $END]

GigabitEthernet0/0    Yes (ldp)    No    No No    Yes

    set ITEM [string range $LDP_INTERFACE_CONFIG 0 $END]
```

Check to see whether **Yes** or **No** is the last parameter in the string **ITEM**. Set the variable **END** to the last item in the string to minus 3 if the last item is **Yes** or minus 2 if the last item is **No**. This accounts for the number of characters in each word. From the previous example, we see the value is **Yes**. Given the following expression, you see that **END** should be set to 56:

```
Router(tcl)#expr [string last Yes $ITEM] - 3
56

    if {[expr [string last Yes $ITEM]] > [expr [string last No $ITEM]]} {
        set END [expr [string last Yes $ITEM] - 3]
        } else {
        set END [expr [string last No $ITEM] -2 ]
    }
```

Replace everything in the string **ITEM** except for the interface name and status, as shown here:

```
Router(tcl)#set ITEM [string replace $ITEM [expr [string first " " $ITEM]] $END]
GigabitEthernet0/0  Yes

    set ITEM [string replace $ITEM [expr [string first " " $ITEM]] $END]
```

Add the line break to the output:

```
Router(tcl)#set ITEM "$ITEM <br />"
GigabitEthernet0/0  Yes
 <br />
    set ITEM "$ITEM <br />"
```

Concatenate the collected information into the **LDP_INTERFACES** string:

```
set LDP_INTERFACES [concat $LDP_INTERFACES $ITEM]
```

Remove the current line in the string, as shown:

```
Router(tcl)#set LDP_INTERFACE_CONFIG [string replace $LDP_INTERFACE_CONFIG 0
  [string first "\n" $LDP_INTERFACE_CONFIG 3]]
GigabitEthernet0/1     Yes           No       No  No      No

    set LDP INTERFACE_CONFIG [string replace $LDP_INTERFACE_CONFIG 0 [string
  first "\n" $LDP_INTERFACE_CONFIG 3]]
}
```

This section pulls the BGP VPNv4 neighbor information and status of the BGP relationship using the **show ip bgp vpnv4 all summary** command:

```
Router(tcl)#set BGP_NEIGHBORS [exec "show ip bgp vpnv4 all summary"]
BGP router identifier 192.168.254.254, local AS number 65065
BGP table version is 7, main routing table version 7

Neighbor        V    AS MsgRcvd  MsgSent  TblVer  InQ OutQ Up/Down   State/PfxRcd
10.93.130.225   4  65065    311      324       7    0    0 05:10:18  0
192.50.50.50    4  65065      0        0       0    0    0 never     Active
192.168.100.1   4  65065      0        0       0    0    0 never     Active
192.168.200.1   4  65065      0        0       0    0    0 never     Active

if [catch {cli_open} RESULT] {
    error $RESULT $errorInfo
} else {
    array set cli1 $RESULT
}
if [catch {cli_exec $cli1(fd) "en"} RESULT] {
    error $RESULT $errorInfo
}
```

```
if [catch {cli_exec $cli1(fd) "show ip bgp vpnv4 all summary" } RESULT] {
    error $RESULT $errorInfo
} else {
    set BGP_NEIGHBORS $RESULT
}
if [catch {cli_close $cli1(fd) $cli1(tty_id)} RESULT] {
    error $RESULT $errorInfo
}
```

Clear the variable **BGP_NEIGHBOR_OUTPUT**:

```
set BGP_NEIGHBOR_OUTPUT ""
```

Set the variable **BEGIN** to the location just beyond the **"PfxRcd"** statement in the variable **BGP_NEIGHBORS**, as shown:

```
Router(tcl)#set BEGIN [expr [string first "PfxRcd" $BGP_NEIGHBORS 1] + 8]
206
set BEGIN [expr [string first "PfxRcd" $BGP_NEIGHBORS 1] + 8]
```

While there is a . in the variable **BGP_NEIGHBORS**, continue processing the subsequent commands:

```
while {[regexp -all {.} $BGP_NEIGHBORS] > 0} {
```

If the value of **BEGIN** is less than 10, set it to 0:

```
if {$BEGIN < 10} {
    set BEGIN 0
}
```

If a new line is present in the **BGP_NEIGHBORS** string, after the location of **BEGIN + 20**, process the subsequent commands, as follows:

```
Router(tcl)#string first "\n" $BGP_NEIGHBORS [expr $BEGIN + 20]
288

    if {[string first "\n" $BGP_NEIGHBORS [expr $BEGIN + 20]]} {
```

Set the variable **END** to the first newline value in the **BGP_NEIGHBORS** string, after the location of **BEGIN + 20**, as shown here:

```
Router(tcl)#set END [string first "\n" $BGP_NEIGHBORS [expr $BEGIN + 20]]
288
        set END [string first "\n" $BGP_NEIGHBORS [expr $BEGIN + 20]]
```

Otherwise (**else**), set the variable **END** to the penultimate value in the string **BGP_NEIGHBORS**:

```
    } else {
    set END [expr [string length $BGP_NEIGHBORS] - 1]
}
```

Set the temporary variable **ITEM** to the string range as follows:

```
Router(tcl)#set ITEM [string range $BGP_NEIGHBORS $BEGIN $END]
10.93.130.225   4       65065       311     324         7   0     0 05:10:18
0
```

```
    set ITEM [string range $BGP_NEIGHBORS $BEGIN $END]
```

If the string length of **ITEM** is less than 0, exit from the while loop:

```
if {[string length $ITEM] < 10} {break}
```

BGP uses the term *active* to convey that it is actively attempting to establish a connection with a neighbor. To minimize confusion, change **Active** to **DOWN**. The following if/else statement verifies the existence of the word **Active** in the variable **ITEM** and changes it to **DOWN**:

```
if {[regexp -all {Active} $ITEM] == 0} {
```

Replace everything in the string with the exception of the BGP neighbor IP address, as shown:

```
Router(tcl)#set ITEM [string replace $ITEM [expr [string first " " $ITEM]] $END]
10.93.130.225
```

```
        set ITEM [string replace $ITEM [expr [string first " " $ITEM]] $END]
```

Add the word **UP** and the HTML command for a line break:

```
set ITEM "$ITEM UP <br />"
```

Concatenate **ITEM** with **BGP_NEIGHBOR_OUTPUT**:

```
 set BGP_NEIGHBOR_OUTPUT [concat $BGP_NEIGHBOR_OUTPUT $ITEM]
} else {
```

If the BGP neighbor is **Active** set the output to **DOWN**, including the appropriate HTML commands:

```
    set ITEM [string replace $ITEM [expr [string first " " $ITEM]] $END]
    set ITEM "$ITEM DOWN <br />"
     set BGP_NEIGHBOR_OUTPUT [concat $BGP_NEIGHBOR_OUTPUT $ITEM]
}
```

Replace the current line in the **BGP_NEIGHBORS** variable, as shown:

```
Router(tcl)#set BGP_NEIGHBORS [string replace $BGP_NEIGHBORS 0 $END]
192.50.50.50    4       65065       0       0         0   0     0 never    Active
192.168.100.1   4       65065       0       0         0   0     0 never    Active
192.168.200.1   4       65065       0       0         0   0     0 never    Active
```

```
    set BGP_NEIGHBORS [string replace $BGP_NEIGHBORS 0 $END]
```

Set the value of the variable **BEGIN** to **-1**. During the beginning of the **while** statement, it will be reset to **0**:

```
set BEGIN -1
}
```

The following portion of code gathers the BGP configuration and displays it within a window. We are using the previous **show running-config** command to reduce the amount of time it takes for the script to run.

To maintain the integrity of the **CONFIG** variable, copy it to the variable **BGP_CONFIG**:

```
set BGP_CONFIG $CONFIG
```

If the string variable **BGP_CONFIG** contains **router bgp**, execute the subsequent command:

```
if {[regexp -all {router bgp} $BGP_CONFIG] > 0} {
```

If the string variable **BGP_CONFIG** contains **address-family**, execute the subsequent command:

```
if {[regexp -all {address-family} $BGP_CONFIG] > 0} {
```

Set the variable **BEGIN** to the first match of **router bgp** in the string variable **BGP_CONFIG**, as shown:

```
set BEGIN [string first "router bgp" $BGP_CONFIG]
```

Set the variable **END** to the last match of **exit-address-family** in the string variable **BGP_CONFIG**, as shown:

```
Router(tcl)#set END [string last exit-address-family $BGP_CONFIG]
1202
       set END [string last exit-address-family $BGP_CONFIG]
```

Collect the BGP configuration information and place the results in the variable **BGP_CONFIG_RESULTS**, as shown:

```
Router(tcl)#set BGP_CONFIG_RESULTS [string range $BGP_CONFIG $BEGIN [expr $END +
  18]]
router bgp 65065
 no synchronization
 bgp log-neighbor-changes
 neighbor 10.93.130.225 remote-as 65065
 neighbor 192.50.50.50 remote-as 65065
 neighbor 192.50.50.50 route-reflector-client
 neighbor 192.168.100.1 remote-as 65065
```

```
 neighbor 192.168.100.1 update-source Loopback0
 neighbor 192.168.100.1 route-reflector-client
 neighbor 192.168.200.1 remote-as 65065
 no auto-summary
 !
 address-family vpnv4
  neighbor 10.93.130.225 activate
  neighbor 10.93.130.225 send-community extended
  neighbor 192.50.50.50 activate
  neighbor 192.50.50.50 send-community extended
  neighbor 192.168.100.1 activate
  neighbor 192.168.100.1 send-community extended
  neighbor 192.168.100.1 route-reflector-client
  neighbor 192.168.200.1 activate
  neighbor 192.168.200.1 send-community extended
 exit-address-family
 !
 address-family ipv4 vrf RED
  no synchronization
 exit-address-family
 !
 address-family ipv4 vrf PURPLE
  no synchronization
 exit-address-family
 !
 address-family ipv4 vrf Orange
  no synchronization
 exit-address-family
 !
 address-family ipv4 vrf GRN
  no synchronization
 exit-address-family
 !
 address-family ipv4 vrf BLU
  no synchronization
 exit-address-family


        set BGP_CONFIG_RESULTS [string range $BGP_CONFIG $BEGIN [expr $END + 18]]
```

The final step is to replace the end of line value with the corresponding HTML break command:

```
regsub -all  {\n} $BGP_CONFIG_RESULTS {<br />} BGP_CONFIG_RESULTS
}
```

The very last step before configuring the HTML section is to collect the BGP ASN. You can do so using the following command:

```
Router(tcl)#set BGP_AS [string range $BGP_CONFIG_RESULTS 11 [expr [string first
  "<br" $BGP_CONFIG_RESULTS] - 1]]
65065
        set BGP_AS [string range $BGP_CONFIG_RESULTS 11 [expr [string first
  "<br" $BGP_CONFIG_RESULTS] - 1]]
    }
```

The Tcl script is now at an end. The remainder of the program is HTML.

Configuring HTML

The following sets the header variable and will display in the title bar of your browser. Notice the quotes?

```
set header "<html>
<head>
<title>MPLS-VPN Configuration Application:</title>
</head>
```

The title of the application, MPLS-VPN Configuration Application, is displayed at the top center of the page, using a font type of Arial and a font size of 6:

```
<div align='center'>
<font face='arial' size='6'>MPLS-VPN Configuration Application</font><br />
</div>
</html>
```

The end quotes signify the end of the header. The header will display using the last line in the configuration, **"puts $httpsock $httpheader$header$config$footer"**:

```
"
```

The next section of HTML code is the "config" portion.

```
set config "
```

The text *VRF Information* is displayed with the following characteristics:

```
<div align='left' style='color: gray; font-family: arial; font-size: 18pt;
  MARGIN: 10px 10px'>
      VRF Information:
</div>
```

Displaying text was the easy part. Now you are going to make the program more interesting by creating a scrolling window for the VRF information. This window is aligned to the left side of the screen, using the following parameters. The variable **ALL_VRF_INFO** is an ordered list using the **<ol>** and **</ol>** options. The output will look similar to Figure 6-4.

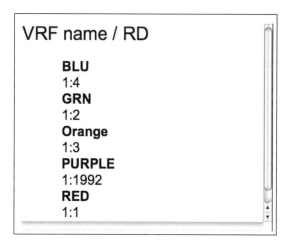

Figure 6-4   *ALL_VRF_INFO Ordered List*

```
<div align='left' style='overflow: scroll; border-right-style: solid; font-fam-
ily: arial; font-size: 10pt; border-right-width:1px; WIDTH: 250px; FLOAT: left;
HEIGHT: 200px; MARGIN: 10px 10px'>
    <font face='arial' size='4'>VRF name / RD</font><br />
    <ol>$ALL_VRF_INFO</ol>
</div>
```

The center scroll window contains the import and export information
IMPORT_EXPORT:

```
<div align='left' style='overflow: scroll; border-right-style: solid; font-fam-
ily: arial; font-size: 10pt; border-right-width:1px; WIDTH: 230px; FLOAT: left;
HEIGHT: 200px; MARGIN: 10px 10px'>
      <font face='arial' size='4'>Import / Export</font><br />
    <ol>$IMPORT_EXPORT</ol>
</div>
```

The right scroll window contains the VRF interface status information
VRF_INTERFACE_OUTPUT:

```
<div align='left' style='overflow: scroll; border-right-style: solid; font-fam-
ily: arial; font-size: 10pt; border-right-width:1px; WIDTH: 300px; FLOAT: left;
HEIGHT: 200px; MARGIN: 10px 10px'>
    <font face='arial' size='4'>VRF Interface Status</font><br />
      <ol>$VRF_INTERFACE_OUTPUT</ol>
</div>
```

The numerous breaks move the position for the next text beyond the scroll windows:

```
<br /><br /><br /><br /><br /><br /><br /><br /><br /><br /><br /><br />
```

Display the *VRF Configuration* text:

```
<div align='left' style='color: gray; font-family: arial; font-size: 18pt;
  MARGIN: 10px 10px'>
        VRF Configuration:
</div>
```

In this section, you need to create multiple text boxes for input of user information:

```
<font face='arial' size='4'>
```

Using the following command, you will send the collected information to the MPLS-CFG.tcl script. This script will be initiated when Submit button is selected:

```
<form name='MPLS-CFG' action='MPLS-CFG.tcl' method='GET' target='_blank'>
```

You need to create an input box that allows the user to add the VRF name. This text box will initially display VRF_Name when selected. The name will clear allowing the user to add information. If the information is deleted, the original VRF_Name is returned to the text box:

```
<input type='text' name='VRF_Name' value='VRF_Name'
onblur='init_field(this,\"VRF_Name\");' onFocus='clear_field(this,\"VRF_Name\");
' style='WIDTH: 200px; font-family: arial; font-size: 10pt'>
```

This text box allows the user to add RD information:

```
        <font face='arial' size='4'>
      <form name='MPLS-CFG' action='MPLS-CFG.tcl' method='GET' target='_blank'>
    <input type='text' name='RD' value='RD' onblur='init_field(this,\"RD\");'
onFocus='clear_field(this,\"RD\");
' style='WIDTH: 200px; font-family: arial; font-size: 10pt'>
```

This text box allows the user to add import information:

```
        <font face='arial' size='4'>
      <form name='MPLS-CFG' action='MPLS-CFG.tcl' method='GET' target='_blank'>
    <input type='text' name='Import' value='Import'
onblur='init_field(this,\"Import\");' onFocus='clear_field(this,\"Import\");
' style='WIDTH: 200px; font-family: arial; font-size: 10pt'>
```

This text box allows the user to add export information:

```
        <font face='arial' size='4'>
      <form name='MPLS-CFG' action='MPLS-CFG.tcl' method='GET' target='_blank'>
    <input type='text' name='Export' value='Export'
onblur='init_field(this,\"Export\");' onFocus='clear_field(this,\"Export\");
' style='WIDTH: 200px; font-family: arial; font-size: 10pt'>
```

Add a break to position the next text box:

```
<br />
```

This text box allows the user to add VRF interface information:

```
<div align='left'>
      <font face='arial' size='4'>
    <color='black'>
      <form name='MPLS-CFG' action='MPLS-CFG.tcl' method='GET' target='_blank'>
  <input type='text' name='Interface' value='Interface'
onblur='init_field(this,\"Interface\");'
onFocus='clear_field(this,\"Interface\");
' style='WIDTH: 250px; font-family: arial; font-size: 10pt'>
```

This text box allows the user to add the IP address of the VRF interface:

```
      <font-family: arial; font-size: 18pt>
    <color='black'>
      <form name='MPLS-CFG' action='MPLS-CFG.tcl' method='GET' target='_blank'>
  <input type='text' name='IP_Address' value='IP_Address'
onblur='init_field(this,\"IP_Address\");'
onFocus='clear_field(this,\"IP_Address\");
' style='WIDTH: 250px; color:#000000; font-family: arial; font-size: 10pt'>
```

This text box allows the user to add IP address mask of the VRF interface:

```
  <input type='text' name='Mask' value='Mask' onblur='init_field(this,\"Mask\");'
onFocus='clear_field(this,\"Mask\");
' style='WIDTH: 250px; color:#000000; font-family: arial; font-size: 10pt'>
```

Add a break to position the next text box:

```
<br />
```

Display a radio button that allows the user to select yes or no as to redistributing routes:

```
<div align='left' style='color: black; font-family: arial; font-size: 12pt;
      MARGIN: 10px 10px'>
  Redistribute Connected:
  <input type='radio' name='Red_Connected' value='yes'  /> yes

  <input type='radio' name='Red_Connected' value='no' checked='checked' /> no
</div>
```

Add two breaks to position the next text box:

```
<br /><br />
```

Display BGP / LDP Information:

```
<div align='left' style='color: gray; font-family: arial; font-size: 18pt;
  MARGIN: 10px 10px'>
    BGP / LDP Information:
</div>
```

This scroll window contains the LDP interface information **LDP_INTERFACES:**

```
<div align='left' style='overflow: scroll; border-right-style: solid; font-fam-
ily: arial; font-size: 10pt; border-right-width:1px; WIDTH: 220px; FLOAT: left;
HEIGHT: 200px; MARGIN: 10px 10px'>
    <font face='arial' size='4'>Label Int / Operational</font><br />
      <ol>$LDP_INTERFACES</ol>
</div>
```

This scroll window contains the BGP neighbor information **BGP_NEIGHBOR_OUTPUT:**

```
<div align='left' style='overflow: scroll; border-right-style: solid; font-fam-
ily: arial; font-size: 10pt; border-right-width:1px; WIDTH: 220px; FLOAT: left;
HEIGHT: 200px; MARGIN: 10px 10px'>
    <font face='arial' size='4'>BGP Neighbors</font><br />
      <ol>$BGP_NEIGHBOR_OUTPUT</ol>
</div>
```

This scroll window contains the BGP configuration information **BGP_CONFIG_RESULTS:**

```
<div align='left' style='overflow: scroll; border-right-style: solid; font-fam-
ily: arial; font-size: 10pt; border-right-width:1px; WIDTH: 340px; FLOAT: left;
HEIGHT: 200px; MARGIN: 10px 10px'>
    <font face='arial' size='4'>BGP Configuration</font><br />
      <ol>$BGP_CONFIG_RESULTS</ol>
</div>
```

Reposition the output to format the display appropriately:

```
<br /><br /><br /><br /><br /><br /><br /><br /><br /><br />
```

Display the BGP Configuration: text:

```
<div align='left' style='color: gray; font-family: arial; font-size: 18pt;
    MARGIN: 10px 10px'>
  BGP Configuration:
</div>
```

This text box will display the BGP ASN if present or allow the user to add or delete the BGP ASN:

```
<div align='left'>
      <font face='arial' size='4'>
      <form name='MPLS-CFG' action='MPLS-CFG.tcl' method='GET' target='_blank'>
      <input type='text' name='BGP_AS' value='$BGP_AS'
onblur='init_field(this,\"$BGP_AS\");' onFocus='clear_field(this,\"$BGP_AS\");
    ' style='WIDTH: 230px; font-family: arial; font-size: 10pt'>
```

This text box provides a location for the user to enter the IP address of the BGP neighbor:

```
  <font face='arial' size='4'>
```

```
    <form name='MPLS-CFG' action='MPLS-CFG.tcl' method='GET' target='_blank'>
    <input type='text' name='Neighbor' value='Neighbor'
onblur='init_field(this,\"Neighbor\");' onFocus='clear_field(this,\"Neighbor\");
' style='WIDTH: 230px; font-family: arial; font-size: 10pt'>
```

This text box provides a location for the user to enter the source interface for the BGP neighbor configured previously:

```
        <font face='arial' size='4'>
        <form name='MPLS-CFG' action='MPLS-CFG.tcl' method='GET' target='_blank'>
        <input type='text' name='Source_Int' value='Source_Int'
onblur='init_field(this,\"Source_Int\");'
onFocus='clear_field(this,\"Source_Int\");
        ' style='WIDTH: 250px; font-family: arial; font-size: 10pt'>
</div>
```

Display Route Reflector Client text:

```
<div align='left' style='color: black; font-family: arial; font-size: 12pt; MAR-
GIN: 10px 10px'>
    Route Reflector Client:
```

Display a radio button that allows the user to select yes or no as to the neighbor being a route-reflector client:

```
    <input type='radio' name='RR_Client' value='yes'  /> Yes
    <input type='radio' name='RR_Client' value='no' checked='checked' /> No
</div>
```

Realign the location of the next display:

```
<br /><br />
```

Display LDP Configuration text:

```
<div align='left' style='color: gray; font-family: arial; font-size: 18pt;
  MARGIN: 10px 10px'>
        LDP Configuration:
</div>
```

This text box provides a location for the user to enter the label interface:

```
<div align='left'>
    <font face='arial' size='4'>
    <form name='MPLS-CFG' action='MPLS-CFG.tcl' method='GET' target='_blank'>
    <input type='text' name='Label_Int' value='Label_Int'
onblur='init_field(this,\"Label_Int\");'
```

```
onFocus='clear_field(this,\"Label_Int\"); ' style='WIDTH: 230px; font-family:
 arial; font-size: 10pt'>
```

This text box provides a location for the user to enter the IP address of the label interface:

```
<font face='arial' size='4'>
 <form name='MPLS-CFG' action='MPLS-CFG.tcl' method='GET' target='_blank'>
 <input type='text' name='IP_Address' value='IP_Address'
onblur='init_field(this,\"IP_Address\");'
onFocus='clear_field(this,\"IP_Address\");' style='WIDTH: 230px; font-family:
 arial; font-size: 10pt'>
```

This text box provides a location for the user to enter the IP address mask of the label interface:

```
     <input type='text' name='Mask' value='Mask'
onblur='init_field(this,\"Mask\");' onFocus='clear_field(this,\"Mask\");'
style='WIDTH: 250px; font-family: arial; font-size: 10pt'>
</div>
```

The following breaks reposition the next location to display information:

```
<br /><br /><br /><br />
```

Display Configuration: text:

```
<div align='left' style='color: black; font-family: arial; font-size: 14pt; MAR-
GIN: 10px 10px'>
    Configuration:
    <input type='radio' name='ADD_REMOVE' value='yes' checked='checked' /> Add
    <input type='radio' name='ADD_REMOVE' value='no'/> Remove
</div>
```

The following break repositions the next location to display information:

```
<br />
```

This quote ends the "config" section:

```
"
```

The following configuration clears and repopulates the text box fields:

```
set footer "
<script>
function clear_field(field, value) {if(field.value == value) field.value = '';}
function init_field(field, value) {if(field.value == '') field.value = value;}
</script>
<br />
<input type='submit' style='color: red value='Deploy Changes'>
"
```

This section sets the HTTP header information.

```
set httpheader "HTTP/1.1 200 OK
Content-Type: text/html; charset=UTF-8
Content-Transfer-Encoding: binary
"
```

This last line of code displays the **httpheader**, **header**, **config**, and **footer** sections of the application:

```
puts $httpsock $httpheader$header$config$footer
```

You must copy the script to the TCL directory on the IOS device (for example, flash:/TCL/).

Using your browser, enter the IP address of the IOS device as follows and check the damage:

> http://192.168.0.186:8082/MPLS-VPN.tcl

If the configuration was re-created correctly, the display will be similar to that shown in Figure 6-5.

Writing Code for the MPLS CFG Script

The MPLS-VPN.tcl application will collect the user input information and pass it to the MPLS-CFG.tcl script.

The following 16 parameters are passed to the MPLS-CFG.tcl script:

- VRF_Name
- Route_Dist
- Import
- Export
- VRF_Interface
- VRF_IP_Address
- VRF_Mask
- Red_Connected
- BGP_AS
- Neighbor
- Source_Int
- RR_Client

- Label_Int
- Lab_IP_Address
- Lab_Mask
- Add_Config

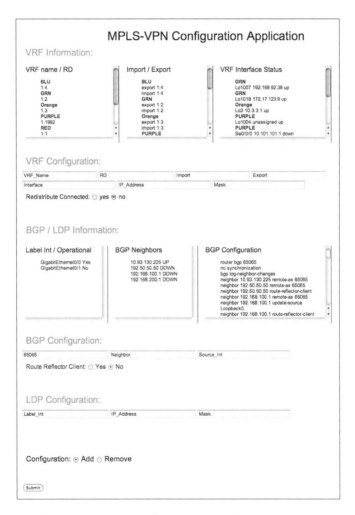

Figure 6-5   *Complete MPLS VPN Configuration Application*

Now that you have all the parameters that will be passed to the configuration script, it is time to create a flowchart that shows how you will use that information. The flowchart shown in Figure 6-6 went through several iterations, thoughtful consideration, and testing of the code before being presented here.

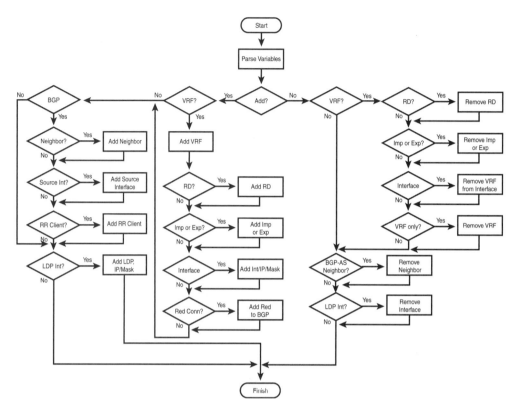

Figure 6-6 *Flowchart for MPLS-CFG.tcl Application*

Tip To minimize your time coding, having a well thought-out flowchart is essential!

The first section of the code parses the variables sent from the MPLS-VPN.tcl application. Each parameter is sent in order and defined in the MPLS-CFG.tcl script as a unique value.

The following command set the variable **COMMANDS** to all the elements in the list for 0 to the end using the **lrange** command:

```
set COMMANDS [lrange $parmlist 0 end]
```

Each parameter is assigned to a unique variable, using variable names representative of each parameter for easy of programming:

```
set VRF_Name [lindex $COMMANDS 1]
set Route_Dist [lindex $COMMANDS 3]
set Import [lindex $COMMANDS 5]
set Export [lindex $COMMANDS 7]
set VRF_Interface [lindex $COMMANDS 9]
set VRF_IP_Address [lindex $COMMANDS 11]
```

```
set VRF_Mask [lindex $COMMANDS 13]
set Red_Connected [lindex $COMMANDS 15]
set BGP_AS [lindex $COMMANDS 17]
set Neighbor [lindex $COMMANDS 19]
set Source_Int [lindex $COMMANDS 21]
set RR_Client [lindex $COMMANDS 23]
set Label_Int [lindex $COMMANDS 25]
set Lab_IP_Address [lindex $COMMANDS 27]
set Lab_Mask [lindex $COMMANDS 29]
set Add_Config [lindex $COMMANDS 31]
```

Initialize the variable for maintaining changes to the configuration:

```
set CONFIG_CHANGES ""
```

Initialize the terminal interface for making configuration changes:

```
if [catch {cli_open} RESULT] {
        error $RESULT $errorInfo
} else {
        array set cli1 $RESULT
}
```

Enter enable mode on the IOS device:

```
if [catch {cli_exec $cli1(fd) "en"} RESULT] {
        error $RESULT $errorInfo
}
```

Enter configuration mode on the IOS device:

```
if [catch {cli_exec $cli1(fd) "config terminal"} RESULT] {
        error $RESULT $errorInfo
}
```

The first decision block in the flowchart is to verify if the changes on the IOS device will be added to or removed from the configuration. If elements are to be added to the configuration, execute the subsequent step:

```
if {[string compare "yes" $Add_Config] == 0} {
```

Continue to execute the subcommands if the parameter in the variable name "VRF_Name" is something other than "VRF_Name". This indicates that the user entered a value in the "VRF_Name" input text box:

```
if {[string compare "VRF_Name" $VRF_Name]} {
```

Add the VRF to the configuration:

```
if [catch {cli_exec $cli1(fd) "ip vrf $VRF_Name" } RESULT] {
        error $RESULT $errorInfo
```

```
} else {
```

To keep track of the configuration changes, the variable string **CONFIG_CHANGES** is used:

```
    set CONFIG_CHANGES [concat $CONFIG_CHANGES "ip vrf $VRF_Name <br />"]
}
```

If an element in the **"RD"** variable is present, execute the subcommands and capture the results in the **CONFIG_CHANGES** variable:

```
if {[string compare "RD" $Route_Dist]} {
    if [catch {cli_exec $cli1(fd) "rd $Route_Dist" } RESULT] {
            error $RESULT $errorInfo
    } else {
        set CONFIG_CHANGES [concat $CONFIG_CHANGES "rd $Route_Dist <br />"]
    }
}
```

If an element in the **"Import"** variable is present, execute the subcommands and capture the results in the **CONFIG_CHANGES** variable:

```
if {[string compare "Import" $Import]} {
    if [catch {cli_exec $cli1(fd) "route-target import $Import" } RESULT] {
            error $RESULT $errorInfo
    } else {
            set CONFIG_CHANGES [concat $CONFIG_CHANGES "route-target import
  $Import <br />"]
    }
}
```

If an element in the **"Export"** variable is present, execute the subcommands and capture the results in the **CONFIG_CHANGES** variable:

```
if {[string compare "Export" $Export]} {
    if [catch {cli_exec $cli1(fd) "route-target export $Export" } RESULT] {
            error $RESULT $errorInfo
    } else {
            set CONFIG_CHANGES [concat $CONFIG_CHANGES "route-target export
  $Export <br />"]
    }
}
```

If an element in the **VRF_Interface** variable is present, execute the subcommands, including adding the IP address and network mask, bringing up the interface and capturing the results in the **CONFIG_CHANGES** variable:

```
if {[string compare "Interface" $VRF_Interface]} {

    if [catch {cli_exec $cli1(fd) "interface $VRF_Interface" } RESULT] {
```

```
                    error $RESULT $errorInfo
    } else {
                set CONFIG_CHANGES [concat $CONFIG_CHANGES "interface $VRF_Interface
  <br />"]
    }
    if [catch {cli_exec $cli1(fd) "ip vrf forwarding $VRF_Name" } RESULT] {
                error $RESULT $errorInfo
    } else {
                set CONFIG_CHANGES [concat $CONFIG_CHANGES "ip vrf forwarding
$VRF_Name <br />"]
    }
    if [catch {cli_exec $cli1(fd) "ip address $VRF_IP_Address $VRF_Mask" }
  RESULT] {
                error $RESULT $errorInfo
    } else {
                set CONFIG_CHANGES [concat $CONFIG_CHANGES "ip address
$VRF_IP_Address $VRF_Mask <br />"]
    }
}
```

If the Redistribute Connected check box is set to **"yes"**, execute the subcommands and capture the results in the **CONFIG_CHANGES** variable:

```
    if {[string compare "yes" $Red_Connected] == 0} {

        if [catch {cli_exec $cli1(fd) "router bgp $BGP_AS" } RESULT] {
                    error $RESULT $errorInfo
        } else {
                    set CONFIG_CHANGES [concat $CONFIG_CHANGES "router bgp $BGP_AS
  <br />"]
        }

        if [catch {cli_exec $cli1(fd) "address-family ipv4 vrf $VRF_Name" }
  RESULT] {
                    error $RESULT $errorInfo
        } else {
                    set CONFIG_CHANGES [concat $CONFIG_CHANGES "address-family ipv4
  vrf $VRF_Name <br />"]
        }

        if [catch {cli_exec $cli1(fd) "redistribute connected" } RESULT] {
                    error $RESULT $errorInfo
        } else {
                    set CONFIG_CHANGES [concat $CONFIG_CHANGES "redistribute
  connected <br />"]
        }
    }
}
```

If an element in the **"BGP_AS"** variable is present, execute the subcommands and capture the results in the **CONFIG_CHANGES** variable. As long as BGP has been configured on the IOS device, the subelements will be executed:

```
if {[string compare "BGP_AS" $BGP_AS]} {
```

The command **mpls ip** is entered on the IOS device to validate that it has been configured. Entering this more that one time will not cause a problem on the IOS device:

```
if [catch {cli_exec $cli1(fd) "mpls ip"} RESULT] {
        error $RESULT $errorInfo
} else {
        set CONFIG_CHANGES [concat $CONFIG_CHANGES "mpls ip <br />"]
}
if [catch {cli_exec $cli1(fd) "router bgp $BGP_AS" } RESULT] {
        error $RESULT $errorInfo
} else {
        set CONFIG_CHANGES [concat $CONFIG_CHANGES "router bgp $BGP_AS <br />"]
}
```

If an element in the **"Neighbor"** variable is present, execute the subcommands and capture the results in the **CONFIG_CHANGES** variable. Notice that the configurations are also applied within the **"vpnv4"** address family:

```
if {[string compare "Neighbor" $Neighbor]} {


    if [catch {cli_exec $cli1(fd) "neighbor $Neighbor remote-as $BGP_AS" }
  RESULT] {
            error $RESULT $errorInfo
    } else {
            set CONFIG_CHANGES [concat $CONFIG_CHANGES "neighbor $Neighbor
  remote-as $BGP_AS <br />"]
    }
    if [catch {cli_exec $cli1(fd) "address-family vpnv4" } RESULT] {
            error $RESULT $errorInfo
    } else {
            set CONFIG_CHANGES [concat $CONFIG_CHANGES "address-family vpnv4 <br
  />"]
    }
    if [catch {cli_exec $cli1(fd) "neighbor $Neighbor activate" } RESULT] {
            error $RESULT $errorInfo
    } else {
            set CONFIG_CHANGES [concat $CONFIG_CHANGES "neighbor $Neighbor
  activate <br />"]
    }
    if [catch {cli_exec $cli1(fd) "neighbor $Neighbor send-community extended" }
  RESULT] {
            error $RESULT $errorInfo
```

```
    } else {
            set CONFIG_CHANGES [concat $CONFIG_CHANGES "neighbor $Neighbor
  send-community extended <br />"]
    }
```

To allow additional changes at the appropriate location in the configuration, it is imperative that you "**exit**" from the address family:

```
    if [catch {cli_exec $cli1(fd) "exit" } RESULT] {
            error $RESULT $errorInfo
    } else {
            set CONFIG_CHANGES [concat $CONFIG_CHANGES "exit <br />"]
    }
}
```

If an element contains a source-interface value, execute the subcommands and capture
the results in the **CONFIG_CHANGES** variable:

```
if {[string compare "Source_Int" $Source_Int]} {
    if [catch {cli_exec $cli1(fd) "neighbor $Neighbor update-source $Source_Int"
  } RESULT] {
        error $RESULT $errorInfo
    } else {
            set CONFIG_CHANGES [concat $CONFIG_CHANGES "neighbor $Neighbor
  update-source $Source_Int <br />"]
    }

}
```

If the neighbor was selected to be a route-reflector client, execute the subcommands and
capture the results in the **CONFIG_CHANGES** variable:

```
    if {[string compare "yes" $RR_Client] == 0} {


        if [catch {cli_exec $cli1(fd) "neighbor $Neighbor route-reflector-
  client" } RESULT] {
                error $RESULT $errorInfo
        } else {
                set CONFIG_CHANGES [concat $CONFIG_CHANGES "neighbor $Neighbor
  route-reflector-client <br />"]
        }
        if [catch {cli_exec $cli1(fd) "address-family vpnv4" } RESULT] {
                error $RESULT $errorInfo
        } else {
                set CONFIG_CHANGES [concat $CONFIG_CHANGES "address-family
  vpnv4 <br />"]
        }
        if [catch {cli_exec $cli1(fd) "neighbor $Neighbor route-reflector-
  client" } RESULT] {
```

```
                error $RESULT $errorInfo
        } else {
                set CONFIG_CHANGES [concat $CONFIG_CHANGES "neighbor $Neighbor
  route-reflector-client <br />"]
        }
    }
}
```

If an element in the **"Label_Int"** variable is present, execute the subcommands and capture the results in the **CONFIG_CHANGES** variable:

```
if {[string compare "Label_Int" $Label_Int]} {
```

In the event that this IOS device is an MPLS VPN "P-type" device only, you need to make sure that MPLS has been added in the global configuration:

```
if [catch {cli_exec $cli1(fd) "mpls ip"} RESULT] {
        error $RESULT $errorInfo
} else {
        set CONFIG_CHANGES [concat $CONFIG_CHANGES "mpls ip <br />"]
}
if [catch {cli_exec $cli1(fd) "interface $Label_Int"} RESULT] {
        error $RESULT $errorInfo
} else {
        set CONFIG_CHANGES [concat $CONFIG_CHANGES "interface $Label_Int <br />"]
}
if [catch {cli_exec $cli1(fd) "mpls ip"} RESULT] {
        error $RESULT $errorInfo
} else {
        set CONFIG_CHANGES [concat $CONFIG_CHANGES "mpls ip <br />"]
}
if [catch {cli_exec $cli1(fd) "no shutdown"} RESULT] {
        error $RESULT $errorInfo
} else {
        set CONFIG_CHANGES [concat $CONFIG_CHANGES "no shutdown <br />"]
}
```

If the IP address and mask are present for the label interface, execute the subcommands and capture the results in the **CONFIG_CHANGES** variable:

```
    if {[string compare "IP_Address" $Lab_IP_Address] && [string compare "Mask"
  $Lab_Mask]} {


        if [catch {cli_exec $cli1(fd) "ip address $Lab_IP_Address $Lab_Mask" }
    RESULT] {
                error $RESULT $errorInfo
        } else {
                set CONFIG_CHANGES [concat $CONFIG_CHANGES "ip address
  $Lab_IP_Address $Lab_Mask <br />"]
```

```
        }
    }
}
```

The **else** section of the configuration is associated with the first decision in the flow-chart: add or remove configuration. Because the script checks only for additions, the only other alternative is removal of elements within the IOS configuration:

```
} else {
```

The following **if** statement looks for an element in the **"VRF_Name"** variable and any value entered in the **"Route_Dist"**, **"Import"**, **"Export"**, or **"VRF_Interface"** and will execute the subcommands and capture the results in the **CONFIG_CHANGES** variable. This statement eliminates the accidental removal of a VRF if any other parameters are entered:

```
    if {[string compare "VRF_Name" $VRF_Name] && [string compare "RD"
$Route_Dist] != 0 || [string compare "Import" $Import] != 0 || [string compare
"Export" $Export] != 0 || [string compare "Interface" $VRF_Interface] != 0} {



        if [catch {cli_exec $cli1(fd) "ip vrf $VRF_Name" } RESULT] {
                error $RESULT $errorInfo
        } else {
            set CONFIG_CHANGES [concat $CONFIG_CHANGES "ip vrf $VRF_Name <br />"]
        }
```

If the variable **Route_Dist** is present, execute the subcommands, which removes the route distinguisher from the VRF and captures the results in the **CONFIG_CHANGES** variable:

```
if {[string compare "RD" $Route_Dist]} {
    if [catch {cli_exec $cli1(fd) "no rd $Route_Dist" } RESULT] {
            error $RESULT $errorInfo
    } else {
        set CONFIG_CHANGES [concat $CONFIG_CHANGES "no rd $Route_Dist <br />"]
    }
}
```

If an element in the **"Import"** variable is present, execute the subcommands and capture the results in the **CONFIG_CHANGES** variable:

```
if {[string compare "Import" $Import]} {
    if [catch {cli_exec $cli1(fd) "no route-target import $Import" } RESULT] {
            error $RESULT $errorInfo
    } else {
            set CONFIG_CHANGES [concat $CONFIG_CHANGES "no route-target import
  $Import <br />"]
    }
}
```

If an element in the **"Export"** variable is present, execute the subcommands and capture the results in the **CONFIG_CHANGES** variable:

```
if {[string compare "Export" $Export]} {
    if [catch {cli_exec $cli1(fd) "no route-target export $Export" } RESULT] {
            error $RESULT $errorInfo
    } else {
            set CONFIG_CHANGES [concat $CONFIG_CHANGES "no route-target export
  $Export <br />"]
    }
}
```

If the **"VRF_Interface"** element variable is present, execute the subcommands and capture the results in the **CONFIG_CHANGES** variable. This sequence of commands removes the VRF from the selected interface and also automatically removes the IP address:

```
    if {[string compare "Interface" $VRF_Interface]} {
        if [catch {cli_exec $cli1(fd) "interface $VRF_Interface" } RESULT] {
                error $RESULT $errorInfo
        } else {
                set CONFIG_CHANGES [concat $CONFIG_CHANGES "interface
  $VRF_Interface <br />"]
        }
        if [catch {cli_exec $cli1(fd) "no ip vrf forwarding $VRF_Name" } RESULT]
{
                error $RESULT $errorInfo
        } else {
                set CONFIG_CHANGES [concat $CONFIG_CHANGES "no ip vrf
  forwarding $VRF_Name  <br />"]
        }
    }
}
```

If the only element in the **"VRF Configuration:"** section is the **"VRF_Name"**, remove the VRF entirely and capture the results in the **CONFIG_CHANGES** variable:

```
if {[string compare "VRF_Name " $VRF_Name] && [string compare "RD" $Route_Dist]
== 0 && [string compare "Import" $Import] == 0 && [string compare "Export"
$Export] == 0 && [string compare "Interface" $VRF_Interface] == 0 } {
    if [catch {cli_exec $cli1(fd) "no ip vrf $VRF_Name " } RESULT] {
            error $RESULT $errorInfo
    } else {
        set CONFIG_CHANGES [concat $CONFIG_CHANGES "no ip vrf $VRF_Name <br />"]
    }
}
```

If the **"BGP_AS"** and **"Neighbor"** variables are present, remove the BGP neighbor and capture the results in the **CONFIG_CHANGES** variable:

```
if {[string compare "BGP_AS" $BGP_AS] && [string compare "Neighbor" $Neighbor]} {
```

```
    if [catch {cli_exec $cli1(fd) "router bgp $BGP_AS" } RESULT] {
            error $RESULT $errorInfo
    } else {
            set CONFIG_CHANGES [concat $CONFIG_CHANGES "router bgp $BGP_AS <br
  />"]
    }
    if [catch {cli_exec $cli1(fd) "no neighbor $Neighbor" } RESULT] {
            error $RESULT $errorInfo
    } else {
            set CONFIG_CHANGES [concat $CONFIG_CHANGES "no neighbor $Neighbor
  <br />"]
    }
}
```

If the variable **"Label_Int"** is present, remove the LDP from the selected interface and capture the results in the **CONFIG_CHANGES** variable:

```
if {[string compare "Label_Int" $Label_Int]} {


    if [catch {cli_exec $cli1(fd) "interface $Label_Int"} RESULT] {
            error $RESULT $errorInfo
    } else {
            set CONFIG_CHANGES [concat $CONFIG_CHANGES "interface $Label_Int <br
  />"]
    }
    if [catch {cli_exec $cli1(fd) "no mpls ip"} RESULT] {
            error $RESULT $errorInfo
    } else {
            set CONFIG_CHANGES [concat $CONFIG_CHANGES "no mpls ip <br />"]
    }
}
}
```

Exit from configuration mode, to capture the running-configuration:

```
if [catch {cli_exec $cli1(fd) "end" } RESULT] {
    error $RESULT $errorInfo
}
```

Capture the running-configuration and store it in the variable **CONFIG**:

```
if [catch {cli_exec $cli1(fd) "show running-config" } RESULT] {
    error $RESULT $errorInfo
} else {
    set CONFIG $RESULT
}
if [catch {cli_close $cli1(fd) $cli1(tty_id)} RESULT] {
    error $RESULT $errorInfo
}
```

Replace all the newline elements with the HTML line break. If this is not done, the configuration will display as a single string:

```
regsub -all {\n} $CONFIG {<br>} CONFIG
```

Begin the HTML section of the script and display Configuration: at the top of the screen:

```
set stats "
<div align='left' style='color: black; font-family: arial; font-size: 18pt;
  overflow: hidden; MARGIN: 10px 10px'>
  Configuration:
</div>
```

Create a scroll window and display all the configuration changes that were completed:

```
<div align='left' style='overflow: scroll; border-right-style: solid; font-fam-
ily: arial; font-size: 10pt; border-right-width:1px; WIDTH: 360px; FLOAT: left;
HEIGHT: 480px; MARGIN: 10px 10px'>
    <font face='arial' size='4'>Configuration Changes</font><br />
    <ol>$CONFIG_CHANGES</ol>
</div>
```

Create a scroll window and display the entire IOS configuration:

```
<div align='left' style='overflow: scroll; border-right-style: solid; font-fam-
ily: arial; font-size: 10pt; border-right-width:1px; WIDTH: 520px; FLOAT: left;
HEIGHT: 480px; MARGIN: 10px 10px'>
     <font face='arial' size='4'>Full Configuration</font><br />
    <ol>$CONFIG </ol>
</div>
"
```

Finally, here is the very last line, which displays the configuration changes and the configuration:

```
puts $httpsock $httpheader$stats
```

Troubleshooting as You Go

If you replicated both the MPLS-VPN.tcl and MPLS-CFG.tcl scripts exactly and placed them on your IOS device, you would miss out on the fun of troubleshooting and the errors you see in Figures 6-7 and 6-8.

There is not much information from the output to direct you where to begin troubleshooting, especially when the only message you receive is "Error in script." Fortunately, you can use another tool. Strategically adding syslog or "puts" messages within your script will provide you with the information necessary to troubleshoot effectively.

Figure 6-7   *Error in Script*

Figure 6-8   *Error in Script: Missing Close Brace*

In this example, we place the following command just before the last line in the configuration, "**puts $httpsock $httpheader$stats**":

```
action_syslog msg "Here are the configuration changes: \n $CONFIG_CHANGES"
```

Open a session to the router (Telnet, in this example) and enable logging for debug messages and turn on terminal monitoring, as shown here:

```
Router#configure terminal
Enter configuration commands, one per line.  End with CNTL/Z.
Router(config)#logging monitor debugging
Router(config)#logging on
Router#terminal monitor
```

The output from the router is captured as shown:

```
Router#
file name:  MPLS-CFG.tcl
Parameters:
VRF_Name=Gray&RD=9%3A9&Import=9%3A9&Export=9%3A9&Interface=Interface&IP_Address=
IP_Address&Mask=Mask&Red_Connected=no&BGP_AS=65065&Neighbor=Neighbor&Source_Int=
Source_Int&RR_Client=no&Label_Int=Label_Int&IP_Address=IP_Address&Mask=Mask&ADD_
REMOVE=yes
*Jan  4 18:58:42.300: %SYS-5-CONFIG_I: Configured from console by  on vty9
  (EEM:Web_Server.tcl)
*Jan  4 18:58:43.812: %HA_EM-6-LOG: Web_Server.tcl: Here are the configuration
  changes:
 ip vrf Gray <br /> rd 9:9 <br /> route-target import 9:9 <br /> route-target
  export 9:9 <br /> mpls ip <br /> router bgp 65065 <br />
```

The output displays the text **Here are the configuration changes:** with the associated parameters.

You can place syslog action messages throughout your script and monitor the status of variables and counters, or to determine whether your script is actually executing a particular set of instructions. This will be an invaluable tool as you write and debug scripts.

Other useful Cisco IOS **debug** commands include the following:

- **debug event manager action cli**
- **debug event manager tcl cli_library**
- **debug event manager tcl commands**

Using Tcl to Troubleshoot Network Problems

Troubleshooting network issues is both an art and a science. It requires skills in knowing where to collect data, gathering the appropriate information, analyzing all the information, and applying the solution to resolve the issue. One of the more time-consuming steps is collecting information. Leveraging Tcl will help to ensure data is collected in a timely manner. You can resolve network challenges significantly faster when information is readily available. This section shows how to use Tcl scripts to troubleshoot network problems.

Syslog messages are generated under specific conditions and used to track the operation of a network device. Detecting syslog messages in a timely manner can result in a proactive approach to solve network problems. The next example provides a script that detects a syslog message indicating a change in an Open Shortest Path First (OSPF) neighbor relationship, collects information from the IOS device, and sends it to a particular e-mail address.

The environment variables used in this script are syslog message, syslog pattern, **show** command output, e-mail, directory, and policy. The script activation and the output can be easily modified by changing the environment variables.

The Tcl script is written as follows:

```
::cisco::eem::event_register_syslog pattern $_syslog_pattern
```

Verify that all the environment variables exist. If any of them are not available, print out an error message and quit:

```
if {![info exists _email_server]} {
    set result \
                "Policy cannot be run: variable _email_server has not been set"
    error $result $errorInfo
}


if {![info exists _email_from]} {
    set result \
                "Policy cannot be run: variable _email_from has not been set"
    error $result $errorInfo
```

```
}

if {![info exists _email_to]} {
    set result \
                "Policy cannot be run: variable _email_to has not been set"
    error $result $errorInfo
}

if {![info exists _email_cc]} {
    #_email_cc is an option, must set to empty string if not set.
    set _email_cc ""
}


if {![info exists _show_cmd]} {
    set result \
        "Policy cannot be run: variable _show_cmd has not been set"
    error $result $errorInfo
}

if {![info exists _syslog_pattern]} {
    set result \
        "Policy cannot be run: variable _syslog_pattern has not been set"
    error $result $errorInfo
}

namespace import ::cisco::eem::*
namespace import ::cisco::lib::*
```

Execute the **show** command and collect the information:

```
if [catch {cli_open} result] {
    error $result $errorInfo
} else {
    array set cli1 $result
}

if [catch {cli_exec $cli1(fd) "en"} result] {
    error $result $errorInfo
}
if [catch {cli_exec $cli1(fd) $_show_cmd} result] {
    error $result $errorInfo
} else {
    set cmd_output $result
}
```

```
if [catch {cli_close $cli1(fd) $cli1(tty_id)} result] {
    error $result $errorInfo
}
```

Generate an e-mail with the output of the **show** command:

```
set routername [info hostname]
if {[string match "" $routername]} {
    error "Host name is not configured"
}

if [catch {smtp_subst [file join $tcl_library email_template_cmd.tm]} result] {
    error $result $errorInfo
}

if [catch {smtp_send_email $result} result] {
    error $result $errorInfo
}
```

The script needs to be copied to the IOS device, and the environment variables are configured in configuration mode, as shown.

Specify where the e-mail should be sent:

`Router(config)#event manager environment _email_to Sent-To@e-mail-server`

Configure the command to be captured when the syslog pattern is seen:

`Router(config)#event manager environment _show_cmd show cdp neighbor`

Specify from whom the e-mail should be sent:

`Router(config)#event manager environment _email_from Sent-From@e-mail-server`

Set the syslog pattern that triggers the script. You will track the state of the OSPF neighbor relationship using the syslog message %OSPF-5-ADJCHG:

`Router(config)#event manager environment _syslog_pattern %OSPF-5-ADJCHG`

Set the environment variable of the e-mail server:

`Router(config)#event manager environment _email_server Sent-From@e-mail-server`
`:password@IP-Address`

Configure the file location of the script:

`Router(config)#event manager directory user policy "flash:/"`

Specify the name of the script:

`Router(config)#event manager policy syslog_email.tcl`

Monitoring the Console for Events

Monitoring the console of the IOS device, you can verify the functionality of the script when the syslog event occurs. The following is the output from our router:

```
TCLRouter#
*Oct 26 00:17:51.048: cli_history_entry_add: free_hist_list size=0,
  hist_list size=7
*Oct 26 00:17:51.048: check_eem_cli_policy_handler: command_string=show ip
  ospf neighbor
*Oct 26 00:17:51.048: check_eem_cli_policy_handler: num_matches = 0,
  response_code = 1
*Oct 26 00:17:52.892: OSPF: 192.168.1.178 address 192.168.0.178 on
  GigabitEthernet0/0 is dead
*Oct 26 00:17:52.892: OSPF: 192.168.1.178 address 192.168.0.178 on
  GigabitEthernet0/0 is dead, state DOWN
```

The OSPF neighbor relationship expired:

```
*Oct 26 00:17:52.892: %OSPF-5-ADJCHG: Process 1, Nbr 192.168.1.178 on
  GigabitEthernet0/0 from FULL to DOWN, Neighbor Down: Dead timer expired
*Oct 26 00:17:52.892: OSPF: Neighbor change Event on interface
  GigabitEthernet0/0
*Oct 26 00:17:52.892: OSPF: DR/BDR election on GigabitEthernet0/0
*Oct 26 00:17:52.892: OSPF: Elect BDR 0.0.0.0
*Oct 26 00:17:52.892: OSPF: Elect DR 192.168.254.254
*Oct 26 00:17:52.892:         DR: 192.168.254.254 (Id)    BDR: none
*Oct 26 00:17:52.892: fh_fd_syslog_event_match: num_matches = 0
*Oct 26 00:17:52.892: fh_fd_data_syslog: num_matches = 0
*Oct 26 00:17:52.892: fh_fd_syslog_event_match: num_matches = 0
*Oct 26 00:17:52.892: fh_fd_data_syslog: num_matches = 0
*Oct 26 00:17:52.892: syslog_pubinfo_enqueue: matched
  pattern="%OSPF-5-ADJCHG", matched message="
*Oct 26 00:17:52.892: %OSPF-5-ADJCHG: Process 1, Nbr 192.168.1.178 on
  GigabitEthernet0/0 from FULL to DOWN, Neighbor Down: Dead timer expired"
```

The syslog event match was detected:

```
*Oct 26 00:17:52.892: fh_fd_syslog_event_match: num_matches = 1
*Oct 26 00:17:52.892: fh_fd_data_syslog: num_matches = 1
*Oct 26 00:17:52.892: fh_fd_syslog_event_match: num_matches = 0
*Oct 26 00:17:52.892: fh_fd_data_syslog: num_matches = 0
*Oct 26 00:17:52.892: fh_fd_syslog_event_match: num_matches = 0
*Oct 26 00:17:52.892: fh_fd_data_syslog: num_matches = 0
*Oct 26 00:17:52.892: fh_fd_syslog_event_match: num_matches = 0
*Oct 26 00:17:52.892: fh_fd_data_syslog: num_matches = 0
*Oct 26 00:17:52.892: fh_fd_syslog_event_match: num_matches = 0
*Oct 26 00:17:52.892: fh_fd_data_syslog: num_matches = 0
```

```
*Oct 26 00:17:52.892: fh_fd_syslog_event_match: num_matches = 0
*Oct 26 00:17:52.892: fh_fd_data_syslog: num_matches = 0
*Oct 26 00:17:52.892: fh_fd_syslog_event_match: num_matches = 0
*Oct 26 00:17:52.892: fh_fd_data_syslog: num_matches = 0
*Oct 26 00:17:52.892: fh_send_server_sig_hndlr: received a pulse from syslog
 on node0/0 with fdid: 3
*Oct 26 00:17:52.892: fh_send_syslog_fd_msg: msg_type=64
*Oct 26 00:17:52.892: fh_send_syslog_fd_msg: sval=0
```

The event is published by the script:

```
*Oct 26 00:17:52.892: fh_send_server_sig_hndlr: received
 FH_MSG_EVENT_PUBLISH
*Oct 26 00:17:52.892: EEM: server processes multi events: timewin=1,
 sync_flag=0, ec_index=0, cmp_occ=1
*Oct 26 00:17:52.892: EEM: ctx=6:(6,1,1)
*Oct 26 00:17:52.892: EEM: server processes multi events: corr_res=1,
 cur_tcnt=1, cmp_tcnt=1
*Oct 26 00:17:52.892: fh_schedule_policy: prev_epc=0x00000000;
 epc=0x49BA816C
*Oct 26 00:17:52.892: EEM server schedules scripts
*Oct 26 00:17:52.892: EEM server schedules one event: policy_type=script
 epc=49BA816C.
*Oct 26 00:17:52.892: EEM: server schedules a policy:
 policyname=tmpsys:/eem_policy/syslog_email.tcl
*Oct 26 00:17:52.892: spawn script tmpsys:/eem_policy/syslog_email.tcl
```

The EEM server policy sends an e-mail:

```
*Oct 26 00:17:52.892: EEM policy tmpsys:/eem_policy/syslog_email.tcl has
 been scheduled to run
*Oct 26 00:17:52.892: fh_spawn: -FMRUN -FMSAFE tmpsys:/lib/tcl/base.tcl
 tmpsys:/eem_policy/syslog_email.tcl
*Oct 26 00:17:52.892: fh_tcl_spawn: argc=5, argstr=-FMRUN,
 stdin=null:/syslog_email.tcl, stdout=syslog:/info/noscan/syslog_email.tcl,
 stderr=syslog:/err/noscan/syslog
_email.tcl, priority=4
*Oct 26 00:17:52.896: pid for spawned process is 312. fdid: 3 sn: 13 jobid:
 18
*Oct 26 00:17:52.900: fh_tcl_esi_open: fd=8
*Oct 26 00:17:52.900: fh_tcl_esi_open: fd=9
*Oct 26 00:17:52.900: fh_tcl_get_mode: mode = 1, StartupScript =
 tmpsys:/lib/tcl/base.tcl, RealScript = tmpsys:/eem_policy/syslog_email.tcl
*Oct 26 00:17:52.900: fh_set_tclpath_global: tcl_library is set to
 tmpsys:/lib/tcl
*Oct 26 00:17:52.900: fh_set_tclpath_global: auto_path is set to
 tmpsys:/eem_lib_user tmpsys:/eem_lib_system
```

```
*Oct 26 00:17:52.916: fh_io_msg: received FH_MSG_API_INIT; jobid=33,
 processid=312, client=23, job name=EEM TCL Proc
*Oct 26 00:17:52.916: fh_register_evreg_cmds: tctx=49BF7FE4, dummy=1
*Oct 26 00:17:52.916: fh_tcl_compile_policy: evaluating policy:
 startup_scriptname=tmpsys:/lib/tcl/base.tcl, real_scriptname=tmpsys:
 /eem_policy/syslog_email.tcl
*Oct 26 00:17:52.920: fh_tcl_slave_interp_init: interp=4937EF34,
 tctx=49BF7FE4, fh_mode=1, real=tmpsys:/eem_policy/syslog_email.tcl,
 curr=syslog_email.tcl
*Oct 26 00:17:52.932: fh_register_evreg_cmds: tctx=49BF7FE4, dummy=1
*Oct 26 00:17:53.328: [fh_cli_debug_cmd]
*Oct 26 00:17:53.328: %HA_EM-6-LOG: syslog_email.tcl : DEBUG(cli_lib) :
 CTL: cli_open called.
*Oct 26 00:17:53.328: [fh_tty_open_cmd]
*Oct 26 00:17:53.332: [fh_sys_reqinfo_routername_cmd]
*Oct 26 00:17:53.344: [fh_tty_read_cmd]
*Oct 26 00:17:53.344: [fh_tty_read_cmd] size= 12
*Oct 26 00:17:53.344: [fh_tty_prompt_cmd]
*Oct 26 00:17:53.392: OSPF: Build router LSA for area 0, router ID
192.168.254.254, seq 0x8000000A, process 1
*Oct 26 00:17:53.392: OSPF: No full nbrs to build Net Lsa for interface
 GigabitEthernet0/0
*Oct 26 00:17:53.392: OSPF: Build network LSA for GigabitEthernet0/0, router
 ID 192.168.254.254
```

The script generates an e-mail, as shown in Figure 6-9.

```
------ Forwarded Message
From: 'Sent-From@e-mail-server' < \Sent-From@e-mail-server >
Date: 25 Oct 2009 16:17:54 PST
To: Sent-To < Sent-To@e-mail-server >
Subject: From router TCLRouter: Periodic show cdp nei Output


Capability Codes: R - Router, T - Trans Bridge, B - Source Route Bridge
               S - Switch, H - Host, I - IGMP, r - Repeater

Device ID     Local Intrfce   Holdtme  Capability Platform  Port ID
3750          Gig0/0          158      R S I   WS-C3750-Fas
1/0/24
TCLRouter
```

Figure 6-9   *Script-Generated E-mail*

Using this script as a foundation, you could write many other scripts to accomplish different troubleshooting tasks. As another example, you could monitor for high CPU usage, which you could detect via a high CPU syslog messages. This detection could then trigger a script to collect **show proc cpu** output and e-mail the results. Besides sending e-mail, you could build a script that makes a configuration change based on a particular error condition. For example, you could shut down a particular interface upon the receipt of a certain number of errors.

You can use Tcl scripts to collect information from a device or perform more intelligent tasks, such as making changes under specific conditions. As you become more familiar with Tcl in IOS, the options will expand almost infinitely.

Creating a Web Application for Remote SNMP Graphing

Earlier chapters examined how to collect information from the local device using Simple Network Management Protocol (SNMP). This next example uses remote SNMP get to collect interface output information from a PIX firewall. This information will be saved to a file on the local IOS device in an Extensible Markup Language (XML) format and displayed in a graphical format using a free charting application.

The script begins with setting variables for the SNMP server or the PIX firewall and the SNMP community string. The use of variables means that whenever you need to make a change to the SNMP server or SNMP community string, you have to make that change in only one location in the code. This could also be accomplished by using environment variables or passing information from another script:

```
set SNMP_SERVER 192.168.0.190
set SNMP_STRING Public
```

The count is used to determine how many samples to collect:

```
set COUNT 0
```

The XML data must be formatted appropriately for display. You will concatenate additional information that will be saved to a file called Data.xml:

```
set XML_Data "<graph caption='Interface Statistics' xAxisName='Time'
yAxisName='PPS' showNames='1' decimalPrecision='0' formatNumberScale='0'> \n"
```

The Data.xml is initially deleted to keep the file size manageable:

```
file delete -force flash:/TCL/Data.xml
```

Setting the **while** count to **13** will enable the collection of 12 samples. This could be another value assigned to a variable to make changes to the script easier:

```
while {$COUNT < 13} {
```

Open the CLI:

```
if [catch {cli_open} RESULT] {
        error $RESULT $errorInfo
    } else {
        array set cli1 $RESULT
}


if [catch {cli_exec $cli1(fd) "en"} RESULT] {
        error $RESULT $errorInfo
}
```

Collect the current count of the interface output statistics (ifOutUcastPkts.2) using a
remote SNMP **get** with version 2c on the PIX firewall and store that information in the
variable **OUT_Packets**:

```
if [catch {cli_exec $cli1(fd) "snmp get v2c $SNMP_SERVER $SNMP_STRING timeout 1
  oid ifOutUcastPkts.2" } RESULT] {
        error $RESULT $errorInfo
    } else {
        set OUT_Packets $RESULT
}
```

Note   This example uses the SNMP Server Manager feature, which is not enabled by
default. To enable the feature, enter the following configuration commands before using
the Tcl script:

```
Router(config)#snmp-server manager
```

Capture the current time and save it in the variable **CLOCK**. This will be used to correlate the time with the output statistic from the PIX firewall:

```
if [catch {cli_exec $cli1(fd) "show clock" } RESULT] {
        error $RESULT $errorInfo
    } else {
        set CLOCK $RESULT
}
```

Close the session:

```
if [catch {cli_close $cli1(fd) $cli1(tty_id)} RESULT] {
        error $RESULT $errorInfo
}
```

Using the **string range** command, you can collect only the (hour:minute:second) parameters necessary for display:

```
set CLOCK [string range $CLOCK 2 9]
```

If the counter is 0, this is the first time through the operation and you need to set a base-
line. Because the SNMP object ifOutUcastPkts.2 is a cumulative count, you will want to
monitor the change:

```
if {$COUNT == 0} {
```

The elaborate use of the **string range** command collects only the numeric value and saves
it in the variable **OUT_Packets_Current**:

```
set OUT_Packets_Current [string range $OUT_Packets [expr [string first "= "
  $OUT_Packets] + 2] [expr [string first "\n" $OUT_Packets [expr [string first "= "
  $OUT_Packets] + 2]] - 1]]
} else {
```

If this is not the first time through the operation, set the previous output counter to the variable **OUT_Packets_Base**:

```
set OUT_Packets_Base $OUT_Packets_Current
set OUT_Packets_Current [string range $OUT_Packets [expr [string first "= "
  $OUT_Packets] + 2] [expr [string first "\n" $OUT_Packets [expr [string first "= "
  $OUT_Packets] + 2]] - 1]]
```

To get the difference or change in the packet counter, you have to subtract the previous count from the current count and store that in the variable **OUT_Packets_Graph**:

```
set OUT_Packets_Graph [expr  $OUT_Packets_Current - $OUT_Packets_Base]
```

The collected time and interface output count information is added to the **XML_Data** variable:

```
    set XML_Data [concat $XML_Data "<set name='$CLOCK' value='$OUT_Packets_Graph'
color='black' /> \n"]
```

```
}
```

Increment the variable **COUNT** to keep track of how many samples are collected:

```
incr COUNT
```

The **after** command is to delay the operation of the script. This example uses a value of 4950 milliseconds. This allows for 50 milliseconds to run through the operation and still collect data every 5 seconds:

```
    after 4950
```

```
}
```

End the string **XML_Data** with "**</graph>**":

```
set XML_Data [concat $XML_Data "</graph>"]
```

Open the file flash:/TCL/Data.xml for reading and writing:

```
set FILE [open flash:/TCL/Data.xml RDWR]
```

Copy the **XML_Data** string into the file:

```
puts $FILE $XML_Data
```

Close the file handle:

```
close $FILE
```

The code that follows is for generating the HTML output.

Set the title and parameters for charting the collected information:

```
set chart "<html>
        <head>
                <title>SNMP Remote Collection of Interface Statistics</title>
        </head>
      <body bgcolor='ffffff'>
```

To display the graph, we are using free charting software by FusionCharts. The file FCF_Line.swf must be saved to a location on the Cisco IOS device and the path to the location of the file must also be specified unless it is placed in the local directory, as in the following example. The data is stored in the file Data.xml (from the script), and a pointer to the file is used for the charting software. Another option includes specifying the size of the chart (in this example, 500 by 900):

```
        <OBJECT classid='clsid:D27CDB6E-AE6D-11cf-96B8-444553540000'
  codebase=http://download.macromedia.com/pub/shockwave/cabs/flash/swflash.cab#
  version=6,0,0,0' width='900' height='500' id='Column3D' >
              <param name='movie' value='FCF_Line.swf' />
              <param name='FlashVars'
  value='&dataURL=Data.xml&chartWidth=900&chartHeight=500'>
              <param name='quality' value='high' />
              <embed src='FCF_Line.swf'
  flashVars='&dataURL=Data.xml&chartWidth=900&chartHeight=500' type='application/
  x-shockwave-flash' pluginspage='http://www.macromedia.com/go/getflashplayer' />
          </object>
      </body>
</html>
"
```

Set the title:

```
set header "<html>
    <head>
        <title>SNMP Remote Collection of Interface Statistics</title>
    </head>
    <div align='left'>
    <font face='arial' size='6'>SNMP Remote Collection of Interface
  Statistics</font><br />
    </div>
</html>
"
```

Empty footer:

```
set footer "
"
```

HTML header information:

```
set httpheader "HTTP/1.1 200 OK


Content-Type: text/html; charset=UTF-8

Content-Transfer-Encoding: binary
"
```

Display the output:

```
puts $httpsock $httpheader$header$chart$footer
```

Copy the script (in this example, it is named Remote-SNMP.tcl and the FCF_Line.swf) file to the IOS device. Using your web browser, using the IP address of your IOS device, enter the following:

> http://192.168.0.186:8082/Remote-SNMP.tcl

It will take approximately 60 seconds for the script to collect the information and display it onscreen. The output should look like Figure 6-10.

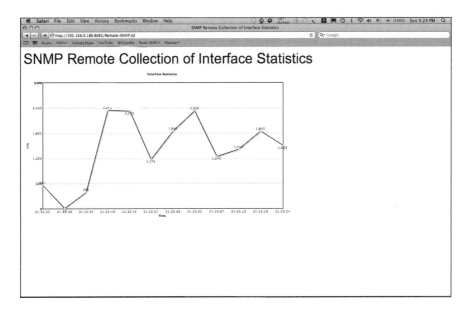

Figure 6-10 *SNMP Remote Collection of Interface Statistics*

Adding charts to your applications can prove very useful. For example, you can combine charts with interface or CPU utilization, error statistics, IP service level agreement (SLA), or whatever your desire. This information can also be used to troubleshoot network problems or for capacity planning.

Summary

In this chapter, you learned how to create an application from start to finish, how to troubleshoot your applications, and how to use your applications for troubleshooting. Using these examples or writing your own, users no longer need to understand command syntax to be able to easily make complex configuration changes or gather information for display in a user-friendly format.

References

RFC 2863: *The Interface Group MIB*

RFC 5424: *The Syslog Protocol*

Cisco Beyond (a repository for user-contributed EEM policies):
http://www.cisco.com/en/US/prod/collateral/iosswrel/ps6537/ps6555/ps6815/product_promotion0900aecd8055c188.html

Cisco Embedded Automation Systems: http://www.cisco.com/go/easy

Charting software: http://www.fusioncharts.com/

## Chapter 7

Security in Tcl Scripts

This chapter covers the following topics:

- Introduction to PKI Infrastructure

- Using Digital Signatures to Sign a Tcl Script

- Tcl Script-Failure Scenario

- Scaling Tcl Script Distribution

From the early days of programming, those with nefarious intent have attempted—and in many cases successfully integrated—additional code into programs that have caused serious consequences to the unsuspecting user. Because a Tcl script is a program running on an IOS-based device, additional code added to the script could potentially send passwords via e-mail, erase the saved configurations or IOS images, cause the device to reload periodically, and so on. The capability to protect scripts against this type of attack is paramount!

Cisco IOS Software Release 12.4(15)T introduced a new feature to improve security for Tcl scripts. The purpose of this security feature is to provide a method for signing a Tcl script that proves the script has not been modified since the time it was signed by the author. It relies on techniques and methods of existing public key cryptography libraries.

Introduction to PKI Infrastructure

Public key infrastructure (PKI) is used to provide a scalable method for certificate/key exchange and is commonly used for secure exchange data (confidentiality), to ensure that the data has not been modified in transit (integrity), to authenticate the origin, and for nonrepudiation.

PKI enables you to send messages with confidentiality and sign messages that are guaranteed to be genuine. Confidentiality allows for conducting secret communication via a public channel; however, it is not needed because the Tcl script is not secret and can be viewed by anyone who has access.

Even though confidentiality is not needed, we do require Tcl scripts to have a digital signature to guarantee they are truly genuine and have not been tampered with. PKI enables you to generate a digital signature that is connected to the Tcl script and guarantees it is genuine.

Because PKI is well established, it can be leveraged to provide the security needed for signing Tcl scripts. Many applications already take advantage of PKI and leverage the security it provides, including SSL/HTTPS, IPsec, and S/MIME. You are probably familiar with purchasing items online, filing tax returns online, and software licensing, all of which use PKI and secure protocols.

Using PKI will provide assurance that a script has not been tampered with and give you the confidence to implement a signed script in a production environment.

PKI Prerequisite

To use PKI, a public/private key pair must first be established. Generally, the longer the key, the higher the level of security provided by that key.

A private key is simply a long string of characters, typically 512. As the name indicates, this key is not to be shared and must always be kept private.

The public key is public and distributed to anyone.

The public/private key pairs are simple to generate and the private key is (nearly) impossible to derive from the public key. Although any security algorithm can be broken given enough time and CPU cycles, longer keys make this task infeasible.

Confidentiality with PKI

When sending messages through a public channel, you can use PKI to encrypt the data so that only the intended recipient can decrypt it. The sender of an encrypted message can encrypt the data but cannot decrypt the data after it has been encrypted. The recipient's public key is used to encrypt the data. The data is sent to the recipient, and once it is received is decrypted with the recipient's private key. This process is unidirectional. For two-way encrypted communication to occur, two key pairs are needed. Each sender encrypts data using the correct public key of the intended recipient. This process is also referred to as *asymmetric encryption*.

As shown in Figure 7-1, Alice will be sending Bob an encrypted message. The process is as follows:

Step 1.   For Alice to send any encrypted information to Bob, she must have Bob's public key.

Step 2.   Alice uses Bob's public key to encrypt the message she wants to send to Bob.

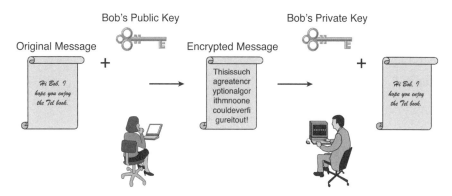

Figure 7-1   *PKI Infrastructure*

Step 3.   Even if someone captures the information in transit, it is undecipherable without Bob's private key, or at least a tremendous number of CPU cycles used to break the private key.

Step 4.   When Bob receives the information, he uses his own private key to decrypt the original message that Alice sent.

Digital Signatures with PKI

Digital signatures enable you to ensure that information is not altered in transit from sender to recipient. You can do so by creating a hash or signature of the original data.

The entire message must remain intact. Even if 1 bit of the data is changed, the entire message integrity is violated. When you sign a check, for example, you are verifying the authenticity with your unique signature. If the amount of the check is changed from your written and numeric values, this represents an obvious violation.

To provide the integrity check, the entire data being sent is run through a hashing function. In simple terms, the hashing function produces a unique result for any given input data, of a known length. Common hashing functions include message digest 4 (MD4), message digest 5 (MD5), and secure hash algorithm (SHA). The hashed data result can be sent using the PKI confidentiality process described earlier. In this way, the message integrity is preserved from sender to recipient.

Figure 7-2 shows how Alice can send a message with a digital signature:

Step 1.   Alice runs the original message through a hash function, creating a unique value.

Step 2.   Alice encrypts the hash value with her private key, resulting in the digital signature.

Step 3.   The signature is attached to the message.

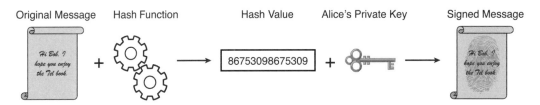

Figure 7-2   *Signing Digital Signatures*

Figure 7-3 shows how Bob can verify the integrity of a message.

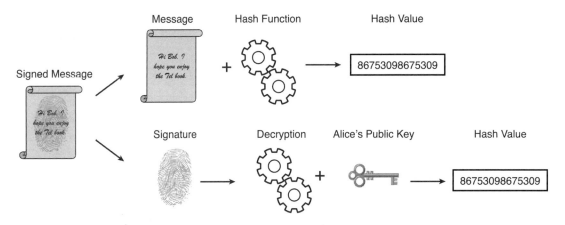

Figure 7-3   *Verifying Digital Signatures*

Step 1.   For Bob to verify that Alice is indeed the originator of the message, Bob must have Alice's public key.

Step 2.   Bob will extract the signature from the message.

Step 3.   The message will be hashed using the same process that Alice used, and a result will be generated.

Step 4.   The signature will also be decrypted using Alice's public key, and a hash value will be generated.

Step 5.   Bob will then compare the message hash value to the signature value. If they match, Bob can be reasonably certain that the message is unaltered.

Using Digital Signatures to Sign a Tcl Script

Two prerequisites must be met to sign a Tcl script:

■   A digital certificate must be made available on the router that will perform the signature check of the Tcl script. The digital certificate is stored in the IOS running-configuration and may also be saved in the nonvolatile random-access memory (NVRAM) of the router.

■   The Tcl script must have been signed with the private key that matches the public key available in the digital certificate. The signature is provided in a special format and is in plain text directly after the Tcl commands in the script.

If Tcl script signature checking is enabled, different actions can take place when a Tcl script is executed. If the signature of the Tcl script matches the digital certificate, the Tcl script will be executed immediately. If the signature fails to be verified, the following choices are available, depending on the IOS configuration:

■   The script can be immediately stopped.

■   The script can be allowed to run even though the signature check failed, in a special "safe" Tcl mode. The "safe" TCL mode has a reduced number of keywords available and is thought to be less dangerous than the full Tcl mode.

■   The script can be allowed to run normally. This can be used for testing purposes, but would rarely be used in an actual *live* network. In effect, this turns off the security check.

To digitally sign a script, an IOS image containing the crypto feature set must be used. This means the image name contains the k9 feature set. For example, the following image contains the crypto feature: c7200-adventerprisek9-mz.

The following example details how to correctly sign a Tcl script with a digital signature, using a UNIX host as the certificate authority (CA) server. As an alternative, a CA can also be created using other operating systems or can be hosted commercially.

A CA is a trusted third party that maintains, verifies, enrolls, distributes, and revokes public keys. It is for that very reason that the CA must be secure.

The previous examples assumed that Bob or Alice had the other's public key. But how does Bob know that the key he has is really from Alice? There are a couple of answers to that question:

■   Alice and Bob exchanged public keys out-of-band. This works fine in a small environment, but when there are hundreds or thousands of devices, manually exchanging keys becomes difficult.

■   A CA is used to maintain all certificates.

This is where a CA really shows its value. The CA maintains the public keys or certificates, usually in an X.509 format. Key exchange is as follows:

Step 1. Before Bob can verify Alice's public key, he must have the CA public key, which should be exchanged out-of-band.

Step 2. When Bob needs Alice's public key, he sends a request to the CA.

Step 3. The CA signs Alice's public key with the CA private key, consequently verifying the origination and sends it to Bob.

Step 4. Bob uses the CA public key to validate Alice's public key.

You must complete the following steps to sign a Tcl script:

Step 1. Decide on the final Tcl script contents (myscript).

Step 2. Generate a public/private key pair.

Step 3. Generate a certificate with the public key.

Step 4. Generate a detached S/MIME pkcs7 signature for the script you created (myscript) using the private key.

Step 5. Modify the format of the signature to match the Cisco style for a signed Tcl script and append it to the end of the script you created (myscript).

Note The name of the script will be referred to as myscript throughout this example.

Step 1: Decide on the Final Tcl Script Contents (Myscript)

Finalize any last-minute changes needed to the script text file. After the Tcl script has been signed, no more changes may be made.

Step 2: Generate a Public/Private Key Pair

The private key must always be kept private! Failure to do so would allow anyone in possession of the private key to sign Tcl scripts as if they were written by the original author.

To generate a key pair, you can use the open source project OpenSSL. Executable versions of the OpenSSL are available for download at http://www.openssl.org

Note The versions of utilities mentioned in this chapter were run on Windows XP in the Cygwin environment. Cygwin is a UNIX-like environment for Windows.

```
$ uname -a
CYGWIN_NT-5.1 joe-wxp01 1.5.25(0.156/4/2) 2008-06-12 19:34 i686 Cygwin
$ openssl version
OpenSSL 0.9.8k 25 Mar 2009
```

```
$ expect -version
expect version 5.26
$ xxd -version
xxd V1.10 27oct98 by Juergen Weigert
```

Using a UNIX host or similar, run the following command to generate a key pair (this example uses a 2048-byte key):

```
$ openssl genrsa -out privkey.pem 2048
Generating RSA private key, 2048 bit long modulus
.......................................+++
............................................................................+
++
e is 65537 (0x10001)
$
```

As you can see from the directory, the following file has been created:

```
$ ls -l
total 5
-rw-r--r-- 1 joe mkgroup-l-d  114 May 28 10:23 myscript
-rw-r--r-- 1 joe mkgroup-l-d 1679 May 28 10:23 privkey.pem
$
```

The new file is called privkey.pem and contains both the private key and public key. The file needs to be kept in a secure location because it holds the private key.

Next, extract the public key from the key pair file:

```
$ openssl rsa -in privkey.pem -pubout -out pubkey.pem
writing RSA key
$
```

As you can see from the directory, the following file has been created:

```
$ ls -l
total 6
-rw-r--r-- 1 joe mkgroup-l-d  114 May 28 10:23 myscript
-rw-r--r-- 1 joe mkgroup-l-d 1679 May 28 10:23 privkey.pem
-rw-r--r-- 1 joe mkgroup-l-d  451 May 28 10:25 pubkey.pem
$
```

Now there are two separate files, one that contains the pair of keys (privkey.pem) and another file that contains only the public key (pubkey.pem).

Step 3: Generate a Certificate with the Key Pair

To create a certificate, we must answer a few questions. These answers will be stored along with the certificate, in case any concerns arise later about where the certificate comes from:

```
$ openssl req -new -x509 -key privkey.pem -out cert.pem -days 1095
```

You are about to be asked to enter information that will be incorporated into your certificate request. What you are about to enter is what is called a distinguished name (DN). There are quite a few fields, but some may be left blank.

For some fields there will be a default value. If you enter a period (.), the field will be left blank:

```
Country Name (2 letter code) [AU]:US
State or Province Name (full name) [Some-State]:California
Locality Name (eg, city) []:San Jose
Organization Name (eg, company) [Internet Widgits Pty Ltd]:Acme Inc.
Organizational Unit Name (eg, section) []:Central Unit
Common Name (eg, YOUR name) []:Joe
Email Address []:joe@xyz.net
```

As you can see from the directory, the following cert.pem file has been added:

```
$ ls -l
total 10
-rw-r--r-- 1 joe mkgroup-l-d 1639 May 28 10:26 cert.pem
-rw-r--r-- 1 joe mkgroup-l-d  114 May 28 10:23 myscript
-rw-r--r- 1 joe mkgroup-l-d 1679 May 28 10:23 privkey.pem
-rw-r--r-- 1 joe mkgroup-l-d  451 May 28 10:25 pubkey.pem
$
```

The certificate has now been generated in the file cert.pem. This certificate will later be transferred to the IOS router for the router to perform the signature check on the signed Tcl script.

Step 4: Generate a Detached S/MIME pkcs7 Signature for Myscript Using the Private Key

When the script is signed, a new file is generated called myscript.pk7, which contains the signature:

```
$ cat myscript
puts hello
puts "argc = $argc"
puts "argv = $argv"
puts "argv0 = $argv0"
puts "tcl_interactive = $tcl_interactive"
```

```
$
$ openssl smime -sign -in myscript -out myscript.pk7 -signer cert.pem -inkey pr
ivkey.pem -outform DER –binary
$
```

The myscript.pk7 file has been added:

```
$ ls -l myscript.pk7
-rw-r--r-- 1 joe mkgroup-l-d 1856 May 28 10:30 myscript.pk7
$
```

To validate that the signature matches the myscript certificate we generated earlier, perform the following:

```
$ openssl smime -verify -in myscript.pk7 -CAfile cert.pem -inform DER -content
myscript
puts hello
puts "argc = $argc"
puts "argv = $argv"
puts "argv0 = $argv0"
Verification successful
puts "tcl_interactive = $tcl_interactive"
$
```

The "Verification successful" message indicates that myscript matches the contents of the signature.

Step 5: Modify the Format of the Signature to Match the Cisco Style for Signed Tcl Scripts and Append It to the End of Myscript

Now that a signature for myscript has been generated, we still need to make some formatting changes to put myscript in the correct format for Cisco IOS to understand.

The format of a signed Tcl script is as follows:

```
Actual Tcl script contents in plain test
...
#Cisco Tcl Signature V1.0
#Actual hex data of the signature
```

The signature portion of myscript is inserted after the hash character (#). Tcl always treats this as a comment. If this script is executed on an IOS router that does not know about Tcl script signature checking, the router will simply ignore these commented lines.

The signature must be converted to a hex format instead of binary:

```
$ xxd -ps myscript.pk7 > myscript.hex
$
```

The directory listing shows that the file was created:

```
$ ls -l myscript.hex
-rw-r--r-- 1 joe mkgroup-l-d 3774 May 28 10:42 myscript.hex
$
```

Next, a helper script is used to place the #Cisco Tcl Signature V1.0 and the # characters in the new signature file.

You can show the contents of the file by using the **cat** command:

```
$ cat my_append
#!/usr/bin/expect
set my_first {#Cisco Tcl Signature V1.0}
set newline {}
set my_file [lindex $argv 0]
set my_new_file ${my_file}_sig
set my_new_handle [open $my_new_file w]
set my_handle [open $my_file r]
puts $my_new_handle $newline
puts $my_new_handle $my_first
foreach line [split [read $my_handle] "\n"]  {
    set new_line {#}
    append new_line $line
    puts $my_new_handle $new_line
}
close $my_new_handle
close $my_handle
$
```

Initiate the helper script using the following syntax:

```
$ ./my_append myscript.hex
$
```

The directory listing shows the myscript.hex and myscript.hex_sig files:

```
$ ls -l myscript.hex*
-rw-r--r-- 1 joe mkgroup-l-d 3774 May 28 10:42 myscript.hex
-rw-r--r-- 1 joe mkgroup-l-d 3865 May 28 10:56 myscript.hex_sig
$
```

Lastly, the signature file and the script file must be concatenated:

```
$ cat myscript myscript.hex_sig > myscript.tcl
$
```

The directory listing shows that the file was created:

```
$ ls -l myscript.tcl
-rw-r--r-- 1 joe mkgroup-l-d 3979 May 28 10:58 myscript.tcl
$
```

The signed Tcl script has finally been generated (myscript.tcl)!

The following script combines many of the preceding steps and will help to automate the process:

```
#!/bin/sh
# the next line restarts using tclsh \
exec tclsh "$0" "$@"

proc PrintUsageInfo {} {
        puts {usage:  signme input_file [-c cert_file] [ -k privkey_file]} }

set cert_file cert.pem
set privkey_file privkey.pem

if {$argc == 0} {
    PrintUsageInfo
    exit -1
}

set state flag
set cnt 0
foreach arg $argv {
    switch -- $state {
        flag {
            switch -glob -- $arg {
                \-c {
                    set state cert
                }
                \-k {
                    set state key
                }
                default {
                    if {$cnt == 0} {
                        set filename $arg
                    } else {
                        PrintUsageInfo
```

```
                                exit -1
                        }
                    }
                }
            }
            cert {
                set cert_file $arg
                set state flag
            }
            key {
                set privkey_file $arg
                set state flag
            }
        }
    }
    incr cnt
}

if {![string equal $state flag]} {
    PrintUsageInfo
    exit -1
}

if {[catch {set commented_signed_hex [exec openssl smime -sign -in $filename \
    -signer $cert_file -inkey $privkey_file -outform DER -binary | xxd -ps \
    | sed s/^/#/ ]} err]} {
    puts stderr "Error signing $filename - $err"
    exit -1
}

set signature_tag "\n#Cisco Tcl Signature V1.0"

if {[catch {set fd [open $filename a+]} err]} {
    puts stderr "Cannot open $filename  - $err"
    exit -1
}

puts $fd $signature_tag
puts $fd $commented_signed_hex
close $fd

puts "$filename signed successfully."
exit
```

To take advantage of the newly signed script, the IOS device must be configured with a certificate.

After logging in to the IOS device and establishing access to configuration mode, complete the following steps:

Step 1. Configure and enroll in a trust point using the cert.pem file. At the prompt, paste the certificate into the terminal. That is, paste the contents of the cert.pem file beginning after "-----BEGIN CERTIFICATE-----"and ending before "-----END CERTIFICATE-----".":

```
PE11(config)#crypto pki trustpoint TCLSecurity
PE11(ca-trustpoint)#enrollment terminal
PE11(ca-trustpoint)#crypto pki authenticate TCLSecurity
Enter the base 64 encoded CA certificate.
End with a blank line or the word "quit" on a line by itself
-----BEGIN CERTIFICATE-----
MIIEjDCCA3SgAwIBAgIJANOb35p5QONbMA0GCSqGSIb3DQEBBQUAMIGKMQswCQYD
VQQGEwJVUzETMBEGA1UECBMKQ2FsaWZvcm5pYTERMA8GA1UEBxMIU2FuIEpvc2Ux
EjAQBgNVBAoTCUFjbWUgSW5jLjEVMBMGA1UECxMMQ2VudHJhbCBVbml0MQwwCgYD
VQQDEwNKb2UxGjAYBgkqhkiG9w0BCQEWC2pvZUB4eXoubmV0MB4XDTA5MDUyODE3
MjY1OVoXDTEyMDUyNzE3MjY1OVowgYoxCzAJBgNVBAYTAlVTMRMwEQYDVQQIEwpD
YWxpZm9ybmlhMREwDwYDVQQHEwhTYW4gSm9zZTESMBAGA1UEChMJQWNtZSBJbmMu
MRUwEwYDVQQLEwxDZW50cmFsIFVuaXQxDDAKBgNVBAMTA0pvZTEaMBgGCSqGSIb3
DQEJARYLam9lQHh5ei5uZXQwggEiMA0GCSqGSIb3DQEBAQUAA4IBDwAwggEKAoIB
AQDXjtFzWDXyHftgy7i75HczyvAFh10E2oB/tTC9WA5mih2L8ZMGTu+705LYP0E+
TlhVadastpYSEEVPOrdWiUuqLIoFKV7LE6KsEcKTuGRQp0tEGhfQrPyBuCcpuzO5
FZv7mpCJMvhXzW/wioAvFLE4vuXHHdAhsdK2dD1nOHmljvsx3hJ+Us6PKTnU1BNU
HpSReM6T9hH321Wakt9D4Q+qXW6T3IE2pD6tzvTZouLKXD7BMXjoNjMe6vIzlwmY
b7E2Txwui6YtPcJK15pRcl1+DozT9iGj43ps6glAIUfjtjCPEoQBblWeqNAHVYWn
WDP4FXg9H7z4xjocDuKJm+bBAgMBAAGjgfIwge8wHQYDVR0OBBYEFOb3HxpTyQcw
7YH4JwE2rdZUx4HnMIG/BgNVHSMEgbcwgbSAFOb3HxpTyQcw7YH4JwE2rdZUx4Hn
oYGQpIGNMIGKMQswCQYDVQQGEwJVUzETMBEGA1UECBMKQ2FsaWZvcm5pYTERMA8G
A1UEBxMIU2FuIEpvc2UxEjAQBgNVBAoTCUFjbWUgSW5jLjEVMBMGA1UECxMMQ2Vu
dHJhbCBVbml0MQwwCgYDVQQDEwNKb2UxGjAYBgkqhkiG9w0BCQEWC2pvZUB4eXou
bmV0ggkA05vfmnlA41swDAYDVR0TBAUwAwEB/zANBgkqhkiG9w0BAQUFAAOCAQEA
F+W1JWf56IJPjYT0f2MForE3/gsKMgUvMh+kyf4Fcgvdh4WuKUEwTVBHpHglOYyL
XfNZe6ILf9e3SgmXsqJOwAu/qK8d5uMwZ4d8TVoZqN1QmJPhvBcp7WZS8EvMVAWU
vwo8SUgDUY1QzXPa5R333T0k1Vo+wxc7c4zftH/gbbqrGGgP5EAlXKvX75Z/dafv
d/jPl4DniOlwz54ieRwjRU7B9w80Oa8EQeGRnsuNBcXRYqNoHJMRQK2xelqBL//8
10TEQeAoN3WjHBkqLXjf6HasnhfnwoNpNEn+ni5xN5uigbmuBzS1TCeevve/Y0ix
NnU3fSYpIOnb1tZLBbYY7A==
-----END CERTIFICATE-----
Certificate has the following attributes:
        Fingerprint MD5: 856A9FF2 23AF24B0 8422B4FC 1E9E4153
        Fingerprint SHA1: 35248814 47468190 4A1A3B6C 9D60C2A8 0B99BB0C
% Do you accept this certificate? [yes/no]: yes
Trustpoint CA certificate accepted.
% Certificate successfully imported
```

Verify that the trust point was accepted correctly:

```
PE11#show crypto pki trustpoints
Trustpoint TCLSecurity:
    Subject Name:
    e=joe@xyz.net
    cn=Joe
    ou=Central Unit
    o=Acme Inc.
    l=San Jose
    st=California
    c=US
            Serial Number: 0x0D39BDF9A7940E35B
    Certificate configured.
```

It looks correct because we see the expected information that was entered when we generated the certificate.

Step 2.   Configure the IOS device to require that all Tcl scripts be verified against the certificate before running. In this example, if a script does not pass the security check, it will not be allowed to execute:

```
PE11(config)#scripting tcl trustpoint name TCLSecurity
PE11(config)#scripting tcl securemode
PE11(config)#scripting tcl trustpoint untrusted terminate
```

All Tcl scripts that are run on the router must now perform a signature check.

Alternatives for executing scripts include the following:

■   **Execute:** Run the script even if the Tcl script fails verification

■   **Safe-execute:** Execute the script in safe mode when the Tcl script fails verification.

Step 3.   After copying the script myscript.tcl to disk0: of the IOS device, you can initiate it using the following command:

```
PE11#tclsh disk0:myscript.tcl
hello
argc = 0
argv =
argv0 = unix:myscript.tcl
tcl_interactive = 0
```

Tcl Script-Failure Scenario

In the event the script has been modified, the signature will detect that there was a change and prevent it from executing.

The following example shows that the script was modified and consequently forbidden from being executed.

The first line of the script has been changed from "puts hello" to "puts hellox," and the file has been copied to the IOS device as myscript-changed1char.tcl. Attempting to run the script elicits the following response:

```
PE11#tclsh disk0:myscript-changed1char.tcl
Invalid Signature
PE11#
*May 28 19:45:28.115: %SYS-6-SCRIPTING_TCL_INVALID_OR_MISSING_SIGNATURE: tcl
  signing validation failed on script signed with trustpoint name TCLSecurity,
  cannot run the signed TCL script.
```

As you can see from the preceding output, the Tcl script security is a valuable feature for protecting the contents of a Tcl script. If any portion of the contents of the Tcl script has been modified by anyone, from the time the script was initially written to the time it is run on the router, the change will be detected and the script will be forbidden from executing.

For smaller company networks, it might be acceptable to have a network administrator manually install the certificate in all routers that need to run the script. The certificate is copied to a local storage such as slot0: or disk0: or any other valid file system attached to the router. In addition, copies of the Tcl script can also copied to these local storage devices attached to the router.

To deploy scripts in a larger network, take advantage of the capability of IOS software to use a TFTP server as a repository and allow all IOS devices to download Tcl scripts from the TFTP server.

Scaling Tcl Script Distribution

In the next example, a central TFTP server has been deployed in the network using an IP address of 192.168.1.81. In this case, the IOS device downloads the Tcl script across the network using TFTP. The signature checking is still performed, thus retaining a high level of security while using an unsecure transfer protocol:

```
PE11#tclsh tftp://192.168.1.81/myscript.tcl
Loading myscript.tcl from 192.168.1.81 (via Serial2/0.111): !
[OK - 4046 bytes]
hello
argc = 0
argv =
argv0 = tftp://192.168.1.81/myscript.tcl
tcl_interactive = 0
```

If the script has been modified, we receive the same results as before:

```
PE11#tclsh tftp://192.168.1.81/myscript-changed1char.tcl
Loading myscript-changed1char.tcl from 192.168.1.81 (via Serial2/0.111): !
[OK - 4047 bytes]
Invalid Signature
```

```
*Mar 27 23:40:35.543: %SYS-6-SCRIPTING_TCL_INVALID_OR_MISSING_SIGNATURE: tcl
  signing validation failed on script signed with trustpoint name TCLSecurity,
  cannot run the signed TCL script.
```

The public certificate is stored locally in the router's NVRAM and consequently is taking up valuable memory space. You may find yourself in a situation where the IOS device is running out of memory. To minimize the impact on NVRAM, you can use the **service compress-config** command to reduce the certificate's overhead on NVRAM:

```
PE11(config)#service compress-config
PE11(config)#end
PE11#write
Warning: Attempting to overwrite an NVRAM configuration previously written
by a different version of the system image.
Overwrite the previous NVRAM configuration?[confirm]
*Mar 27 23:47:45.323: %SYS-5-CONFIG_I: Configured from console by console
[confirm]
Building configuration...
Compressed configuration from 5689 bytes to 3535 bytes[OK]
```

Caution　You might also need to erase the NVRAM and rewrite it, to further reduce the amount of data stored in NVRAM. Do so with extreme caution, because you might lose the entire configuration!

Instead of using a central TFTP server as a repository for Tcl scripts, you can use other protocols to transmit the Tcl Scripts from a central server, including FTP, RCP, SCP, HTTP, and HTTPS.

Summary

Ensuring that Tcl scripts have not been modified is critical to maintaining the integrity of the network infrastructure. If a script is changed, the ramifications could be disastrous! Fortunately, digitally signing a Tcl script is not a difficult task and offers a mechanism from which you can be confident in the integrity of the script.

References

SUN public key infrastructure overview:
http://www.sun.com/blueprints/0801/publickey.pdf

OpenSSL documentation: http://www.openssl.org/docs/apps/openssl.html

Cygwin home page: http://www.cygwin.com/

Signed Tcl scripts:
http://www.cisco.com/en/US/docs/ios/12_4t/netmgmt/configuration/guide/sign_tcl.html

Appendix A

Cisco IOS Tcl Commands Quick Reference

This appendix includes only those Tcl commands *specific* to Cisco IOS. If a command is not mentioned, it indicates the command acts identically in Cisco IOS Tcl as Tcl running on other operating systems.

Tcl Cisco IOS Commands

The sections that follow describe the parameters, output, usage, and examples of Tcl Cisco IOS commands.

hostname **Command**

Required parameters: None

Optional parameters: None

Returns: A string

Usage: Returns a string with the current Cisco IOS device hostname

Example:

```
Router(tcl)#hostname
Router
```

Note   The hostname can only be retrieved, but not changed using **hostname** command. Use the **ios_config** command to change the hostname.

ios_config **Command**

Required parameters: "*configuration command*"

Optional parameters: None

Returns: Nothing

Usage: Modify the Cisco IOS running-configuration using any valid configuration command

Example:

```
Router(tcl)#ios_config "hostname Router"
```

Note   For deeper levels of subcommands, simply continue to add additional commands in a new set of quotation marks. For example:

```
Router(tcl)#ios_config "ip sla 1" "icmp-echo 10.2.3.4" "frequency 30" "end"


Router(tcl)#show running-config | begin ip sla
ip sla 1
 icmp-echo 10.2.3.4
 frequency 30
 !
```

You should always complete the command sequence with the **end** statement. This will minimize locking of the configuration.

log_user **Command**

Required parameters: None

Optional parameters: 0 or 1

Returns: The current value, either 0 or 1

Usage: Control whether Tcl displays the returned value for each command. If you want to see the returned value, set **log_user** to **1** by entering **log_user 1**. If you do not want to see the returned value for each command, set **log_user** to **0** by entering **log_user 0**. If you want to display the current value of **log_user** and not modify it, enter **log_user**.

Example:

```
Router(tcl)#set a 100
100
Router(tcl)#log_user 0
0
Router(tcl)#set a 101

Router(tcl)#
```

snmp_getbulk **Command**

Required parameters: *community_string*, *non_repeaters*, *max_repetitions oid*

Optional parameters: *oid2*, *oid3*, ...

Returns: The value of SNMP Management Information Base (MIB) object values, with Extensible Markup Language (XML) tags

> **Note**   The **snmp** commands were introduced in Cisco IOS Software Release 12.3.(7)T.

Usage: Query the local Cisco IOS router SNMP MIB object values, getting a large block of data with a single command. The **snmp_getbulk** command speeds the process of gathering MIB object data. The *community_string* variable acts as a primitive password mechanism and needs to match the currently configure Simple Network Management Protocol (SNMP) community string.

The parameter *non_repeaters* should be set to 0, and *max_repetitions* should be set to the number of object identifiers (OIDs) you want to gather. Keep in mind that there is a hard limit of 2700 characters of data retrieval. The *oid* is the SNMP object identifier to be queried. XML tagging is used to clarify the OID number being returned with *oid* versus the actual contents being returned with *val*.

Example: Query a single OID:

```
Router(tcl)#snmp_getbulk public 0 10 ifDescr.0
{<obj oid='ifDescr.1' val='Ethernet0/0'/>}
{<obj oid='ifDescr.2' val='Ethernet0/1'/>}
{<obj oid='ifDescr.3' val='Ethernet0/2'/>}
{<obj oid='ifDescr.4' val='Ethernet0/3'/>}
{<obj oid='ifDescr.5' val='Ethernet1/0'/>}
{<obj oid='ifDescr.6' val='Ethernet1/1'/>}
{<obj oid='ifDescr.7' val='Ethernet1/2'/>}
{<obj oid='ifDescr.8' val='Ethernet1/3'/>}
{<obj oid='ifDescr.9' val='Serial2/0'/>}
{<obj oid='ifDescr.10' val='Serial2/1'/>}
Router(tcl)#
```

Example: Query multiple OIDs, start from middle of table instead of beginning:

```
Router(tcl)#snmp_getbulk public 0 4 ifDescr.6 ifSpeed.6
{<obj oid='ifDescr.7' val='Ethernet1/2'/>}
{<obj oid='ifSpeed.7' val='10000000'/>}
{<obj oid='ifDescr.8' val='Ethernet1/3'/>}
{<obj oid='ifSpeed.8' val='10000000'/>}
```

```
{<obj oid='ifDescr.9' val='Serial2/0'/>}
{<obj oid='ifSpeed.9' val='1544000'/>}
{<obj oid='ifDescr.10' val='Serial2/1'/>}
{<obj oid='ifSpeed.10' val='1544000'/>}
Router(tcl)#
```

snmp_getid **Command**

Required parameters: *community_string*

Optional parameters: None

Returns: The value of SNMP MIB object under the system branch

Usage: Query specific local Cisco IOS device SNMP MIB object values, which can be used as a quick identifier for the IOS device. The values returned are System.1.0 through System.6.0 from SNMPv2 MIB:

```
- — system (1) object Details
|     |
|     |  --      sysDescr (1)
|     |
|     |  --      sysObjectID (2)
|     |
|     + --      sysUpTime (3)
|     |
|     |  --      sysContact (4)
|     |
|     |  --      sysName (5)
|     |
|     |  --      sysLocation (6)
```

The *community_string* variable acts as a primitive password mechanism and needs to match the currently configure SNMP read community string.

Note   At the time of this writing, SNMPv3 will not function and is currently being addressed.

Example:

```
Router(tcl)#snmp_getid public
{<obj oid='system.1.0' val='Cisco IOS Software, 2800 Software (C2800NM-ADVENTER-
    PRISEK9-M), Version 12.3(14)T7, DEVELOPMENT TEST SOFTWARE
Technical Support: http://www.cisco.com/techsupport
Copyright (c) 1986-2007 by Cisco Systems, Inc.
Compiled Fri 29-Jun-07 22:48 by prod_rel_team'/>}
{<obj oid='system.2.0' val='products.1'/>}
{<obj oid='sysUpTime.0' val='5078'/>}
```

```
{<obj oid='system.4.0' val=''/>}
{<obj oid='system.5.0' val='Router'/>}
{<obj oid='system.6.0' val=''/>}
Router(tcl)#
```

snmp_getnext **Command**

Required parameters: *community_string*, *oid*

Optional parameters: *oid2*, *oid3*, ...

Returns: The value of the next SNMP MIB object value

Usage: Query the local Cisco IOS router SNMP MIB object values, getting the next OID value after the supplied OID. Allows for querying of one or more MIB objects at a time. The *community_string* variable acts as a primitive password mechanism and needs to match the currently configure SNMP community string. The *oid* is the SNMP object identifier to be queried. XML tagging is used to clarify the OID number being returned with *oid* versus the actual contents being returned with *val*.

Example: Query a single OID:

```
Router(tcl)#snmp_getnext public ifDescr.1
{<obj oid='ifDescr.2' val='Ethernet0/1'/>}
Router(tcl)#
```

Example: Query multiple OIDs:

```
Router(tcl)#snmp_getnext public ifDescr.1 ifSpeed.1
{<obj oid='ifDescr.2' val='Ethernet0/1'/>}
{<obj oid='ifSpeed.2' val='10000000'/>}
Router(tcl)#
```

snmp_getone **Command**

Required parameters: *community_string*, *oid*

Optional parameters: *oid2*, *oid3*, ...

Returns: The value of the requested SNMP MIB object values, with XML tags

Usage: Query the local Cisco IOS router SNMP MIB object values, getting the value of the requested OID. Allows for querying of one or more MIB objects at a time. The *community_string* variable acts as a primitive password mechanism and needs to match the currently configure SNMP community string. The *oid* is the SNMP object identifier to be queried. XML tagging is used to clarify the OID number being returned with *oid* versus the actual contents being returned with *val*.

Example: Query a single OID:

```
Router(tcl)#snmp_getone public ifDescr.1
{<obj oid='ifDescr.1' val='Ethernet0/0'/>}
Router(tcl)#
```

Example: Query multiple OIDs:

```
Router(tcl)#snmp_getone public ifDescr.1 ifSpeed.1
{<obj oid='ifDescr.1' val='Ethernet0/0'/>}
{<obj oid='ifSpeed.1' val='10000000'/>}
Router(tcl)#
```

snmp_setany **Command**

Required parameters: *community_string*, *oid*, enter, *val*

Optional parameters: *oid2*, enter2, *val2*, ...

Returns: The new changed value of the specified SNMP MIB object values if successfully changed; otherwise, an error message is generated.

Usage: Change the value of local Cisco IOS router SNMP MIB object values, if they can be written. Allows for the changing of one or more MIB object at a time.

The *community_string* variable acts as a primitive password mechanism and needs to match the currently configure SNMP community string. For a set to work properly, the supplied *community_string* must be configured to allow write access, such as the **RW** access string, which indicates **read-write** access. In addition, the individual OID that you are attempting to change must also support write access. Not every MIB object supports being written to or changed.

The *oid* is the SNMP object identifier to be changed.

The *type* parameter is one of the choices outlined in Table A-1.

> **Note**   The valid range can be further limited, depending on the specific MIB object definition.

Example: Change the value of a single-integer OID, change the state of an interface from shutdown to up:

```
Router(tcl)#snmp_setany public ifAdminStatus.7 -i 1
{<obj oid='ifAdminStatus.7' val='1'/>}
Router(tcl)#
*Jan 19 00:30:02.595: %LINK-3-UPDOWN: Interface Ethernet1/2, changed state to up
*Jan 19 00:30:03.595: %LINEPROTO-5-UPDOWN: Line protocol on Interface
   Ethernet1/2, changed state to up
Router(tcl)#
```

Table A-1 snmp_setany *Valid Types, Meanings, and Valid Ranges*

Supplied Type	Meaning	Valid Range
-i	32-bit signed numeric value	-2147483648 to 2147483647
-u	32-bit unsigned numeric value	0 to 4294967295
-c	32-bit unsigned numeric value, must always increase	0 to 4294967295
-g	32-bit unsigned numeric value, can increase or decrease	0 to 4294967295
-o	Octet string, in hex, separated by spaces and enclosed in " "	00 to FF
-ipv4	IPv4 address, separated by . and enclosed in " "	0.0.0.0 to 255.255.255.255
-oid	Object identifier, number separated by . and enclosed in " "	Any numeric values

Example: Change the value of a single display string OID, change the description of an interface:

```
Router(tcl)#snmp_setany public ifAlias.1 -d "this is a new description for e0/0"
{<obj oid='ifAlias.1' val='this is a new description for e0/0'/>}
Router(tcl)#show running-config interface ethernet 0/0
Building configuration...

Current configuration : 117 bytes
!
interface Ethernet0/0
 description this is a new description for e0/0
 no ip address
 shutdown
 no cdp enable
end

Router(tcl)#
```

tcl_trace **Command**

Required parameters: {variable | vdelete | vinfo}:

- variable *variable-name* {r | w | u} *command*

- vdelete *variable-name* {r | w | u} *command*

- vinfo *variable-name*

Optional parameters: None

Returns:

- **tcl_trace variable:** Returns nothing
- **tcl_trace vdelete:** Returns nothing
- **tcl_trace vinfo:** Returns one or more lists of commands that will be called when the variable is accessed

Usage for tcl_trace variable: Calls a procedure when a variable is read, written, or unset. The procedure can be used in debugging a Tcl script. If a large or complicated script is being developed, insert **tcl_trace** in the script as needed. It will provide information about the variable being accessed or changed.

Usage for tcl_trace vdelete: Delete the linkage to a procedure called when a variable is read, written, or unset. Only the linkage previously created with the **tcl_trace** variable is deleted, not the actual procedure.

Usage for tcl_trace vinfo: Show the linkage between a variable and what procedure will be called when the variable is read, written, or unset. The return value contains one or more lists. The first list, if present, shows the procedure called when the variable is read. The second list, if present, shows the procedure called when the variable is written. The third list, if present, shows the procedure called when the variable is unset.

Example: Create a user procedure whenever a variable is read, written, or unset, as follows.

This procedure will be called whenever the variable is read:

```
proc myReading {var1 var2 var3} {
```

Display the variable name being read:

```
    #var1 will contain the variable name
    #var3 will contain either "r" if $var1 is being read
    #                         "w" if $var1 is being written
    #                   or "u" if $var1 is being unset
    if {[string eq $var3 "r"]} {puts "reading $var1"}
}
```

This procedure will be called whenever the variable is written:

```
proc myWriting {var1 var2 var3} {
```

Display the variable name being read:

```
    #var1 will contain the variable name
    #var3 will contain either "r" if $var1 is being read
    #                         "w" if $var1 is being written
    #                   or "u" if $var1 is being unset
    if {[string eq $var3 "w"]} {puts "writing $var1"}
}
```

This procedure will be called whenever the variable is unset:

```
proc myUnset {var1 var2 var3} {
```

Display the variable name being read:

```
    #var1 will contain the variable name
    #var3 will contain either "r" if $var1 is being read
    #                         "w" if $var1 is being written
    #                      or "u" if $var1 is being unset
    if {[string eq $var3 "u"]} {puts "unset $var1 "}
}
```

Now enter them into the Cisco IOS device in Tcl mode:

```
Router#tclsh
Router(tcl)#proc myReading {var1 var2 var3} {
+>      if {[string eq $var3 "r"]} {puts "reading $var1"}
+>}
Router(tcl)#proc myWriting {var1 var2 var3} {
+>      if {[string eq $var3 "w"]} {puts "writing $var1"}
+>}
Router(tcl)#proc myUnset {var1 var2 var3} {
+>      if {[string eq $var3 "u"]} {puts "unset $var1 "}
+>}
```

Next, specify the variable to trace:

```
Router(tcl)#tcl_trace var a r myReading


Router(tcl)#
Router(tcl)#tcl_trace var a w myWriting


Router(tcl)#
Router(tcl)#tcl_trace var a u myUnset
```

You can now check which procedure will be called under what conditions:

```
Router(tcl)#tcl_trace vinfo a
{u myUnset} {w myWriting} {r myReading}
```

Next, read, write, and unset the variable:

```
Router(tcl)#set a 11
writing a
11
Router(tcl)#set b $a
reading a
11
Router(tcl)#unset a
unset a
```

Finally, delete one aspect of the tcl_trace linkage to the procedure:

```
Router(tcl)#tcl_trace vinfo a
{u myUnset} {w myWriting} {r myReading}
Router(tcl)#tcl_trace vdelete a r myReading

Router(tcl)#tcl_trace vinfo a
{u myUnset} {w myWriting}
Router(tcl)#
```

tclsh **Command**

Required parameters: None

Optional parameters: *script_name*

Returns: Execution of the script

Usage: Runs the specified Tcl script if included; otherwise, the interactive Tcl shell will be invoked.

Example: The following example creates a Tcl script that sorts the interfaces and defines an **alias** command to facilitate operation.

The script sorts the output of the **show ip int brief** command:

```
set a [split [exec "show ip int brief"] "\n"]
set b [lsort $a]
set c [llength $b]
set d 0
while {$d < $c} {
 puts [lindex $b $d]
 incr d
}
```

The **alias** command will minimize the number of characters required to run the command:

```
Router#configure terminal
Router(config)#alias exec sorted tclsh flash:INT_LIST.tcl
Router(config)#end
Router#sorted
GigabitEthernet0/0      192.168.0.186      YES NVRAM  up              up
GigabitEthernet0/1      10.0.0.1           YES NVRAM  up              down
Interface               IP-Address         OK? Method Status          Protocol
Loopback0               192.168.254.254    YES NVRAM  up              up
```

```
Loopback1001            172.18.134.3        YES NVRAM  up              up
Serial0/0/0             10.101.101.1        YES NVRAM  down            down
Serial0/0/1             10.25.24.2          YES NVRAM  down            down
```

tclquit **Command**

Required parameters: None

Optional parameters: None

Returns: Nothing

Usage: Exits out of tclsh mode

Example:

```
Router(tcl)#tclquit
Router#
```

Note   The **exit** command can be used as an alternative to **tclquit**.

typeahead **Command**

Required parameters: A string of characters enclosed in double quotes (" ")

Optional parameters: None

Returns: Nothing

Usage: Characters are inserted in front of the current cursor position.

Example: The following is a script that will clear the interface counters and automatically type "enter" at the prompt:

```
typeahead "\n"
exec {clear counters}
```

The current cursor position has been prefilled with the text that was typed and passed into the **typeahead** command. The file has been saved as CLEAR.tcl to the flash: file system. On initiating the script, the counters are cleared:

```
Router#tclsh flash:CLEAR.tcl


Router#
000105: Feb  1 04:41:51.607: %CLEAR-5-COUNTERS: Clear counter on all interfaces
   by rablair on vty1
```

Example: The following is a script that will delete a file provided as an input parameter to the script and automatically type "enter" at each prompt:

```
typeahead "\n\n"
exec "delete [lindex $argv 0]"
```

The current cursor position has been prefilled with the text that was typed and passed into the **typeahead** command. The file has been save as delete.tcl to the flash: file system. On initiating the script, the file named "flash:test" is deleted:

```
Router#dir flash:test
Directory of flash:/test

    8  -rw-          72   Apr 7 2010 02:41:32 +00:00  test

64008192 bytes total (4575232 bytes free)
Router#tclsh flash:delete.tcl flash:test

Router#dir flash:test
%Error opening flash:/test (File not found)
Router#
```

Cisco Tcl Default Variables

This section covers the variables with default values found only in the Tcl interpreter built in to Cisco IOS Software. If a variable is not mentioned, it indicates the variable has the same purpose in Cisco IOS Tcl as Tcl running on other operating systems.

sys_type **Variable**

Type: Array

Meaning: Contains the operating system information

Example contents:

```
Router(tcl)#array get sys_type
os ios
Router(tcl)#
```

tclDefaultLibrary **Variable**

Type: String

Meaning: Unused variable, can be ignored

Example contents:

```
Router(tcl)#puts $tclDefaultLibrary
NULL
```

tcl_traceExec **Variable**

Type: Numeric

Meaning: Used for debugging Tcl scripts. If it is set to **2**, it will display the Tcl command-level debugging. If it is set to **3**, it will show the operation of the Tcl script compilation during script execution. Table A-2 outlines the different numeric values and their meanings.

Table A-2   tcl_traceExec *Variable Numeric Values*

tcl_traceExec **Value**	**Meaning**
0	No debugging is displayed (the default).
1	Print the names of procedures as the are being called.
2	Print the name of any command being called and it is input variables.
3	Print the result of each byte-code being executed.

Example contents and usage:

Using the following script named count-to-one.tcl on the local storage of the Cisco IOS device:

```
set b 2
set c 0

proc count {b c} {
 while {$c < $b} {
  puts "$c "
  incr c
 }
}

count $b $c
```

Set the **tcl_traceExec** to **0** and run the script as normal:

```
Router(tcl)#set tcl_traceExec 0
0
Router(tcl)#source flash:count-to-one.tcl
0
1
Router(tcl)#
```

Next, set **tcl_traceExec** to **2** and run the script. You can see the name of the procedure (**count**) being executed:

```
Router(tcl)#set tcl_traceExec 1
1
Router(tcl)#source flash:count-to-one.tcl
Calling proc count
0
1

Router(tcl)#
```

Next, set **tcl_traceExec** to **2** and run the script. You can see the name of the procedure (**count**) being executed and any Tcl command, such as **puts**:

```
Router(tcl)#set tcl_traceExec 2
2
Router(tcl)#source flash:count-to-one.tcl
Calling proc count
3: (15) invoking puts
0
3: (15) invoking puts
1

Router(tcl)#
```

Next, set **tcl_traceExec** to **3** and run the script. You can see the same information provided by setting **tcl_traceExec** to **2** and the results of Tcl byte-code compilation. Variables are shown as they are being accessed. The output could be used to track down problems with the byte-code compiler:

```
Router(tcl)#set tcl_traceExec 3
3
Router(tcl)#source flash:count-to-one.tcl
Calling proc count
3 : 0   (0) loadScalar1 1         # var "c"
3 : 1   (2) loadScalar1 0         # var "b"
3 : 2   (4) lt
3 : 1   (5) jumpFalse1 19         # pc 24
3 : 0   (7) push1 0         # "puts"
3 : 1   (9) loadScalar1 1         # var "c"
3 : 2   (11) push1 1       # " "
3 : 3   (13) concat1 2
3 : 2   (15) invokeStk1 2
3: (15) invoking puts
0
3 : 1   (17) pop
```

```
3 : 0   (18) incrScalar1Imm 1 1
3 : 1   (21) pop
3 : 0   (22) jump1 -22    # pc 0
3 : 0   (0) loadScalar1 1        # var "c"
3 : 1   (2) loadScalar1 0        # var "b"
3 : 2   (4) lt
3 : 1   (5) jumpFalse1 19        # pc 24
3 : 0   (7) push1 0       # "puts"
3 : 1   (9) loadScalar1 1        # var "c"
3 : 2   (11) push1 1      # " "
3 : 3   (13) concat1 2
3 : 2   (15) invokeStk1 2
3: (15) invoking puts
1
3 : 1   (17) pop
3 : 0   (18) incrScalar1Imm 1 1
3 : 1   (21) pop
3 : 0   (22) jump1 -22    # pc 0
3 : 0   (0) loadScalar1 1        # var "c"
3 : 1   (2) loadScalar1 0        # var "b"
3 : 2   (4) lt
3 : 1   (5) jumpFalse1 19        # pc 24
3 : 0   (24) push1 2      # ""
3 : 1   (26) done

Router(tcl)#
```

Tcl Variables Identical in IOS and Other Operating Systems

This section contains variables found in IOS that might also be found in other operating systems.

argc, argv, argv0 **Variables**

Type:

- Numeric: argc
- String: argv, argv0

Meaning: Provide access to arguments passed into the script as parameters. Parameters make writing Tcl scripts more flexible because they allow the user to provide the input data rather than hard-coding the data values. By using argument variables, you get access to user input variables:

- **argc** provides a count of how many arguments were passed in.

- **argv** provides a string representation of all incoming arguments, not including the name of the Tcl script.

- **argv0** provides access to the name of the Tcl script being executed, if the script is run noninteractively.

Example contents and usage:

Use the following Tcl script named arg-demo.tcl on the local storage of the Cisco IOS device:

```
puts "argc = $argc"
puts "argv = $argv"
puts "argv0 = $argv0"
```

Run the script from the Router# prompt, as follows:

```
Router#tclsh flash:arg-demo.tcl arg1 arg2 arg3
argc = 3
argv = arg1 arg2 arg3
argv0 = flash:arg-demo.tcl
```

Next, explore the same variables from within tclsh mode:

```
Router#tclsh
Router(tcl)#puts $argc
0

Router(tcl)#puts $argv

Router(tcl)#puts $argv0
tclsh

Router(tcl)#
```

tcl_interactive **Variable**

Type: Numeric

Meaning: Represents the current mode of operation, either interactive or noninteractive. If the variable is **1**, the user is in Tcl shell mode typing commands one by one. If the variable is **0**, the user is running a Tcl script directly with no user interaction. Changing the value with **set** has no effect.

Example contents and usage:

If the following Tcl script named int.tcl is on the local storage of the Cisco IOS router

```
puts "tcl_interactive = $tcl_interactive"
```

You can execute the script from the Router# prompt:

```
Router#tclsh flash:int.tcl
tcl_interactive = 0
```

Explore the **tcl_interactive** variable from within tclsh mode:

```
Router#
Router(tcl)#puts $tcl_interactive
1
```

> **Note**   The output of 0 indicates that the script was initiated outside the Tcl shell, and an output of 1 indicates the command was initiated from the Tcl shell.

tcl_patchlevel **Variable**

Type: String

Meaning: Shows the version of Tcl that is running. Currently, the latest version is 8.3.4. The variable can be changed, but has no effect.

Example contents and usage:

```
TCL1(tcl)#puts $tcl_patchLevel
8.3.4
```

tcl_pkgPath **Variable**

This is an unused variable and can be ignored. Cisco IOS does not use this variable for locating packages. See the section "Package Example" for a workaround for using packages with Cisco IOS.

Type: String

Meaning: Used to set the path that is searched looking for packages when a Tcl script uses "package require."

Example contents and usage:

```
TCL1(tcl)#puts $tcl_pkgPath
NULL

TCL1(tcl)#set tcl_pkgPath "flash:/TCL"
flash:/TCL
TCL1(tcl)#puts $tcl_pkgPath
flash:/TCL

TCL1(tcl)#
```

tcl_platform **Variable**

Type: Array

Meaning: Contains the operating system version, byte order, hardware, and operating system information

Example contents and usage:

```
TCL1(tcl)#array get tcl_platform
osVersion 12.4 byteOrder bigEndian machine Router platform ios os {Cisco IOS}
user Cisco
```

tcl_version **Variable**

Type: String

Meaning: Shows the version of Tcl that is running. Currently, the latest version of Tcl that is supported in Cisco IOS is 8.3.4. The variable can be changed, but has no effect.

Example contents and usage:

```
Router(tcl)#puts $tcl_version
8.3
```

Package Background

In a Tcl interpreter running in a UNIX environment, you can use the **package** command to automatically load packages of Tcl code as needed. The purpose of the package system is to allow modular code and code reuse. Groups of logically related procedures can all be combined into one package. By combining functions together in a *package*, the code author can quickly build a library of functions that can be easily inserted into programs as needed.

In addition to the code grouping, it provides the benefit of code versioning. Packages specify what version of code they provide. It is typically represented as *major-version.minor-version*. Because the code might change over time, every modification can be tracked with a new version number. If the change is internal only and does not impact the incoming parameters used, the author might increment the minor version from 1.0 to 1.1. If a major change is done to the package, such that the incoming parameters are modified, it is wise to increment the major version from 1.1 to 2.0. Another reason to increment the major version is the removal or addition of procedures.

Code that provides functionality can declare the package name it provides with a call to the **package** command:

package provide *packagename major.minor*

To include a package in a Tcl script, use the following command syntax:

package require *packagename*

If a Tcl script requires a particular version of a package, you can specify the version:

```
package require packagename major.minor
```

Package Example

In this example, you will create packages to compute the area of different shapes. The packages are each in separate files, one for a circle, triangle, and a square. Whenever you are writing a Tcl script that needs to deal with circle computations, you can simply include the circle library with a call to **package require circle**. If the Tcl script is modified to later handle squares, you can make a call to **package require square**. In this way, you can have modular Tcl scripts that allow for code to be reused.

When building a package, it is a good practice to create the procedures in their own namespace. Any new procedures and variables being defined by the package should not be in the global namespace. That way it avoids naming collisions which could lead to errors.

You now write the packages for computing the area of different shapes, in separate files named circle.tcl, square.tcl, and triangle.tcl.

Circle.tcl Script

The circle.tcl script is as follows:

```
package provide circle 1.0
```

Create the namespace:

```
namespace eval ::circle {
```

Export commands:

```
    namespace export circle
}

proc ::circle::area {radius} {
  set pi 3.14159265
  return [expr $pi * $radius * $radius]
}
```

Square.tcl Script

The square.tcl script is as follows:

```
package provide square 1.0
```

Create the namespace:

```
namespace eval ::square {
```

Export commands:

```
    namespace export square
}
proc ::square::area {height} {
  return [expr $height * $height]
}
```

Triangle.tcl Script

The triangle.tcl script is as follows:

```
package provide triangle 1.0
```

Create the namespace:

```
namespace eval ::triangle {
```

Export commands:

```
    namespace export triangle
}

proc ::triangle::area {base height} {
  return [expr 0.5 * $base * $height]
}
```

Creating the pkgIndex.tcl Script

Now that you have written the three package files, you can create a pkgIndex.tcl script. This allows the Tcl command **package require** to find the correct Tcl scripts.

In this example, you will perform the steps in a UNIX environment, because of some limitations of the Tcl interpreter in Cisco IOS, which are discussed later.

To create the pkgIndex.tcl file, make sure to start tclsh in the same directory where you have created circle.tcl, square.tcl, and triangle.tcl:

```
<sjc-lds-019$-~/tcl/mypackages>% ls
circle.tcl  square.tcl  triangle.tcl
```

Enter the Tcl interpreter:

```
<sjc-lds-019$-~/tcl/mypackages>% tclsh
%
```

Now you will create the pkgIndex.tcl script with the Tcl command **pkg_mkIndex**. The only required parameter is the directory path. If needed, you could specify a pattern to search for. However, in this case, you accept the default and allow all packages to be created:

```
% pkg_mkIndex .
% ls
circle.tcl  pkgIndex.tcl  square.tcl  triangle.tcl
%
```

The following shows the contents of the newly created pkgIndex.tcl:

```
package ifneeded circle 1.0 [list source [file join $dir circle.tcl]]
package ifneeded square 1.0 [list source [file join $dir square.tcl]]
package ifneeded triangle 1.0 [list source [file join $dir triangle.tcl]]
```

The Tcl package index file, version 1.1 is generated by the **pkg_mkIndex** command and sourced either when an application starts up or by a **package unknown** script. It invokes the **package ifneeded** command to set up package-related information. Consequently, packages will be loaded automatically in response to **package require** commands. When this script is sourced, the variable **$dir** must contain the full path name of this file's directory.

To use the file to automatically load the correct package, use the **auto_path** global variable command. The **auto_path** variable should point to one directory level higher than the directory containing pkgIndex.tcl. The pkgIndex.tcl is located in /users/mydir/tcl/packages directory. Make sure the **auto_path** is set correctly:

```
% set auto_path "/users/mydir/tcl"
/users/mydir/tcl
%
```

The Tcl shell will automatically search all subdirectories below the **auto_path** level to check for packages. To verify what packages are currently available, use the following command:

```
% package names
Tcl
%
```

As expected, the Tcl package is the only one that is currently available and is built in to the Tcl interpreter.

Now that you have created pkgIndex.tcl and set **auto_path** correctly, you can load the *circle* package. Use the **package require** command to require the Tcl interpreter to automatically use pkgIndex.tcl to find it:

```
% package require circle
1.0
%
```

As you can see, the *circle* package has been successfully loaded, and Tcl confirms the version that was loaded. To verify what package names are available, use the following command:

```
% package names
square triangle circle Tcl
%
```

The Tcl shell has now become aware of all the packages you created. To use a function within the *circle* package, use the following command:

```
% ::circle::area {6}
113.0973354
%
```

Using Packages in Cisco IOS

In Cisco IOS, a few limitations apply to packages:

- First, the **auto_path** is ignored in Cisco IOS. When **package require** is entered in the Cisco IOS Tcl shell, it will not search subdirectories below the **auto_path**, as was the case in the UNIX Tcl shell.

- Another issue that occurs in Cisco IOS Tcl shell is that the Tcl command **pkg_mkIndex** is not available. As a result of this limitation, you have to create the pkgIndex.tcl file in a UNIX environment, and then copy the pkgIndex.tcl from UNIX over to Cisco IOS.

- You also need to modify the pkgIndex.tcl file slightly to point to the local storage directory of the Cisco IOS router where the package files are going to be stored.

- Finally, you make use of a Cisco IOS **config** command to have the packages automatically made available.

This section demonstrates how to load the packages created earlier into a Cisco IOS environment.

Decide the path on the Cisco router where the packages will be stored. In this case, you will store them in the flash:/packages/ directory. Now modify the previously generated pkgIndex.tcl to contain the directory variable.

The Tcl package index file, version 1.1, is generated by the **pkg_mkIndex** command and sourced either when an application starts or by a **package unknown** script. It invokes the **package ifneeded** command to set up package-related information. Packages will be loaded automatically in response to the **package require** commands. When the script is sourced, the variable **$dir** must contain the full pathname of this file's directory:

```
set dir "flash:/package/"
package ifneeded circle 1.0 [list source [file join $dir circle.tcl]]
```

```
package ifneeded square 1.0 [list source [file join $dir square.tcl]]
package ifneeded triangle 1.0 [list source [file join $dir triangle.tcl]]
```

Copy all three packages and pkgIndex.tcl to the Cisco IOS device to the flash:/package/ directory. After you have done so, you can enter a configuration command into Cisco IOS to load the pkgIndex.tcl script, whenever the Tcl interpreter is started:

```
Router#config terminal
Enter configuration commands, one per line.  End with CNTL/Z.
Router(config)#scripting tcl init flash:/package/pkgIndex.tcl
Router(config)#end
Router#
```

Start the Tcl shell and verify which packages are available:

```
Router#tclsh
Router(tcl)#package names
square tbcload triangle circle Tcl
Router(tcl)#
```

To verify that you can call a procedure from within the newly added packages, use the following command:

```
Router(tcl)#package require square
1.0
Router(tcl)#::square::area { 5 }
25
Router(tcl)#
```

By following the preceding steps, you can successfully use packages with the Cisco IOS Tcl shell.

load **Command Removed in Cisco IOS**

In Cisco IOS, Tcl does not support the **load** command to extend the Tcl interpreter. In UNIX, compiled C language functions can be loaded into the Tcl shell. The reason for the removal in Cisco IOS is due to the lack of dynamic linking and the security implications of combining C code in the Tcl interpreter. As a result, the **load** functionality has been disabled in Cisco IOS. Using the **load** command results in an error message, as shown here:

```
Router(tcl)#load myfile
dynamic loading is not currently available on this system
Router(tcl)#
```

Compiling Tcl Scripts into Byte-Codes

The Tcl interpreter in Cisco IOS supports the use of byte-code compiled scripts. Tcl scripts consist of interpreted commands that can run on many different platforms, consequently, machine-independent byte-code was developed to allow compilation to take place on one machine and then later execute the code on another machine.

The only advantage to compiling the Tcl script is to hide the implementation details of a Tcl script. Compiling byte-code helps limit access to the implantation details or source code to the original author's Tcl script.

If you develop a script and want to distribute it without revealing the contents, compiling will reduce the chance that others can see the script. This is not foolproof. A determined hacker could possibly derive the original Tcl code from the compiled byte-code version.

There is no significant performance gained at runtime by converting Tcl scripts to byte-code.

To compile your Tcl script to byte-code format, obtain the free TCLPro compiler along with the optional C language development kit. As of this writing, it is available from two websites:

http://www.tcl.tk/software/tclpro/eval

http://sourceforge.net/projects/tclpro/files

If you are using Windows as a development platform, obtain version 1.5, because it does not have a license check. Do not obtain the ActiveState version; it will produce byte-code that is incompatible with Cisco IOS.

Note   TCLPro 1.5 is also supported on Solaris and Linux.

Install tclpro141.exe and the optional C language development kit file named tclprodev141.zip. Once installed, enter a command prompt and set the current directory to the location of the Tcl script you want to compile. The following example compiles the simple script named count-to-ten.tcl, the contents of which are as follows:

```
set b 11
set c 0
while {$c < $b} {
 puts "$c "
 incr c
}
```

Invoke the Tcl byte-code compiler:

```
C:\Documents and Settings\user\My Documents\tcl\book>procomp count-to-ten.tcl
TclPro Compiler -- Version 1.4.1
Copyright (C) Ajuba Solutions 1998-2010. All rights reserved.
This product is registered to: John Lautmann


C:\Documents and Settings\user\My Documents\tcl\book>dir count-to-ten.*
 Volume in drive C is System
 Volume Serial Number is 8C49-4519

 Directory of C:\Documents and Settings\user\My Documents\tcl\book

01/24/2010  11:30 PM                 445 count-to-ten.tbc
01/24/2010  11:28 PM                  87 count-to-ten.tcl
               2 File(s)             532 bytes
               0 Dir(s)   120,945,922,048 bytes free

C:\Documents and Settings\user \My Documents\tcl\book>
```

A new file has now been created, with the same name as the original script, but ending in a .tbc extension rather than a .tcl extension.

Here are the contents of count-to-ten.tbc. Note that this is unreadable code:

```
# TclPro::Compiler::Include

if {[catch {package require tbcload 1.3} err] == 1} {
    error "The TclPro ByteCode Loader is not available or does not support the
    correct version"
}
tbcload::bceval {
TclPro ByteCode 1 0 1.3 8.3
5 0 43 7 1 0 20 1 3 5 5 -1 -1
43
w0E<!:B`W!;btt!1#T=!-c,8-<E`<!5#|Tv0|8X!E?cW*.msrj(3!!
5
6SLm#-!
5
WT#mw%!
7
x
1
.v
i
11
x
1
```

```
/v
i
0
x
4
DP)*F
x
1
A!
x
0

1
L  1  21  16  40  12  -1
0
}
```

You transfer both files to the Cisco IOS router and verify they both work correctly:

```
Router(tcl)#source flash:count-to-ten.tcl
0
1
2
3
4
5
6
7
8
9
10

Router(tcl)#source flash:count-to-ten.tbc
0
1
2
3
4
5
6
7
8
9
10

Router(tcl)#
```

Both scripts provide identical results. If you look at the contents of count-to-ten.tbc, you can see the contents are unreadable. As you can see using the TCLPro byte-code compiler, it enables you to easily hide the contents of any Tcl script and still be able to run the script on a Cisco IOS device.

Index

X-Y-Z

FREE Online Edition

Your purchase of **Tcl Scripting for Cisco IOS** includes access to a free online edition for 45 days through the Safari Books Online subscription service. Nearly every Cisco Press book is available online through Safari Books Online, along with more than 5,000 other technical books and videos from publishers such as Addison-Wesley Professional, Exam Cram, IBM Press, O'Reilly, Prentice Hall, Que, and Sams.

SAFARI BOOKS ONLINE allows you to search for a specific answer, cut and paste code, download chapters, and stay current with emerging technologies.

Activate your FREE Online Edition at
www.informit.com/safarifree

> **STEP 1:** Enter the coupon code: DFCRSZG.

> **STEP 2:** New Safari users, complete the brief registration form.
> Safari subscribers, just log in.

If you have difficulty registering on Safari or accessing the online edition, please e-mail customer-service@safaribooksonline.com